THE HISTORY OF AL-ṬABARĪ

AN ANNOTATED TRANSLATION

VOLUME VII

The Foundation of the Community

MUHAMMAD AT AL-MADINA

A.D. 622–626/HIJRAH–4 A.H.

The History of al-Ṭabarī

Editorial Board

Ihsan Abbas, University of Jordan, Amman

C. E. Bosworth, The University of Manchester

Jacob Lassner, Wayne State University, Detroit

Franz Rosenthal, Yale University

Ehsan Yar-Shater, Columbia University (*General Editor*)

SUNY

SERIES IN NEAR EASTERN STUDIES

Said Amir Arjomand, Editor

Bibliotheca Persica
Edited by Ehsan Yar-Shater

The History of al-Ṭabarī
(Ta'rīkh al-rusul wa'l-mulūk)

VOLUME VII

The Foundation of The Community

translated and annotated
by

W. Montgomery Watt

University of Edinburgh, Emeritus

and

M. V. McDonald

University of Edinburgh

State University of New York Press

The preparation of this volume was made possible by a grant from the Program for Research Tools and Reference Works of the National Endowment for the Humanities, an independent federal agency; and in part by the Persian Heritage Foundation.

Published by
State University of New York Press, Albany

Printed in the United States of America

For information, address State University of New York Press, State University Plaza, Albany, N.Y. 12246

Library of Congress Cataloging in Publication Data

Ṭabarī, 838?–923.
The foundation of the community.

(The history of al-Ṭabarī = Ta'rīkh al-rusul wa'l-mulūk; v. 7) (Bibliotheca Persica)
Translation of extracts from: Ta'rīkh al-rusul wa-al-mulūk.
Bibliography: p.
Includes index.
1. Islamic Empire—History—622–661. 2. Medina (Saudi Arabia)—History. I. Watt, W. Montgomery (William Montgomery) II. McDonald, M. V. (Michael V.) III. Title. IV. Series: Ṭabarī, 838?–923. Ta'rīkh al-rusul wa-al-mulūk. English; v. 7. V. Series: Bibliotheca Persica (Albany, N.Y.)
DS38.1.T322513 1987 909'.097671 87-12940
ISBN 0-88706-344-6
ISBN 0-88706-345-4 (pbk.)

Acknowledgements

In 1971 the General Editor proposed to the UNESCO to include a translation of al-Ṭabarī's *History* in its Collection of Representative Works. UNESCO agreed, but the Commission in charge of Arabic works favored other priorities. Deeming the project worthy, the Iranian Institute of Translation and Publication, which collaborated with UNESCO, agreed to undertake the task. After the upheavals of 1979, assistance was sought from the National Endowment for the Humanities. The invaluable encouragement and support of the Endowment is here gratefully acknowledged.

The General Editor wishes to thank sincerely also the participating scholars, who have made the realization of this project possible; the Board of Editors for their selfless assistance; Professor Franz Rosenthal for his many helpful suggestions in the formulation and application of the editorial policy; Professor Jacob Lassner for his painstaking and meticulous editing; and Dr. Susan Mango of the National Endowment for the Humanities for her genuine interest in the project and her advocacy of it.

Preface

The History of Prophets and Kings (*Ta'rīkh al-rusul wa'l-mulūk*) by Abū Ja'far Muḥammad b. Jarīr al-Ṭabarī (839–923), here rendered as the *History of al-Ṭabarī*, is by common consent the most important universal history produced in the world of Islam. It has been translated here in its entirety for the first time for the benefit of non-Arabists, with historical and philological notes for those interested in the particulars of the text.

Ṭabarī's monumental work explores the history of the ancient nations, with special emphasis on biblical peoples and prophets, the legendary and factual history of ancient Iran, and, in great detail, the rise of Islam, the life of the Prophet Muḥammad, and the history of the Islamic world down to the year 915. The first volume of this translation will contain a biography of al-Ṭabarī and a discussion of the method, scope, and value of his work. It will also provide information on some of the technical considerations that have guided the work of the translators.

The *History* has been divided here into 38 volumes, each of which covers about two hundred pages of the original Arabic text in the Leiden edition. An attempt has been made to draw the dividing lines between the individual volumes in such a way that each is to some degree independent and can be read as such. The page numbers of the original in the Leiden edition appear on the margins of the translated volumes.

Al-Tabarī very often quotes his sources verbatim and traces the chain of transmission (*isnād*) to an original source. The chains of transmitters are, for the sake of brevity, rendered by only a dash (—) between the individual links in the chain. Thus, According to Ibn Ḥumayd—Salamah—Ibn Isḥāq means that al-Ṭabarī received the report from Ibn Ḥumayd who said that he was told by Salamah, who said that he was told by Ibn Isḥāq, and so on. The numerous subtle and important differences in the original Arabic wording have been disregarded.

The table of contents at the beginning of each volume gives a brief survey of the topics dealt with in that particular volume. It also includes the headings and subheadings as they appear in al-Ṭabarī's text, as well as those occasionally introduced by the translator.

Well-known place-names, such as, for instance, Mecca, Baghdad, Jerusalem, Damascus, and the Yemen, are given in their English spellings. Less common place-names, which are the vast majority, are transliterated. Biblical figures appear in the accepted English spelling. Iranian names are usually transcribed according to their Arabic forms, and the presumed Iranian forms are often discussed in the footnotes.

Technical terms have been translated wherever possible, but some, such as dirham and imām, have been retained in Arabic forms. Others that cannot be translated with sufficient precision have been retained and italicized as well as footnoted.

The annotation aims chiefly at clarifying difficult passages, identifying individuals and place-names, and discussing textual difficulties. Much leeway has been left to the translators to include in the footnotes whatever they consider necessary and helpful.

The bibliographies list all the sources mentioned in the annotation.

The index in each volume contains all the names of persons and places referred to in the text, as well as those mentioned in the notes as far as they refer to the medieval period. It does not include the names of modern scholars. A general index, it is hoped, will appear after all the volumes have been published.

Ehsan Yar-Shater

Contents

Acknowledgments / v

Preface / vii

Translator's Foreword / xv

The Events of the Year 1 (622–623) / 1

The First Friday Prayer / 1
The Sermon of the Messenger of God at the First Friday Prayer / 2
The Choice of a Site for Mosque and House / 4
Deaths and Minor Events / 5
The Marriage with ʿĀ'ishah / 6
Further Reports Concerning This / 8
Muslim Women Brought to Medina / 8
Prayers of Travellers / 9
Births / 9
Expedition Led by Ḥamzah / 10
Expedition Led by ʿUbayadah / 10
Expedition Led by Saʿd b. Abī Waqqāṣ / 11
Expedition Led by Muḥammad to al-Abwā' / 11
Further Details About Expeditions / 12
Expeditions Led by Muḥammad / 13
Affair of Abū Qays / 14

The Events of the Year 2 (623–624) / 15

Expeditions Led by the Messenger of God / 15
ʿAlī and the Name Abū Turāb / 16
A Variant Account / 17
ʿAlī Marries Fāṭimah / 18
Expedition to Nakhlah / 18
Questions After the Return to Medina / 20
Expedition of Nakhlah—Another Account / 21
Further Details About the Expedition of Nakhlah / 22

Other Events of the Second Year of the Hijrah / 24

The Change of Qiblah / 24
Arrangements About Fasting / 25
The Battle of Badr—the Date / 26
The Account of the Greater Battle of Badr in the Letter of ʿUrwah / 28
Another account / 32
Account of Badr by Ibn Isḥāq / 34
The Dream of ʿĀtikah, and the Relief Force / 35
The Number of Muslims at Badr / 38
The Advance of the Muslims to Badr / 40
Abū Sufyān Takes Evasive Action / 44
The Advance of Quraysh / 45
Preparations and Discussions of Quraysh / 48
The Fighting Begins / 52
Abū Jahl and Other Meccan Dead / 61
The Division of the Booty / 63
The Return of the Muslims to Medina / 64
News of Defeat Reaches Mecca / 67
The Treatment of the Captives / 69
The Release of Zaynab's Husband / 73
Zaynab's Journey to Medina / 75
The Conversion of Abū al-ʿĀṣ / 76
The Conversion of ʿUmayr b. Wahb / 78
Discussions About the Lawfulness of Taking Captives / 80
The Campaign Against the Banū Qaynuqāʿ / 85
Celebration of the First ʿĪd al-Aḍḥā / 87
Minor Expeditions—Dating / 88

The Expedition of al-Sawīq (the Barley-Meal) / 89
Other Events of the Year / 91

The Events of the Year 3 (624–625) / 93

The Story of Kaʿb b. al-Ashraf / 94
The Expedition to al-Qaradah / 98
The Killing of Abū Rāfiʿ the Jew / 99
The Prophet Marries Ḥafṣah / 105
The Expedition to Uḥud / 105
The Fighting Begins / 113
The Muslims Retreat / 120
Mutilation of the Muslim Dead / 129
Various Accounts Concerning Uḥud / 134
The Expedition of Ḥamrā' al-Asad / 138
The Sons of ʿAlī / 142

The Events of the Year 4 (625–626) / *143*

The Expedition of al-Rajīʿ / 143
The Mission of ʿAmr b. Umayyah Against Abu Sufyān / 147
Muḥammad's Marriage to Zaynab bt. Khuzaymah / 150
The Story of Bi'r Maʿūnah / 151
The Expulsion of the Banū al-Naḍīr / 156
Other Events / 161
The Expedition of Dhāt al-Riqāʿ / 161
The Expedition of al-Sawīq (or Badr al-Mawʿid) / 165
Other Events / 167

Abbreviations / 168

Bibliography of Cited Works / 169

Index / 171

Translator's Foreword

This volume deals with the history of the Islamic community at Medina between the Hijrah and the end of year 4 A.H. This was a time of critical importance both for Islam as a religion and for the political community in which it was embodied. Muḥammad and those Meccan Muslims who chose to accompany him (the Emigrants) took up their residence in Medina on the basis of the agreement known as the Constitution of Medina. The document of this name preserved by Ibn Hishām is probably of a later date but appears to incorporate the essential provisions of the original agreement.[1] It was an agreement to form a federation for mutual support between the "clan" of Emigrants with Muḥammad as their chief and eight clans of Medina. The federation was conceived on traditional Arab lines; however, because the nine clans were Muslims and Muḥammad was recognized as Messenger of God, it was in effect an Islamic polity, even though it contained Jewish groups as secondary members. Muḥammad had no special political authority, but it was stated that serious disputes were to be referred to him. Since this body politic was a new venture for all concerned and details of organization would be somewhat fluid, many decisions must have been taken in these early years;

1. IH, 341-4; see also Watt, *Medina*, 221-8, text and discussion; further discussion and analysis by R.B. Serjeant in *Bulletin of the School of Oriental and African Studies*, xli (1978), 1-42.

but al-Ṭabarī gives only a few glimpses of such matters, presumably because there were no specific datable events connected with them.

The first Friday prayer (1256–8) (pages 1256-8 of the Leiden edition)

It was important not only to make political arrangements for the community of Muslims but also to establish its religious observances. The unanimous testimony of the sources is that Muḥammad and the Muslims at Mecca did not make anything special of the Friday midday prayer before the Hijrah. However, there may have been some observance at Medina, and it is to be noted that al-Ṭabarī says it was the first Friday prayer which Muḥammad himself observed. Friday had become a market day in Medina, probably at first to enable Jews to lay in provisions for the sabbath; but it was also observed by the Arabs. It was doubtless because of these facts that the Muslims of Medina had made something special of the Friday prayer, and Muḥammad was ready to accept their practice. Indeed, it was eventually made obligatory for adult male Muslims to be present on this occasion in the mosque, preferably the *jāmiʿ* or central mosque of the town.[2]

Details of other liturgical arrangements are mentioned on pages 9 and 24–6.

The sermon or *khuṭbah* is an essential feature of the Friday prayer. It seems unlikely that the sermon given here by al-Ṭabarī was actually delivered by Muḥammad on this occasion. One of the verses quoted (8.42) is generally held to have been revealed over a year later at the time of the battle of Badr, while Muḥammad himself would hardly have used the phrase "I bear witness that Muḥammad is his servant and Messenger." A different sermon is reproduced by Ibn Hishām for this occasion.

The choice of a site for mosque and house (1258–60)

From other references it is clear that what was built at this time was a house or series of apartments for Muḥammad and his dependants. The mosque was the courtyard of the private dwell-

2. See art. Djumʿa (S.D.Goitein) in EI^2.

ing, perhaps demarcated by a wall. The "building" of the mosque at Qubā' was probably no more than marking off a piece of ground with a wall or fence. At this time Muḥammad had only one wife, Sawdah bt. Zamʿah, the widow of a Muslim who had died in Abyssinia, since ʿĀ'ishah still lived with her parents; he had also two unmarried daughters in his household.[3] Accommodation would be required for these and also, after the consummation of her marriage, for ʿĀ'ishah. Later when Muḥammad had several wives, each had her own apartment opening off the courtyard, and he spent his nights with them in turn.

The choice of a site belonging to the Banū al-Najjār was probably deliberate. Muḥammad was aware that one of the reasons for his invitation to Medina was that people hoped he would be able to put an end to the blood-feuds which had been increasing in violence; and he was careful not to ally himself by marriage with any of the clans of Medina. Al-Najjār was a numerous but not particularly powerful clan, divided into several subclans. The fact that Muḥammad had as great-grandmother a woman of al-Najjār, Salmā bt. ʿAmr, could have been the justification for his decision to live among them. They were also in a fairly central position.

Various deaths (1260f.)

About Kulthūm b. Hidm nothing else appears to be known. The three men mentioned at the end were prominent Meccan pagans of the older generation.

Asʿad b. Zurārah was one of the first group of six men from Medina to contact Muḥammad, probably in 620, and he also made both the First Pledge of al-ʿAqabah in 621 and the Second in 622. He is further credited with being mainly responsible for the conversion of some of the leading men of Medina to Islam; and it was he who, in the year before the Hijrah, had given hospitality to Muḥammad's envoy to Medina, Muṣʿab b. ʿUmayr.[4] His death must have been a serious loss for Muḥammad. The remark that it is bad for the Jews and Hypocrites implies that it will discourage them from believing in God.

At the second meeting at al-ʿAqabah, when the Muslims of

---

3. See 1263 below.
4. IH, 286-93.

Medina had pledged themselves to defend and protect Muḥammad and the Emigrants, Muḥammad had asked for twelve *nuqabāʾ* or representatives to be appointed, perhaps as a kind of council or senate for Medina. The men selected were the leading men in each clan of those present. Asʿad b. Zurārah was the representative of al-Najjār. Though the names of the men are recorded, there is no record of them having met or decided anything. Muḥammad's decision to become himself the replacement for Asʿad may have been made to prevent ill feeling between different sections of the clan, and he may also have realized, now that he had firsthand experience of conditions in Medina, that the institution of *nuqabāʾ* was not going to serve any useful purpose.

The marriage with ʿĀʾishah (1261–3)

All Muḥammad's marriages and those he arranged for his daughters were made for political reasons. Abū Bakr was his chief lieutenant and aide, and he is reputed to have had an excellent knowledge of the inner politics of the nomadic tribes; thus, he was able to advise Muḥammad in his dealings with those tribes. Muḥammad's betrothal to Abū Bakr's daughter ʿĀʾishah was made despite her tender age in order to cement the relationship between the two men. Muḥammad was similarly married in 625 to Ḥafṣah, the daughter of his other prominent lieutenant ʿUmar; she was then eighteen, and her first husband had been killed at Badr.[5] Another important Emigrant, ʿUthmān b. ʿAffān, later the third caliph, was married first at Mecca to Muḥammad's daughter Ruqayyah, and then, after her death at the time of the battle of Badr, to another daughter, Umm Kulthūm.[6] What seems properly to be a betrothal was apparently called a marriage by the Arabs, as may be seen in the case of Muḥammad's daughters and the two sons of Abū Lahab.[7] The mention of the special features in ʿĀʾishah may have been circulated to offset the extravagant praise by Shīʿites of Muḥammad's daughter Fāṭimah. According to the ideas of the times, the age of nine was seemingly not too young for marriage.

5. See 1383 below.
6. See 1358 and 1373 below.
7. See 1347 below.

The early expeditions (1265–73)

One of the outstanding features of the period between the Hijrah and the death of Muḥammad was a long series of "expeditions" of a warlike character. In a sense, these grew out of the nomadic custom of the razzia, the sudden raid in which one tried with superior force to surprise an enemy and drive off his camels. Al-Wāqidī's main surviving work on the career of Muḥammad is called "The Expeditions" (*al-Maghāzī*), and expeditions provide the main structure of the *Sīrah* of Ibn Isḥāq. The term, which is used in English for several Arabic words, has a wide range of application; it may be used for the action of a single individual, for an expedition that is mainly a battle (like Badr or Uḥud), for a defensive battle (like the siege of Medina), or for a three-month expedition with thirty thousand men (to Tabūk).

Not surprisingly, there is some uncertainty about the dating and order of the earliest relatively small expeditions. Three small expeditions led by Emigrants are placed by al-Wāqidī in year 1 and by Ibn Isḥāq in year 2. Al-Ṭabarī's arrangement is somewhat curious. He first gives an account of these three expeditions based mainly on al-Wāqidī, and then, after remarking that Ibn Isḥāq places them in year 2, proceeds to give the latter's account of an expedition led by Muḥammad and two of the previous three. He follows this with Ibn Isḥāq's account of three further expeditions led by Muḥammad himself, which according to both sources are in year 2. Yet all this comes under the heading of year 1, which closes with a paragraph based on al-Wāqidī about Abū Qays b. al-Aslat. Year 2 opens with a version from al-Wāqidī of the four expeditions led by Muḥammad. A table in al-Wāqidī's order and with his dating may make the arrangement clearer.

Month/year	*Destination*	*Leader*	*References in Ṭ*	
9/1	Sīf al-Baḥr	Ḥamzah	1265	: 1267–8
10/1	Rābigh/Aḥyā'	'Ubaydah	1265	: 1267
11/1	al-Kharrār	Sa'd	1265–6	: 1270
2/2	al-Abwā'/Waddān	Muḥammad	1266	: 1270
3/2	Buwāṭ	"	1268	: 1270–1
3/2	Safawān	"	1269–70	: 1271
6/2	al-'Ushayrah	"	1268–9	: 1271

The question of years could be tidied up if the paragraph about Abū Qays were placed immediately after al-Wāqidī's accounts of the three Emigrant expeditions, and if the heading for year 2 were inserted at this point. From the middle of page 1266, the events belong to year 2 apart from that one paragraph.

Some further points may be noted about these expeditions. All except that of Safawān, which was punitive, seem to have had the aim of intercepting a Meccan caravan and gaining booty. All, however, were unsuccessful. Sometimes the Muslim force may have been too weak to have any prospect of success against the men conducting the caravan. On the other hand, Muḥammad had two hundred men for the expedition of Buwāt, and there were only one hundred Meccans with the caravan of twenty-five hundred camels. In light of the new strategy which led to the success of the expedition of Nakhlah (sending out a party with sealed orders), it seems that the earlier failures were due to the ability of the Meccans to gain information from Medina; they doubtless had agents who gave them prior notice of Muslim plans, so that they could either increase the party with the caravan or vary the route.

It is also to be noted that none but Emigrants took part in these early expeditions. Before he encouraged his Meccan followers to join him in making the Hijrah, Muḥammad must have considered how they would make their living at Medina. They could hardly expect to be permanent guests of the Anṣār, the Muslims of Medina, and they probably had no inclination to become farmers, though land seems to have been available. They had some expertise in trade with Gaza and Damascus, but attempts to trade would almost certainly lead to conflict with the Meccans. Therefore, the intercepting of Meccan caravans and disrupting of Meccan trade must have been seen at least as a possibility. The Anṣār presumably acquiesced in these expeditions of Emigrants, but too much reliance should not be placed on the statements that such and such a person (often one of the Anṣār) was left in charge of Medina in Muḥammad's absence, since it is unlikely that at this period Muḥammad himself was in any sense in charge of Medina.

The expedition of Nakhlah (1273-9)

Although only eight men, or at most twelve, took part in this expedition, it was an important stage in the worsening of relations between the Muslims and the pagan Meccans. It was the first occasion on which a Meccan was killed by a Muslim and the first occasion on which the Muslims seized Meccan goods.

The first point to be noted is that the party was sent out eastwards for two days' march, but the sealed orders given to the leader told them to proceed south from there to Baṭn Nakhlah on the road from al-Ṭā' if to Mecca. The exact location is not known, but it must have been to the southeast of Mecca, and the members of the expedition were obviously going to be in considerable danger. All the Muslims professed themselves ready to carry on, but at some point two remained behind the rest of the party, allegedly looking fot a straying camel; but this sounds like an excuse. It is not clear whether Muḥammad knew there would be a caravan at this date making for Mecca or merely thought it a probability. The Muslim party did meet a small caravan, probably only a local one, since it was carrying raisins and leather and had only four men attending it. One of the Muslims had his head shaved, and this made the Meccans think they were a group performing the *'umrah* or lesser pilgrimage.

In the accounts of Ibn Isḥāq and al-Wāqidī, the Muslims now found themselves faced with a problem. It was the last day of the "sacred month" of Rajab, during which hostilities were forbidden; but by the following day the caravan would have entered the "sacred territory" of Mecca, where hostilities were equally forbidden. They decided to attack at once. One of the Meccans was killed by an arrow, two were taken prisoner, and one escaped to Mecca. Despite this escape, the Muslims were able to return safely to Medina with the prisoners and the caravan. The version of al-Suddī, which al-Ṭabarī gives subsequently, suggests that the fighting occurred on the first day of Rajab. The verse of the Qur'ān quoted (2.217) makes it clear that the fighting was in the month of Rajab, but gives no indication whether it was at the beginning or end.

On reaching Medina safely, the members of the successful party were surprised to find that they were not nearly so well received as they had expected. The ostensible reason was that they had killed a man during a sacred month. It seems unlikely that this weighed much with Muḥammad himself, since the sacred month was part of the false religion he was attacking. The matter is more complex than this, however. The Qur'ān itself (2.125; 3.97) acknowledges the sacredness of Meccan territory; but the sacredness of the four months (Rajab, Dhū al-qa'dah, Dhū al-ḥijjah, Muḥarram) may not have been acknowledged until after the abolition of the intercalary month (*nasī*), usually said to be in the year 10/632.[8] It is almost certain, however, that the fundamental reason for the disquiet in Medina over this matter was the fear that it would lead to Meccan reprisals against the whole city. It has to be remembered that the Anṣār had not taken part in any expedition against the Meccans, but they had undertaken to protect the Emigrants if these were attacked, and to this extent were deeply involved in the consequences of the expedition to Nakhlah.

The raiding party is said to have offered Muḥammad a share of the booty as chief of their tribe. The pre-Islamic custom was that the chief should receive a quarter of any booty captured by the tribe in order to offset what he had to expend on behalf of the tribe. The later Islamic norm was that Muḥammad received a fifth, but it is doubtful if anything so precise had yet been decided. Since acceptance of a share of the booty would have implied approval of what the Muslim party had done, Muḥammad at first declined. Eventually, however, the matter was settled by a revelation (2.217): "They ask you about the sacred month, fighting in it; fighting in it is a great (sin), but barring from the ways of God, and disbelieving in him and in the sacred mosque, and expelling its people from it, are greater (sins) in God's sight." After this Muḥammad accepted a share of the booty, presumably now satisfied that the Anṣār would support him whatever the Meccans did. The kinsmen of the man killed would doubtless attempt to avenge him, but the Meccans in general could not ignore the loss of face caused by the capture of the caravan almost, as it were, from under their noses.

---

8. Qur'ān, 9.36f.

The break with the Jews (1279-81)

The change of Qiblah (direction faced in prayer) and the institution of the fast of Ramaḍān are not purely questions of religious observance but are linked with political matters. Muḥammad had from an early date become convinced that the revelations he received were identical in essence to those which were the basis of Judaism and Christianity; he therefore expected that the Jews of Medina would accept him as a prophet. Consequently, when he came to Medina, he was disappointed to find that the Jews there, far from accepting his prophethood, were mostly inclined to poke fun at his revelations. Only one or two formally became Muslims.

The Muslims of Medina appear to have adopted a number of practices from their Jewish neighbours. They kept the Jewish fast of the ʿĀshūrā'; most, but not all, of them faced Jerusalem in prayer; and they made something special of the prayer at midday on Fridays. Muḥammad seems at first to have encouraged all these practices. The Qur'ān (5.5) makes it lawful for Muslims to eat Jewish food and to marry Jewish women. After some sixteen or eighteen months in Medina, however, it became clear to Muḥammad that such concessions were not going to win over the Jews, and a series of events occurred to which Western scholars have given the label of "the break with the Jews." The two points here mentioned by al-Ṭabarī are central to this change, namely, the change of Qiblah and the institution of the fast of Ramaḍān.

A later source has a story of how Muḥammad, while leading prayers, received a revelation bidding him face Mecca instead of Jerusalem, upon which he and all the other participants turned round and faced south instead of north; the place where this is said to have happened became known as the Mosque of the Two Qiblahs. No verse in the Qur'ān exactly fits this story, and a careful study of the whole passage (2.142-52) suggests that there may have been a period of uncertainty before a revelation prescribed the new Qiblah. The date of the change of Qiblah is about 11 February 624.

The essential point about the fast of Ramaḍān is that it was to replace the Jewish ʿĀshūrā', which the Muslims of Medina had been observing before the Hijrah, and in which Muḥammad and the Emigrants probably shared. The brief paragraph in al-Ṭabarī suggests that the fast of Ramaḍān was meant to celebrate the deliverance of the Muslims at Badr just as the 'Āshūrā' commemorated the deliverance of the Israelites at the Red Sea. Although al-Ṭabarī records the institution in year 2, it seems impossible that the Muslims could have kept the full fast in this year, since the battle of Badr occurred on or about 19 Ramaḍān. It is conceivable that some days of fasting were observed after the return to Medina, and that this justified the celebration of the 'īd al-fiṭr, the feast of the breaking of the fast.

It seems likely that the events mentioned marked not only the rejection of Jewish practices but also some political realignments among the Muslims. It is from about this period that we hear of the Hypocrites, the nominal Muslims opposed to many of Muḥammad's policies. Their leader was 'Abd Allāh b. Ubayy, who had for long had close relations with some of the Jews and had hoped they would help him to become prince of Medina. On the other hand, Sa'd b. Mu'ādh, possibly the strongest man in Medina, now put himself wholeheartedly behind Muḥammad and was instrumental in persuading about two hundred of the Anṣār to join the expedition to Badr—the first time any of the Anṣār had taken part in an expedition. There are various small points which suggest that Sa'd b. Mu'ādh might be described as pro-Arab and anti-Jewish. In 627 it was he who decided that all the men of the Jewish clan of Qurayẓah were to be put to death.

The battle of Badr (1279-1359)

The amount of material about the battle of Badr collected by the historians is a mark of its importance. Perhaps its most significant result was the upsurge of confidence among the Muslims. During the later years at Mecca, the Qur'ānic revelations had been showing how God protected his prophets against those who opposed them and rejected the revelations, and how in the end the prophets and the believers were triumphant and the opponents were punished. The victory of Badr was the way in which God had vindicated his prophet Muḥammad against the Meccan pagans, just as he had vindicated other prophets in other ways. For the ordinary believer it was a powerful confirmation of Muḥammad's claim to be a prophet. The belief that God and his angels worked for them during the battle raised the morale of the Muslims to such a point that it became overconfidence.

Muḥammad himself must have been deeply moved by the confirmation of his prophethood, but he must also have been aware that there were many problems ahead. For even if the Meccans had lost a dozen of their most senior men, Abū Sufyān and a few others were still around, and some capable younger men were coming up; so Meccan power must still be feared. Besides, in addition to the loss of leading men there was a serious loss of prestige, and prestige was necessary for the Meccans if they were to maintain their commercial empire. They were thus bound to attempt to reverse the result, and Muḥammad must have been aware of the fact.

With regard to the expedition itself, as previously noted, this was the first occasion on which men of the Anṣār joined Muḥammad. This doubtless came about largely because of the new understanding between Sa'd b. Mu'ādh and Muḥammad. The majority of the Anṣār had probably decided to support and defend Muḥammad against any Meccan reprisals for the attack at Nakhlah. With the contingent of Anṣār the Muslim force would easily have been strong enough to overpower the men accompanying the caravan, and Muslim intentions probably did not go beyond booty. Muḥammad and Sa'd, however, probably realized that things could become more serious.

The excellence of the Meccan information service is shown by the fact that Abū Sufyān knew about the Muslim expedition to Badr in sufficient time to take evasive action and that the people in Mecca knew in time to send out a relief force. The possibility of such a force may have occurred to Muḥammad, but he probably had no definite information until he was in the vicinity of Badr. On this point the view of 'Urwah in his letter (1286) is to be preferred to that of Ibn Isḥāq (1300). Had the Muslims in general known earlier they might have wanted to withdraw, for it was no dishonour to an Arab to avoid an engagement with a superior force. At Badr, however, when the two forces found themselves so close to one another, neither could honourably have retreated. On the other hand, it could be argued that Qur'ān 8.7—God's promise of one of the two companies, the caravan or the relief force—implies that Muḥammad knew something about a relief force before he knew that the caravan had eluded him. It is just conceivable, then, that he deliberately manoeuvred the Muslims into a situation in which they could not honourably avoid a conflict with the Meccans.

On the Meccan side, Abū Jahl was clearly a "hawk" intent on teaching Muḥammad a lesson and restoring Meccan prestige. It was he who taunted with cowardice those who wanted to withdraw while that was still an option. The right of commanding the Meccans in war belonged to Abū Sufyān, but, because he was absent with the caravan, Abū Jahl was temporarily in command; and it may be that he wanted to make the most of this opportunity. Once the Meccans realized the close proximity of the Muslims, there could be no question of retreating.

Some reasons for the Muslim victory can be discerned. The plan adopted by Muḥammad on the suggestion of one of his followers, namely, blocking up all the wells except one and so depriving the Meccans of water, certainly contributed. It is likely, too, that the Anṣār, because they gained a livelihood by cultivating date-palms and cereal crops, were in better condition physically than the Meccans, whose lives as merchants were probably much more sedentary. Even when they accompanied caravans, they presumably did so on camel-back. The Anṣār, moreover, had gained experience of fighting in the feuds which had been endemic in the oasis. Some of the Emigrants also proved successful fighters, possibly because they were in general younger men than their opponents, while their belief in God and in the life of Paradise doubtless increased their confidence.

The accounts of the treatment of prisoners and other events of the period after the battle give interesting insights into the outlook and moral attitudes of the people of the time. The first and lengthiest part of al-Ṭabarī's material comes from Ibn ʿAbbās through his disciple ʿIkrimah, that is, from authorities on the exegesis of the Qur'ān, not authorities on Muḥammad's career. The critical verse is 8.67: "It is not for any prophet to have captives until he has made slaughter in the land . . . (or "until he has subdued the land")." Some of the surrounding verses belong to the period of the battle of Badr but others belong to that of Uḥud, and it is difficult to distinguish the two. It seems likely that 8.67 was not revealed until after Uḥud and is perhaps part of the attempt to explain why that was so disastrous. On this assumption the verse is saying: "If you had not been so keen on ransoms after Badr and had not taken prisoners, these losses would not have befallen you." It is probably not coincidence that in some sources the number of prisoners at Badr and the number of Muslim dead at Uḥud are both stated to be seventy. It should not be supposed, however, that killing instead of taking prisoners was thought of chiefly as a way of weakening the enemy militarily. It was seen rather as inflicting a punishment and something of a moral duty, in line with the *lex talionis.*

Modern Westerners are inclined to think of the principle of "an eye for an eye and a tooth for a tooth" as barbaric,[9] but in actuality the *lex talionis* is a primitive way of maintaining security for life and property. It is indeed almost the only way of doing this when there is no strong central authority capable of punishing wrong-doers. The basis is the solidarity of the group of kinsmen. A person is less likely to kill or injure another without serious cause if he knows that the victim's kin-group will inflict a like injury on his own kin-group. All the groups recognized that it was essential that injuries and deaths should be avenged, and usually ended the blood-feud when proper vengeance had been taken, though it was sometimes difficult to agree on what was proper and equal vengeance. This meant that the system was only effective when the next of kin saw it as a sacred duty to avenge a death. When it became the practice to accept a blood-wit of camels instead of a life, the conservative moralists taunted those who did so with being content with milk instead of blood. It is noteworthy that in al-Ṭabarī's second account (on page 1356) ʿUmar says that the Meccans had called Muḥammad a liar and driven him out, and so deserved to die; and this has the implication that in not having them put to death Muḥammad was failing to perform his duty.

The expulsion of Banū Qaynuqāʿ (1360-2)

One of the limitations of al-Ṭabarī's method of writing history is to be seen in the fact that this is the first reference to the Jews of Medina. The title "the break with the Jews" was given above to the section on the change of Qiblah and the institution of the fast

9. *Exodus* 21.23-5; *Leviticus* 24.17-21.

of Ramaḍān, but al-Ṭabarī himself did not mention the Jews there. Yet from the Qur'ān it is clear that the Jews were a serious problem for Muḥammad from the day of his arrival in Medina. From the little he knew previously about the Jewish religion, he expected the Jews to receive him as a prophet. To the generality of the Jews, however, it was inconceivable that there could be a prophet who did not come from the chosen people, that is, themselves. To make things worse for Muḥammad and the Muslims, the Jews did not merely refuse to recognize Muḥammad as a prophet but made fun of him in various ways and tried to discredit his prophethood by showing that some of the Qur'ānic assertions about Biblical matters were incorrect.

The expulsion of the Banū Qaynuqāʿ is probably to be seen as a corollary of the break with the Jews. It is possible that Muḥammad and Saʿd b. Muʿādh had agreed that they would get rid of the Jews as opportunities presented themselves. According to al-Wāqidī, the immediate occasion of the siege of Qaynuqāʿ was a trick played by a Jew on an Arab woman as she sat in their market. An Arab killed this Jew, and then another Jew killed the Arab. At this, the Jews took refuge in their strongholds, and the Muslims came and besieged them. This incident was no more than a pretext, and by omitting it al-Ṭabarī seems to have judged it so. The very life of the Islamic religio-political community at Medina depended on wholehearted belief that Muḥammad was a prophet and the Qur'ān the word of God; but this belief was endangered by some of the criticisms made by the Jews. This was the fundamental reason for the attacks on the three main Jewish clans in Medina and on particular individuals. Muḥammad was doubtless aware that the Jews were relatively wealthy, and the Muslims benefited from the seizure of their wealth; but that was not the primary reason for attacking them.

Banū Qaynuqāʿ were goldsmiths and armourers, and also conducted a market. They had been confederates of ʿAbd Allāh b. Ubayy, and when they surrendered after a fortnight's siege, he pleaded for them, though without much success. The statement quoted by al-Ṭabarī from al-Wāqidī that Muḥammad wanted to kill them seems to be mistaken. It was against their expulsion that ʿAbd Allāh b. Ubayy argued on the ground that Muḥammad might some day be in need of their skill as armourers; but Muḥammad was not to be moved. On leaving Medina, they are said to have gone first to Wādī al-Qurā, where there were Jewish settlements, then to Syria.

The expulsion of Banū Qaynuqā' was only the first of a series of attacks on Jewish groups and individuals. A few months later, five men of the Anṣār (of the tribe of al-Aws) killed Ka'b b. al-Ashraf, who counted as a Jew because his mother was Jewish, although his father was a pagan Arab from a nomadic tribe. He was a noted poet who after Badr went to Mecca and did his best to discredit the Muslim cause and create dissension. Two of those involved in the killing were his milk-brothers (1368–72). Al-Ṭabarī follows this almost immediately (1375–83) with the account of the killing of Abū Rāfi' Sallām b. Abī al-Ḥuqayq; but this probably occurred considerably later, after the siege of Medina in the year 8/627. He had seconded the efforts of Ka'b b. al-Ashraf against the Muslims and later had helped to persuade nomadic tribes to take part in military operations against Medina.

Minor expeditions between Badr and Uḥud (1362–8; 1373–5)

Apart from the "expedition" against Ka'b b. al-Ashraf, there were four between Badr and Uḥud led by Muḥammad himself and one led by his adoptive son, Zayd b. Ḥārithah. The early Muslim scholars discussed the dating of these expeditions at length without coming to any firm conclusions. Furthermore, so little information is given about them that it is difficult to know the precise aim of some, much less to determine the exact dates.

The first was the so-called "barley-meal raid" (*sawīq*) in which the Muslims were responding to a challenge from the Meccans. Abū Sufyān probably intended to do no more than make a gesture which might help to restore Meccan prestige among the nomads, but his two hundred horsemen could have inflicted heavy casualties on any Muslims fighting on foot—and the Muslims had only one or two horses. His retreat when a Muslim force came out against him seems to show that he was not looking for a confrontation. Significant points are the apparent ease with which he entered Medina and the fact that a leading man of a Jewish clan was prepared to converse with him. (The fact that the nickname of "barley-meal raid" was also given to what is otherwise known as Badr al-Maw'id[10] indicates the difficulties the historians had with the small early expeditions.)

The other expeditions led by Muḥammad were against nomadic tribes and were perhaps chiefly intended to convince potentially hostile nomads that the Muslims could not be attacked with impunity. The expedition led by Zayd to al-Qaradah was, like that to Badr, aimed at a caravan. The Meccan leaders realized the difficulty they were in after Badr, since any caravan following the normal coastal route northwards could easily be attacked by raiders from Medina. They therefore sent a small but wealthy caravan by a more easterly route through Najd. Muḥammad must have learnt about this, for he sent out Zayd with a force of a hundred men, more than sufficient to overawe the Meccans and make them abandon their caravan. Al-Ṭabarī, following Ibn Isḥāq, says the caravan was led by Abū Sufyān, but al-Wāqidī makes the leader Ṣafwān b. Umayyah, supported by Abū Zam'ah al-Aswad b. al-Muṭṭalib.[11]

The battle of Uḥud (1383–1430)

The Meccan defeat at Badr, along with subsequent events such as the loss of a caravan at al-Qaradah, had made it clear to all that if Mecca was to survive as a commercial power it must somehow reduce Muḥammad to impotence and restore its own prestige among the Arabs generally. To the achievement of this end the Meccans directed strenuous efforts in the months after Badr under the forceful leadership of Abū Sufyān b. Ḥarb. By the spring of 625, he was able to mobilize three thousand men from the men of Mecca and the allied tribes in the neighbourhood; of these, 700 had coats of mail and two hundred were mounted on horses. They set out about 11 March and reached the oasis of Medina on Thursday, 21 March, entering it from the northwest corner and pasturing their animals in the fields of cereals there.

Muḥammad's first plan was that the people of Medina should retire to the strongholds or fortified houses (*āṭām*), of which each

10. See 1457-9 below.

11. Abū Sufyān is mentioned by al-Ṭabarī in his report from al-Wāqidī, but he is not mentioned at all in al-Wāqidī, 197f.

clan had several. The Meccans would find these virtually impregnable and would be unable to use their cavalry if there was fighting in the confined spaces between the strongholds. Some of the Anṣār, however, could not bear to see their fields devastated by the Meccans and insisted on marching out to confront them. Somewhat against his better judgement, Muḥammad agreed. He set out with a thousand men and, using a guide with local knowledge, slipped past the Meccans and took up a position to the north of their camp on the lower slopes of the hill of Uḥud, where he could not be attacked by the Meccan cavalry. Before he reached this position, however, ʿAbd Allāh b. Ubayy with three hundred men had returned to the strongholds in the centre of the oasis, leaving only seven hundred men with Muḥammad. Presumably he acted in this way because he disagreed with Muḥammad's policies, though there are divergent views on the point. From this time on, ʿAbd Allāh b. Ubayy is known as the leader of the Hypocrites (*munāfiqūn*), the nominal Muslims opposed to Muḥammad.

Al-Ṭabarī's method of presenting without comment a series of slightly different reports about incidents in the battle does not produce a clear picture but suggests rather a long, confused melée. By following the more coherent accounts and making use of the references in the Qur'ān, the course of the battle may be outlined somewhat as follows.

It possibly began with an unsuccessful attack by the Meccan cavalry. Muḥammad's main defence against them is usually taken to be his archers, posted on his left flank. The report from Ibn ʿAbbās (page 1394) most probably does not mean that al-Zubayr and his men had to move against the cavalry but that they were posted in such a way that they could deflect a cavalry charge in cooperation with the archers. Apart from this, the chief Meccan assault seems to have been an advance by the infantry against the main body of Muslims, who may have begun to move down from the hill slopes. The references to the carrying of the Meccan standard by men of the clan of ʿAbd al-Dār (and the deaths of eleven of them) seem to imply that they led this advance. Fierce fighting ensured, of which the Muslims had the better. The Meccans retreated towards their camp, perhaps even took to flight and abandoned their camp (as is suggested by the mention of the women running away). It is doubtful whether the Muslims actually began to plunder the camp, but some sections of the Muslim force saw opportunities for plunder, and in particular some of the archers left their positions.

When these movements were observed by Khālid b. al-Walīd, commanding the right wing of the cavalry, he caused consternation by charging the Muslim flank and rear. It was at this point that Muḥammad was personally involved in fighting and was wounded. However, he was able to rally a number of Muslims round him and to regain the slopes of Uḥud. They may have been a little higher than previously, and they beat off Meccan attacks without much difficulty. One body of Muslims, however, instead of making for the hill, tried to reach a stronghold to the south of the Meccan camp, and it was probably they who suffered the severest casualties. The figure is given of seventy Muslims killed, four Emigrants and sixty-six of the Anṣār.[12] As soon as Abū Sufyān realized that it would be impossible to dislodge the Muslims from their position on the hill, he decided to leave Medina and return to Mecca. The whole Meccan army moved off to Ḥamrā' al-Asad, eight miles to the south.

To understand this surprising denouement, it is necessary to assess carefully the significance of the battle for the two sides. The fact that there were seventy Muslim casualties as against twenty-two Meccan suggests a serious defeat for the Muslims, and both Muslim and Western scholars have often interpreted it in this way. Yet, a little reflection shows that it was far from being a victory for the Meccans. They had boasted that they would exact several Muslim lives for every Meccan life lost at Badr, whereas, on the assumption that seventy Meccans fell at Badr, the Muslim losses in the two battles were less than those of the Meccans, and so they had not even achieved a life for a life. More seriously, the Meccans had completely failed in their strategic aim of breaking Muḥammad's power. These facts point to the conclusion that in the early stage of the fighting, before the reversal of fortune brought about by the cavalry charge, the Meccan infantry had had much the worse of it; many of the horses, too, may have been wounded by the Muslim arrows. Abū Sufyān must

12. IH, 607-9; W, 300-7.

have reckoned that despite the Muslim casualties the Meccans were not capable of attacking the strongholds of Medina. He may also have hoped that those of the inhabitants of Medina who were least enthusiastic about Muḥammad and his religion would now turn against him and expel him; and he would not want to do anything to antagonize such people.

From a strictly military point of view, then, Muḥammad had not been seriously defeated; apart from the possibility of increased disaffection towards him in Medina, he had come out of the battle at least as well as the Meccans. What Abū Sufyān could not have realized, however, was that the happenings at Uḥud were for Muḥammad and the Muslims a serious spiritual reverse. After the victory of Badr, the Muslims had thought that they were practically invincible, since God and his angels were helping them. In the Qur'ān (8.66), Muḥammad was told to encourage the Muslims to fight, for "if there are twenty steadfast men among you, they will overcome two hundred, and if a hundred, they will overcome a thousand." To the ordinary Muslim, conscious of so many comrades dead, it must have seemed that God was not supporting them after all. Muḥammad's own faith may have been shaken, at least briefly. In due course the Qur'ān made it clear that the discomfiture did not indicate withdrawal of God's support but was caused by the Muslims' own disobedience and excessive desire for plunder.

Whatever Muḥammad's inmost feelings in the immediate aftermath of Uḥud, he publicly put a brave face on things, and on the following day led out about nine hundred men to Ḥamrā' al-Asad, from which the Meccans had now moved on to al-Rawḥā'. This expedition was really a kind of gesture of defiance intended, as Ibn Isḥāq put it, "to lower the morale of the enemy . . . and to give them the impression that his strength was unimpaired." To heighten the show of strength, Muḥammad told the men to gather wood by day and to light a large number of fires at night—a matter mentioned by al-Wāqidī but not thought worthy of inclusion by al-Ṭabarī. A friendly nomad, Ma'bad al-Khuzā'ī, also helped by exaggerating the size and warlike attitude of the Muslim force. At the same time, Abū Sufyān was using comparable means to scare the Muslims into withdrawing, while some of the Meccans wanted to attack Medina again. It is unlikely, however, that either side thought seriously of again engaging the enemy; and both soon returned to base.

The expeditions of year 4 (1431–59)

For an adequate understanding of the events of year 4, which were relatively minor, it is necessary to appreciate more of the general background than is made clear in the materials presented by al-Ṭabarī.

The key is to be found in the activities of the Meccans after Uḥud. Despite the casualties inflicted on the Muslims, the Meccans had failed to dislodge Muḥammad or even, as things turned out, to seriously weaken him. Yet this was what they had to do if they were to preserve their commerce and their wealth. It must have been clear to Abū Sufyān, too, that the army he had managed to collect from Mecca itself and the small neighbouring tribes was not sufficient to achieve their aim. For complete success they would have to have the support of some of the great nomadic tribes; and for the next two years the Meccans were making strenuous efforts to gain this support, using all possible means from promises of booty to straight bribes.

In consequence of this, Muḥammad's general strategy during these years, apart from restoring confidence among the Anṣār and strengthening his position in Medina, was to take all possible measures to counteract what the Meccans were doing. There was an expedition shortly after Uḥud (not mentioned by al-Ṭabarī) into regions friendly to the Meccans in order to counteract their propaganda about Muḥammad's weakness and display something of the Muslims' military power. The expedition to Dhāt al-Riqāʿ (1453–7) was somewhat similar. Muḥammad also hoped to persuade groups from the nomadic tribes to accept Islam and toward this end was prepared to take calculated risks. Examples of this, in which the gamble did not come off, were the expeditions of al-Rajīʿ (1431–7) and Biʾr Maʿūnah (1441–8). Muḥammad's prestige was apparently now such that one group or faction within a tribe might hope to improve its standing in the tribe by being first to embrace Islam. Something of this sort may have been at the root of the attack on the Muslims at al-Rajīʿ. It was certainly present in the disaster at Biʾr Maʿūnah.

In the latter case, the chief of the tribe of ʿĀmir, Abū Barāʾ

ʿĀmir b. Mālik, seems to have wanted to improve his position in the tribe against a rival faction led by his nephew, ʿĀmir b. al-Ṭufayl. Abū Barā' gave his formal protection to the Muslim party, and this should have been respected by all the tribe; and it was in fact respected by all despite the pleas of his nephew to disregard it. Foiled at this point, the nephew suggested to nearby clans of the tribe of Sulaym, with whom he must have been on good terms, that they could attack the Muslims with impunity. All the Muslims were killed except a nomadic confederate who was able to claim that he was protected by some oath. What happened next is puzzling to the Westerner. On his way back to Medina this confederate met two men of the tribe of ʿAmir and killed them; as a result Muḥammad had to pay blood-money to ʿĀmir for these two men, although he was unable to claim blood-money for the forty or more Muslims who had been killed. The explanation is that the actual killing had been done by men of Sulaym, so that in Arab eyes they alone were responsible (and Muḥammad was not in a position to demand blood-money from Sulaym, which was friendly to Mecca). ʿĀmir b. al-Ṭufayl had suggested the killing and so in Western eyes was morally responsible, but he had not been physically involved in it, and so he and his tribe of ʿĀmir were not liable for blood-money. The nomadic confederate was a powerful and brutal man who a little earlier had gone to Mecca in an attempt to kill Abū Sufyān (1437–41).

In the case of the last expedition of the year, that of Badr al-Mawʿid (1457–9), it seems clear that neither side really meant to engage the other in battle, but both put on a show of brinkmanship to convince the tribes of the region that they themselves had no fear, whereas the opponents were on the point of running away.

The expulsion of Banū al-Naḍīr (1448–53)

The main underlying reason for the expulsion of the clan of al-Naḍīr was the same as in the case of Qaynuqāʿ, namely, that Jewish criticisms endangered the ordinary Muslim's belief in Muḥammad's prophethood and in the Qur'ān as revelation from God. It should also be kept in mind that the attack was made only a few weeks after the Muslim loss of life at al-Rajīʿ and Bi'r Maʿūnah, when many people in Medina must have been entertaining gloomy feelings. Some of the details are obscure. The clan of al-Naḍīr had some sort of alliance with the tribe of ʿĀmir, but it is not clear how this affected the question of blood-money. Again, while it is possible that some men of al-Naḍīr really planned to drop a stone on Muḥammad and kill him, it is also possible that the allegation was no more than an excuse to justify the attack. Even if there is some truth in the story, however, the incident was only the occasion for the attack, not the fundamental reason. Apart from the general hostility of the Jews to Muḥammad and Islam, a chief of al-Naḍīr had given hospitality and information to Abū Sufyān at the time of the "barley-meal raid" in 624, and Muḥammad may have been aware of this. The result of the Meccan attack was similar to that on Qaynuqāʿ, except that some of the clan of al-Naḍīr remained at the oasis of Khaybar where they had lands.

Muḥammad's family

During year 4 (about October 625), Muḥammad lost his eldest grandson, ʿAbd Allāh, the son of ʿUthmān and Muḥammad's daughter Ruqayyah. A few months later, however, in January 626, ʿAlī and Fāṭimah had a second son, al-Ḥusayn (1453).

Muḥammad married Zaynab bt. Khuzaymah about February 626 (1441). Her first husband al-Ṭufayl b. al-Ḥārith had divorced her and then she had married his brother ʿUbaydah, who had been killed at Badr. Muḥammad may have felt that he had an obligation to her, since her two husbands had been from the clan of al-Muṭṭalib, which was virtually part of his own clan of Hāshim; she herself belonged to the tribe of ʿĀmir, with which he was cultivating good relations.

About a month later he took another wife, Umm Salamah, the widow of Abū Salamah, who had died from wounds received at Uḥud after apparently recovering. Both were from the Meccan clan of Makhzūm, the clan of Abū Jahl, with which it was important for Muḥammad to have good relations.

Al-Ṭabarī and his Sources

Al-Ṭabarī's main source for the first four years of the Hijrah was the *Sīrah* or biography of the Prophet by Ibn Isḥāq (d.150/767). A form of this is still extant and is available in scholarly printed editions and in an English translation by Alfred Guillaume. The extant form of the *Sīrah* is the recension of it by another scholar, Ibn Hishām (d. 218/833), who added some small items of information but also omitted a few passages. In the present volume, the most notable omissions are those of how the Prophet's uncle al-ʿAbbās took part in the battle of Badr as a pagan and was captured. Though not found in Ibn Hishām's recension, these have been reproduced by al-Ṭabarī.[13] Guillaume places Ibn Hishām's additions in an appendix but includes in his main text passages of Ibn Isḥāq's work from al-Ṭabarī and others. While al-Ṭabarī retains most of the strictly narrative parts of Ibn Isḥāq, he omits some matters only incidental to the main account, as well as the lists of names, the detailed references to Qur'ānic texts about Badr, Uḥud and the like, and most of the poetry.

To the material from Ibn Isḥāq, al-Ṭabarī adds divergent accounts from a large number of sources. The most important of these is al-Wāqidī (d. 207/823), whose *Kitāb al-Maghāzī* ("Book of the Expeditions") has been excellently edited. He seems to have studied questions of dating more thoroughly than Ibn Isḥāq, and al-Ṭabarī always notes where his conclusions differ from the latter's. Apart from this, however, al-Ṭabarī only reproduces material from al-Wāqidī where it is significantly different from Ibn Isḥāq, but he does not reproduce material found only in al-Wāqidī.

Another source worthy of mention is an early document, the letter of ʿUrwah b. al-Zubayr (d.94/712) to the Umayyad caliph ʿAbd al-Malik.[14] Ibn Isḥāq uses material from ʿUrwah but does not seem to have known of this document.

Al-Ṭabarī also has a small amount of material for which he gives no source, such as statements about births, deaths, and marriages. These were possibly regarded as matters of common knowledge.

Problems of Chronology

For the first ten years of the Hijrah there are special difficulties about the correlation of Islamic dates with Christian. The "stan-

13. See pp. 1290, 1323, 1339f, 1344, and notes 65 and 101.
14. See pp. 1284-9 and notes 16 and 56.

dard" correlation (as found in *Wüstenfeld-Mahler'sche Vergleichungs-Tabellen*, ed. Bertold Spuler, Wiesbaden 1961) has been followed here. This is based on the assumption that the strict Islamic calendar, without intercalary months, was followed from the beginning of year 1. This assumption, however, is almost certainly wrong, since the Qur'ānic verse (9.37) forbidding the use of the intercalary month (*nasī*) was revealed at the Pilgrimage of the year 10 (March 632). There is thus a presumption that before that date three or four intercalary months had been observed by the Muslims since the Hijrah. There is no record, however, of how many such months there had been, nor in what years. This leads to discrepancies about the day of the week on which certain events happened. Thus Muḥammad is said to have arrived at Qubā' in the oasis of Medina on Monday, 12 Rabī' al-awwal; but according to the "standard" correlation, this was a Friday. Attention has not been called to discrepancies of this type except in note 1. The alternative method of dating events as so many months after the Hijrah is a useful check, but does not solve the problems.

While Dr. Michael McDonald and I have cooperated closely in this volume, the primary work of translation has been his and that of annotation and introduction mine. The rendering of Qur'ānic verses is from *The Meaning of the Glorious Koran* by Marmaduke Pickthall.

W. Montgomery Watt

The Events of the Year I [1256]

(July 16, 622–July 4, 623)

Part 2: The Period After the Hijrah

Abū Ja'far (al-Ṭabarī) states: We have already mentioned the date of the Prophet's arrival in Medina, the place in which he stayed when he arrived, the man with whom he stayed, the length of his stay in that place and his departure from it. We shall now mention the other noteworthy events of this year, the first year of the Hijrah.

The First Friday Prayer

Among these is his holding the Friday prayer with his companions on the day on which he left Qubā' for Medina. This was on Friday,[1] and the time for prayer—the Friday prayer—overtook

1. IH, 333, says that the Messenger reached Qubā' on the outskirts of the oasis of Medina on Monday, 12 Rabī' al-Awwal (September 24, 622), and stayed there until Friday of that week. According to the standard calendar, 12 Rabī' al-Awwal is itself a Friday; but the standard calendar is based on the assumption that from year 1 the Muslims observed a lunar year without intercalary months, whereas it is almost certain that some intercalary months had been observed before the revela-

him in the territory of the Banū Sālim b. ʿAwf in the bed of a wadi belonging to them, and this was used as a mosque that day.[2] This
[1257] was the first Friday prayer which the Messenger of God held in Islam. On this Friday he delivered a sermon, the first sermon he preached in Medina.

The Sermon of the Messenger of God at the First Friday Prayer[3]

According to Yūnus b. ʿAbd al-Aʿlā—Ibn Wahb— Saʿīd b. ʿAbd al-Raḥmān al-Jumaḥī: The sermon of the Messenger of God at the first Friday prayer which he led at Medina in the territory of the Banū Sālim b. ʿAwf was as follows:

> Praise be to God. I praise him, and call on him for help, forgiveness and guidance. I believe in him, do not deny him and am an enemy of whoever denies him. I bear witness that there is no deity but God alone, without partner, and that Muḥammad is his servant and his Messenger, whom he has sent with guidance, light and exhortation after an interval (*fatrah*)[4] in the appearance of messengers, at a time when

---

tion of the verse (Qur. 9.7) abolishing them; because of this, some slight discrepancies of dating are only to be expected and will not be further commented on here. It is generally agreed in many sources that so long as Muḥammad was at Mecca there was no special observance of the Friday midday prayer.

2. According to IH, 335, the wadi is Wādī Ranūnah; see map in Watt, *Medina*, 152. Banū Sālim b. ʿAwf was a small but important clan in Medina, usually known as Qawāqilah. The clan system at Medina is very complex. Eight large clans are mentioned in the document known as the Constitution of Medina (IH, 341–4), but sixteen subclans seem to have functioned to some extent as independent units, and at least as many more are occasionally mentioned. A form of the genealogical table is given in Watt, *Medina*, 154, and this shows the nominal place of other clans to be mentioned later by al-Ṭabarī. Many of the names in the table appear to be fictitious, perhaps due to the persistence in Medina until about this period of a matrilineal kinship system. It should also be noted that the term *banū*, "sons of," is used for kinship groups of all sizes, from single families to the largest tribes; the use of words like "clan" and "tribe" depends on scholars' estimates of the size of the group.

3. IH, 340, gives a different sermon. The text here cannot be an exact reproduction of the original, since it contains a verse of the Qur'ān revealed at the time of the battle of Badr.

4. It is unlikely that Muḥammad himself would have used the words "I bear witness that Muḥammad is his servant and his Messenger." For *fatrah*, see *EI*[2], s.v. The word was used for the interval or period between any two prophets or

knowledge is scarce, men are led astray, time is cut short, the Last Hour is at hand and the End is close. Whoever obeys God and his Prophet has been rightly guided; whoever disobeys them has erred, been remiss and gone far astray. I recommend to you the fear of God, for the best thing which a Muslim can enjoin upon a Muslim is that he should exhort him to seek the Other World and command him to fear God. Beware of what God has warned you against concerning himself. There is no better advice than this and no better admonition. The fear of God, for whoever acts according to it in fear and dread of his Lord, is a trusty aid to what you desire of the Other World. He who sets aright what is between him and his Lord in secret and in public, seeking nothing thereby but the face of God, will be remembered in this world, and will have a treasure in that which is after death. Then a man will have need of that good which he has done previously; and as for that which is otherwise, he will wish that there was a great distance between him and it. God warns you to beware of himself, but God is merciful to his servants and to those who believe his word and fulfil their promises. God says: [1258]
"The sentence that cometh from me cannot be changed, and I am in no wise a tyrant unto the slaves."[5] Fear God, then, in this world and the next, in secret and in public. He who fears God will have his evil deeds forgiven and his reward magnified; he will achieve a great success. The fear of God will ward off God's hatred and retribution and wrath. The fear of God will make people blameless in the sight of God, will please the Lord and will raise their degree. Seize hold of your portion, and do not be remiss with regard to God. God has caused you to know his Book and has opened his path before you in order that he may know those who speak the truth and those who lie. Act well, then, as God has acted well with you. Be enemies of his enemies, and strive on God's behalf in the way to which he is entitled. He has chosen you and named you Muslims, "that he who perished (on that day)

---

messengers, but more particularly for that between Jesus and Muḥammad. It may also suggest a slackening of the previous prophet's religion.

5. Qur. 50.29; the "slaves" or "servants" (of God) are human beings generally.

might perish by a clear proof (of his sovereignty) and he who survived might survive by a clear proof."[6] There is no power but with God. Remember God frequently and act for the sake of that which is after today; for he who sets aright that which is between him and God will have that which is between him and other men taken care of by God. That is because God pronounces judgement upon men whereas they do not pronounce judgement upon him, and because God rules men whereas they do not rule him. God is most great. There is no might but with God the great.

The Choice of a Site for Mosque and House

According to Ibn Ḥumayd—Salamah—Ibn Isḥāq: The Messenger of God mounted his she-camel and let her reins hang loose. The inhabitants of every settlement of the Anṣār (the Muslims of Medina) which she went past invited him to stay with them, saying, "Come, O Messenger of God, to a settlement which has many defenders and is well-provisioned and impregnable." He would say to them, "Let go her reins, for she is commanded (by God)." Finally he reached the present site of his mosque, and his
[1259] camel knelt down where the door of his mosque is. At that time this place was a drying-floor for dates and belonged to two orphan boys of Banū al-Najjār under the guardianship of Mu'ādh b. 'Afrā'; their names were Sahl and Suhayl, sons of 'Amr b. 'Abbād b. Tha'labah b. Ghanm b. Mālik b. al-Najjār. When the camel knelt down, the Messenger of God remained on her. After a little she got up and went a short distance, while the Messenger of God let go her reins and did not direct her with them. Then she turned round, went back to the place where she had knelt first, and there knelt and laid down her neck. When the Messenger of God dismounted from her, Abū Ayyūb took his saddle into his house. Others of the Anṣār invited him to stay with them but the Messenger of God said to them, "The man goes with his saddle," and stayed with Abū Ayyūb Khālid b. Zayd b. Kulayb among the Banū Ghanm b. al-Najjār.

---

6. Qur. 8.42; generally held to have been revealed about the time of the battle of Badr.

According to Abū Ja'far (al-Ṭabarī): The Messenger of God asked to whom the drying-floor belonged, and Mu'ādh b. 'Afrā' told him, "It belongs to two orphans under my guardianship, whom I will compensate for it." The Messenger of God ordered that a mosque should be built there, and stayed with Abū Ayyūb until the mosque and his living-quarters had been completed.[7]

It is said that the Messenger of God bought the site of his mosque and then built upon it, but the correct version in our opinion is this, according to Mujāhid b. Mūsā—Yazīd b. Hārūn—Ḥammād b. Salamah—Abū al-Tayyāḥ—Anas b. Mālik: The site of the mosque of the Prophet belonged to Banū al-Najjār and contained palm trees, cultivated land and pre-Islamic graves. The Messenger of God said to them, "Ask me a price for it," but they said, "We do not want a price for it, but only the reward we [1260]
shall receive from God." The Messenger of God then gave orders concerning the site; the palm trees were cut down, the cultivated land levelled, and the graves dug up. Before this mosque was completed the Messenger of God used to pray in sheep-enclosures or wherever the time of prayer overtook him.

According to Abū Ja'far (al-Ṭabarī): He himself joined in the work of building his mosque, together with his companions from the Emigrants and the Anṣār.

Deaths and Minor Events

In this year the mosque of Qubā' was built.

The first Muslim to die after the Prophet's arrival in Medina, it is said, was Kulthūm b. al-Hidm, in whose house in Qubā' he had lodged; his death occurred shortly afterwards. There followed in the same year of the Prophet's arrival the death of Abū Umāmah As'ad b. Zurārah, which occurred before the Messenger of God had finished building his mosque; it resulted from diphtheria and a rattling in the throat.

According to Ibn Ḥumayd—Salamah—Muḥammad b. Isḥāq—'Abd Allāh b. Abī Bakr—Yaḥyā b. 'Abd Allāh b. 'Abd al-Raḥmān: The Messenger of God said, "The death of Abū Umā-

7. What was built was primarily the living quarters for Muḥammad and his wives. At first, the mosque was presumably only the courtyard beside these.

mah is an evil thing for the Jews and the Arab Hypocrites. They say, 'If Muḥammad were a prophet, his companion would not have died'; but I have no power with God either for myself or for my companion."

According to Muḥammad b. ʿAbd al-Aʿlā—Yazīd b. Zurayʿ—Maʿmar—al-Zuhrī—Anas: The Messenger of God cauterised Asʿad b. Zurārah for a whitlow (*shawkah*).[8]

According to Ibn Ḥumayd—Salamah—Ibn Isḥāq—ʿĀṣim b.
[1261] ʿUmar b. Qatādah: Abū Umāmah Asʿad b. Zurārah had been the representative (*naqīb*)[9] of Banū al-Najjār, and when he died they came as a group to the Messenger of God and said, "O Messenger of God, you know what position this man held among us; appoint one of us to his place to perform for us the functions he used to perform." The Messenger of God replied, "You are my maternal uncles,[10] and I am one of you; I will be your representative." The Messenger of God was unwilling to single out any one of them for this honour to the disadvantage of others. As a result, it was counted a distinction for the people of Banū al-Najjār that the Messenger of God was their representative.

In this year there died Abū Uḥayḥah in al-Ṭā'if with all his wealth, and al-Walīd b. al-Mughīrah and al-ʿĀṣ b. Wā'il al-Sahmī in Mecca.[11]

The Marriage with ʿĀ'ishah

In this year also the Messenger of God consummated his marriage with ʿĀ'ishah.[12] This was in Dhū al-Qaʿdah (May–June 623) eight

---

8. The identification of *shawkah* with "whitlow" is based on Hava's Dictionary. Elsewhere it is said to be a redness of face or body (Lane; Lisān al-ʿarab; s.v.).

9. At the second meeting at al-ʿAqabah (June 622) twelve men were appointed as *nuqabā'* (sing. *naqīb*) or "representatives" of the Anṣār, the Muslims from Medina. They were leading men in their clans, but their function is obscure; see Watt, *Mecca*, 145–8; *Medina*, 248.

10. He is referring to the fact that his great-grandmother, Salmā bt. ʿAmr, wife of Hāshim, was of Banū al-Najjār.

11. These were three powerful Meccan leaders of an older generation who had opposed Muḥammad; see Watt, *Mecca*, index.

12. ʿĀ'ishah was the daughter of Abū Bakr, Muḥammad's chief lieutenant, and the marriage was important in cementing the relationship of the two men. According to the statements given below, the original marriage, which could be considered rather a betrothal, must have been about April or May, 620 or 621, since

months after his arrival in Medina according to some accounts, or in Shawwāl (April–May 623) seven months after his arrival according to others. He had married her in Mecca three years before the Hijrah, after the death of Khadījah. At that time she was six or, according to other accounts, seven years old.

According to ʿAbd al-Ḥamīd b. Bayān al-Sukkarī—Muḥammad b. Yazīd—Ismāʿīl (that is, Ibn Abī Khālid)—ʿAbd al-Raḥman b. Abī al-Ḍaḥḥāk—a man from Quraysh—ʿAbd al-Raḥmān b. Muḥammad: ʿAbd Allāh b. Ṣafwān together with another person came to ʿĀ'ishah, and ʿĀ'ishah said (to the latter), "O so-and-so, have you heard what Hafṣah has been saying?"[13] He said, "Yes, O Mother of the Faithful." ʿAbd Allāh b. Ṣafwān asked her, "What is that?" She replied, "There are nine special features in me that have not been in any woman, except for what God bestowed on Maryam bt. ʿImrān.[14] By God, I do not say this to exalt myself over any of my companions." "What are these?" he asked. She replied, "The angel brought down my likeness; the Messenger of God married me when I was seven; my marriage was consummated when I was nine; he married me when I was a virgin, no other man having shared me with him; inspiration came to him when he and I were in a single blanket; I was one of the dearest people to him; a verse of the Qur'ān was revealed concerning me when the community was almost destroyed;[15] I saw Gabriel when none of his other wives saw him; and he was taken (that is, died) in his house when there was nobody with him but the angel and myself." [1262]

According to Abū Jaʿfar (al-Ṭabarī): The Messenger of God married her, so it is said, in Shawwāl, and consummated his marriage to her in a later year, also in Shawwāl.

---

intercalary months presumably kept Shawwāl about the same time of the solar year.

13. Daughter of the second caliph ʿUmar; married Muḥammad in 3/625. "Mother of the Faithful" was a title conferred on Muḥammad's wives in 9/630 probably; and this incident must have occurred later; see Watt, *Medina*, 286f.

14. That is, Mary the mother of Jesus (see Qur. 3.35f.; 66.12); but hardly any of the special features apply to her.

15. This refers to the scandal about ʿĀ'ishah after the raid on the tribe of al-Muṣṭaliq in 5/627. The verse is held to be Qur. 24.11.

Further Reports Concerning This

According to Ibn Bashshār—Yaḥyā b. Saʿīd—Sufyān—Ismāʿīl b. Umayyah—ʿAbd Allāh b. ʿUrwah—his father (ʿUrwah)[16]—ʿĀʾishah: The Messenger of God married me in Shawwāl and consummated his marriage to me in Shawwāl. ʿĀʾishah liked her women's marriages to be consummated in Shawwāl.

According to Ibn Wakīʿ—his father—Sufyān—Ismāʿīl b.
[1263] Umayyah—ʿAbd Allāh b. ʿUrwah—ʿUrwah—ʿĀʾishah: The Messenger of God married me in Shawwāl and consummated his marriage to me in Shawwāl, and which of the Messenger of God's wives did he favour more than me? ʿĀʾishah liked her women's marriages to be consummated in Shawwāl.

According to Abū Jaʿfar (al-Ṭabarī): It is said that the Messenger of God consummated his marriage to her on a Wednesday in Shawwāl in the house of (her father) Abū Bakr in al-Sunḥ.[17]

Muslim Women Brought to Medina

In this year the Prophet sent Zayd b. Ḥārithah and Abū Rāfiʿ to his daughters and his wife Sawdah bt. Zamʿah, and they brought them from Mecca to Medina.[18] It is said that when ʿAbd Allāh b. Urayqiṭ[19] returned to Mecca he informed ʿAbd Allāh b. Abī Bakr of the situation of his father Abū Bakr, and the latter brought his father's family to him. The party included Umm Rūmān, the mother of ʿĀʾishah, (ʿĀʾishah herself) and ʿAbd Allāh b. Abī Bakr, and they were accompanied to Medina by Ṭalḥah b. ʿUbayd Allāh.

16. ʿUrwah, a son of al-Zubayr, had access to ʿAʾishah because she was his maternal aunt. His important collection of historical material was known to al-Ṭabarī, partly through Ibn Isḥāq and partly through other channels. See n. 56 below.

17. Al-Sunḥ was a district of Medina where Abū Bakr lodged in the house of one of the local Muslims (IH, 334).

18. Zayd b. Ḥārithah was Muḥammad's adoptive son and Abū Rāfiʿ his *mawlā* or client. It is usually said that they escorted to Medina his two unmarried daughters, Umm Kulthūm and Fāṭimah, as well as his wife Sawdah, whom he had married after Khadījah's death.

19. Or b. Arqaṭ. He was a pagan who had guided Muḥammad and Abū Bakr on their Hijrah from Mecca to Medina.

Prayers of Travellers

In this year, it is said, two *rak'ahs* were added to the prayers of those who were not travelling; up till now the prayers of those not travelling and of those travelling had both been of two *rak'ahs*. This change took place a month after the arrival of the Messenger of God in Medina, that is, on 12 Rabī' al-Ākhir (October 24, 622). Al-Wāqidī asserts that there is no difference of opinion among the people of Ḥijāz on this point.

Births

In this year also, some say, 'Abd Allāh b. al-Zubayr was born;[20] but according to al-Wāqidī, he was born in the second year of the Messenger of God's residence in Medina, in Shawwāl (April 624).

According to Al-Ḥārith—Ibn Sa'd—Muḥammad b. 'Umar al-Wāqidī: Ibn al-Zubayr was born in Medina twenty months after the Hijrah.

According to Abū Ja'far (al-Ṭabarī): He was the first child born to the Emigrants in the abode of the Hijrah. It is said that the [1264] Messenger of God's companions cried, "Allāh Akbar" ("God is very great"), when he was born. This was because a story was current among the Muslims that the Jews claimed that they had bewitched the Muslims so that no children would be born to them. The Muslims praised God in joy that he had shown the Jews' claim to be false. His mother, Asmā' bt. Abī Bakr, is said to have been pregnant with him when she emigrated to Medina.

It is also said that al-Nu'mān b. Bashīr was born in this year and that he was the first child born to the Anṣār after the Emigration of the Prophet to them.

Al-Wāqidī denies that this (happened in year 1).

According to Al-Ḥārith—Ibn Sa'd—al-Wāqidī—Muḥammad b. Yaḥyā b. Sahl b. Abī Ḥathmah—his father—his grandfather: The first child born to the Anṣār was al-Nu'mān b. Bashīr, who was born fourteen months after the Hijrah (about October–

---

20. Son of the prominent Companion al-Zubayr. He attempted to set himself up as caliph in Mecca from 64/684 to 73/692. 'Urwah (n.16) was his full brother.

November 623); the Messenger of God died when he was aged eight or a little more. Al-Nu'mān was born three or four months before Badr.

According to Al-Ḥārith—Ibn Sa'd—Muḥammad b. 'Umar (al-Wāqidī)—Muṣ'ab b. Thābit—Abū al-Aswad: Al-Nu'mān b. Bashīr was mentioned in the presence of Ibn al-Zubayr, and he said, "He is six months older than I."

According to Abū al-Aswad: Ibn al-Zubayr was born exactly twenty months after the Hijrah of the Messenger of God, and al-Nu'mān was born in Rabī' al-Ākhir, year 2 (October 623), fourteen months after the Hijrah.

According to Abū Ja'far (al-Ṭabarī): It is said that al-Mukhtār b. Abī 'Ubayd al-Thaqafī and Ziyād b. Sumayyah were born in this year.

Expedition Led by Ḥamzah

[1265] Al-Wāqidī asserts that in this year, in Ramaḍān, seven months after the Hijrah (about March 623), the Messenger of God entrusted a white banner to Ḥamzah b. 'Abd al-Muṭṭalib with the command of thirty men of the Emigrants. Their aim was to intercept the caravans of Quraysh. Ḥamzah met Abū Jahl at the head of three hundred men. Majdī b. 'Amr al-Juhanī intervened between them, and they separated without a battle. The banner of Ḥamzah was carried by Abū Marthad.[21]

Expedition Led by 'Ubaydah

(He also says that) in this year, eight months after the Hijrah, in Shawwāl (April 623), the Messenger of God entrusted a white banner to 'Ubaydah b. al-Ḥārith b. al-Muṭṭalib b. 'Abd Manāf and ordered him to march to Baṭn Rābigh. His banner was carried by Misṭaḥ b. Uthāthah. He reached the pass of al-Marah, which is near al-Juḥfah, at the head of sixty Emigrants without a single Anṣārī (Muslim of Medina) among them. They met the polythe-

21. This is usually known as the expedition of Sīf al-Baḥr; cf. IH, 419–21; W, 9f. Ḥamzah was Muḥammad's uncle.

ists at a watering place called Aḥyā'; they shot arrows at one another but there was no hand-to-hand fighting.

There is a difference of opinion as to who was the commander of the (Meccan) expedition; some say that it was Abū Sufyān b. Ḥarb and some that it was Mikraz b. Ḥafṣ.

Al-Wāqidī says: I consider the true account to be that it was Abū Sufyān b. Ḥarb, and that he was at the head of two hundred polytheists.[22]

Expedition Led by Sa'd b. Abī Waqqāṣ

In this year, in Dhū al-Qa'dah, the Messenger of God entrusted to Sa'd b. Abī Waqqāṣ a white banner (for an expedition) to al-Kharrār. It was carried by al-Miqdād b. 'Amr.[23]

According to Abū Bakr b. Ismā'īl—his father—'Āmir b. [1266]
Sa'd—his father: I set out on foot at the head of twenty men (or, twenty-one men). We used to lie hidden by day and march at night, until we reached al-Kharrār on the fifth morning. The Messenger of God had enjoined me not to go beyond al-Kharrār, but the caravan had got to al-Kharrār a day before me; there were sixty men with it. Those who were with Sa'd were all from the Emigrants.

According to Abū Ja'far (al-Ṭabarī): Ibn Isḥāq's[24] account of all these expeditions differs from that of al-Wāqidī, which I have just related, and places them all in year 2.

Expedition Led by Muḥammad to al-Abwā'

According to Ibn Ḥumayd—Salamah b. al-Faḍl—Muḥammad b. Isḥāq: The Messenger of God came to Medina on the twelfth of

22. The expedition of Rābigh, placed before Sīf al-Baḥr by IH, 416–8; cf. W, lof. Abū Sufyān of the clan of 'Abd Shams/Umayyah was one of the leading men in Mecca, and played an important part in later events. Art. Abū Sufyān in *EI*²; Watt, *Medina*, index.

23. See IH, 422f.; W, 11.

24. Muḥammad b. Isḥāq (d. 150/767) is the author of the *Sīrah* (biography) of the Prophet, which is the primary source for his career. It has been preserved and published in the recension of Ibn Hishām (d. 218/833), and was also used by al-Ṭabarī in a different recension (see n.99). The other extant early source is the *Maghāzī* of al-Wāqidī (d. 207/823), which was also used by al-Ṭabarī. See Sezgin, *GAS*, i.288–90; 294–9.

Rabīʿ al-Awwal (September 24, 622), and remained there for the rest of Rabīʿ al-Awwal, Rabīʿ al-Ākhir, the two Jumādās, Rajab, Shaʿbān, Ramaḍān, Shawwāl, Dhū al-Qaʿdah, Dhū al-Ḥijjah—the pilgrimage in that month was directed by the polytheists—and Muḥarram. In Ṣafar (which began August 4, 623), nearly twelve months after his arrival in Medina on the twelfth of Rabīʿ al-Awwal, he went out on a raid as far as Waddān, searching for Quraysh and the Banū Ḍamrah b. Bakr b. ʿAbd Manāt b. Kinānah. This was the expedition of al-Abwā',[25] in the course of which the Banū Ḍamrah made a treaty of friendship with him; their fellow-tribesman and chief, Makhshī b. ʿAmr, acted on their behalf. Then the Messenger of God returned to Medina without any
[1267] fighting, and remained there for the rest of Ṣafar and the beginning of Rabīʿ al-Awwal.

Further Details About Expeditions

During this stay he sent ʿUbaydah b. al-Ḥārith b. al-Muṭṭalib at the head of eighty or sixty horsemen from the Emigrants without a single Anṣārī among them. He got as far as Aḥyā', a watering place in Ḥijāz, below the pass of al-Marah.[26] There he met a great band of Quraysh, but there was no fighting between them, except that Saʿd b. Abī Waqqāṣ shot an arrow on that day, which was the first arrow shot in Islam. Then the two groups separated from one another, the Muslims leaving a rearguard. Al-Miqdād b. ʿAmr al-Bahrānī, the confederate (*ḥalīf*) of the Banū Zuhrah, and ʿUtbah b. Ghazwān b. Jābir, the confederate of the Banū Nawfal b. ʿAbd Manāf, fled from the polytheists to the Muslims. They were Muslims, but they had gone to try to effect a reconciliation between the unbelievers and the Muslims. The commander of the Meccan detachment was ʿIkrimah b. Abī Jahl.

Muḥammad (b. Isḥāq) says: The banner of ʿUbaydah, I have heard, was the first banner which the Messenger of God entrusted to a Muslim in Islam.

According to Ibn Ḥumayd—Salamah—Muḥammad b. Isḥāq: Some of the scholars assert that the Messenger of God sent him

---

25. See IH, 415f.; W, 11f.; see also 1270f. below.
26. Apparently the same expedition as that reported 1265 above.

out while he was returning from the raid of al-Abwā', before he reached Medina.

During this stay he sent Ḥamzah b. ʿAbd al-Muṭṭalib at the head of thirty horsemen from the Emigrants, without a single Anṣārī among them, to Sīf al-Baḥr, near al-ʿĪṣ, which is in the territory of Juhaynah. He met Abū Jahl b. Hishām on the coast there at the head of three hundred Meccan horsemen. Majdī b. ʿAmr al- [1268]
Juhanī intervened between them, being on friendly terms with both parties, and the two sides separated without a battle.[27]

Some say that the banner of Ḥamzah was the first banner which the Messenger of God entrusted to a Muslim. This is because he sent him and ʿUbaydah b. al-Ḥārith at the same time, so that there is confusion on this point.

What we have heard from scholars to whom we have spoken is that the banner of ʿUbaydah b. al-Ḥārith was the first banner to be entrusted in Islam.

Expeditions Led by Muḥammad

Then the Messenger of God led an expedition in Rabīʿ al-Ākhir (which began October 2, 623) in search of Quraysh. He went as far as Buwāṭ in the region of Raḍwā and then returned without any fighting.[28]

He stayed in Medina for the rest of Rabīʿ al-Ākhir and part of Jumādā al-Ūlā (which began October 31, 623) and then led another expedition in search of Quraysh.[29] He took the mountain track of the Banū Dīnār b. al-Najjār (of Medina) and then crossed the desert of al-Khabār, halting beneath a tree in the Baṭḥā' Ibn Azhar called Dhāt al-Sāq. He prayed there, and his mosque is there. Food was prepared for him there, and he and those with him ate. The site there of the stones on which his cooking-pot was supported is still well-known. Water was brought to him from water called al-Mushayrib. Then he set off, leaving al- [1269]
Khalā'iq on the left and going through a pass, now called Shuʿbat ʿAbd Allāh. From that point, he went down to the left until he

27. Apparently the same expedition as the one reported 1265 above before that led by ʿUbaydah.

28. Expedition to Buwāṭ: IH, 421; W, 12. See also 1271 below.

29. Expedition of al-ʿUshayrah: IH, 421f.; W, 12f. See also 1271 below.

reached Yalyal, halting where Yalyal adjoined al-Ḍabūʿah. Water was brought to him from a well at al-Ḍabūʿah. Next, he went through the plain of Malal until he joined the road at Ṣukhayrāt al-Yamām, then kept to the road until he halted at al-ʿUshayrah in the Baṭn Yanbuʿ. He stayed there for the rest of Jumādā al-Ūlā and a few days of Jumādā al-Ākhira (which began November 30, 623). During this time, the Banū Mudlij and their confederates from the Banū Ḍamrah made a treaty of friendship with him. Then he went back to Medina without any fighting. In the course of this expedition he made certain remarks to ʿAlī b. Abī Ṭālib.

The Messenger of God had only spent a few days in Medina, less than ten, after coming back from the expedition to al-ʿUshayrah, before Kurz b. Jābir al-Fihrī raided the herds of Medina. The
[1270] Messenger of God went out in pursuit of him and reached a valley called Safawān in the region of Badr, but Kurz eluded him and was not caught. This was the first expedition of Badr.[30]

Then the Messenger of God returned to Medina and stayed there for the rest of Jumādā al-Ākhirah, Rajab and Shaʿbān (December 623 to February 25, 624). Among other expeditions he sent out at this time was one under Saʿd b. Abī Waqqāṣ at the head of eight men.[31]

Affair of Abū Qays

Al-Wāqidī asserts that in this year, the first year of the Hijrah, Abū Qays b. al-Aslat came to the Messenger of God;[32] the Messenger of God proposed Islam to him, and he said, "How excellent is that to which you call me! I will settle my affairs and then return to you." ʿAbd Allāh b. Ubayy[33] met him and said to him, "By God, you are unwilling to fight the Khazraj!" So Abū Qays said, "I will not become a Muslim for a year." He died, however, in Dhū al-Qaʿdah (which began May 7, 623).

---

30. Expedition of Safwān or Badr I: IH, 423; W,12. See also 1271 below.

31. Possibly another version of the expedition to al-Kharrār. See also 1265 above and n.23.

32. Abū Qays had been a prominent man in the struggles in Medina before the Hijrah, as chief of the clan of Wāʾil and leader of the wider group known as Aws Manāt; cf. Watt, *Medina*, index.

33. Leader of the Munāfiqūn or Hypocrites, who were nominally Muslims but opposed Muḥammad in various ways.

The Events of the Year 2

(July 5, 623–June 23, 624)

Expeditions Led by the Messenger of God

In this year, according to all the *Sīrah*-writers, the Messenger of God personally led the expedition of Al-Abwā', or, as it is sometimes called, Waddān; the two places are six miles apart and opposite one another.[34] When he went there, the Messenger of God left Sa'd b. 'Ubādah b. Dulaym in command of Medina.[35] On this expedition his banner was carried by Ḥamzah b. 'Abd al-Muṭṭalib, and was, it is said, white.

Al-Wāqidī asserts that he stayed there for fifteen days and then returned to Medina.

According to Al-Wāqidī: Then the Messenger of God went on an expedition at the head of two hundred of his companions in the month of Rabī' al-Ākhir (which began October 2, 623), and
reached Buwāṭ. His intention was to intercept the caravan of [1271]

---

34. See 1266 above and n. 25.
35. Sa'd b. 'Ubādah of the clan of Sā'idah was a leader of the whole tribe of al-Khazraj, and in Muḥammad's closing years became leader of all the Anṣār.

Quraysh, led by Umayyah b. Khalaf with a hundred men of Quraysh and two thousand five hundred camels.[36] In the end he returned to Medina without fighting. His banner was carried by Sa'd b. Abī Waqqāṣ, and he left Sa'd b. Mu'ādh in command of Medina during this expedition.[37]

Earlier, in Rabī' al-Awwal (which began September 2, 623), he went on an expedition at the head of the Emigrants in pursuit of Kurz b. Jābir al-Fihrī.[38] This man had raided the flocks of Medina which were pastured in al-Jammā' and had driven them off; the Messenger of God pursued him as far as Badr but failed to catch up with him. His banner was carried by 'Alī b. Abī Ṭālib, and he left Zayd b. Ḥārithah in command of Medina.

In this year the Messenger of God set forth at the head of the Emigrants to intercept the caravan of Quraysh when it set off for Syria. This was the expedition of al-'Ushayrah,[39] and it went as far as Yanbu'. He left Abū Salamah b. 'Abd al-Asad in command of Medina. His banner was carried by Ḥamzah b. 'Abd al-Muṭṭalib.

'Alī and the Name Abū Turāb

According to Sulaymān b. 'Umar b. Khālid al-Raqqī—Muḥammad b. Salamah—Muḥammad b. Isḥāq[40]—Muḥammad b. Yazīd b. Khuthaym—Muḥammad b. Ka'b al-Quraẓī—Yazīd b. Khuthaym (father of Muḥammad b. Yazīd b. Khuthaym)—'Ammār b. Yāsir: I and 'Alī were companions with the Messenger of God on the expedition of al-'Ushayrah. We halted on one occasion and saw some men of the Banū Mudlij working in one of their
[1272] date groves, and I said, "Why don't we go and watch how they are working?" So we went and watched them for a while; then we felt drowsy and went to a date grove and went to sleep on some

36. See 1268 above and n. 28.

37. Sa'd b. Mu'ādh of the clan of 'Abd al-Ashhal was leader of the whole tribe of al-Aws and in effect of all the Anṣār.

38. See 1269f. above and n. 30.

39. See 1268 above and n. 29.

40. IH, 422; but only the second *isnād* is given; there is confusion about whether Yazīd was the son of Khuthaym and Muḥammad the grandson, or vice versa. Abū Turāb is literally "father of dust"; see also n.166 below.

dusty ground under the trees. The Messenger of God himself woke us up, coming to us as we were covered in dust. He stirred ʿAlī with his foot and said, "Arise, O dusty one! (*Abū Turāb*). Shall I tell you who are the most wretched of men? Aḥmar of Thamūd[41] who slaughtered the she-camel, and the person who will strike you on this"—indicating the side of his head—"and will stain this from it,"—and he took hold of his beard.

According to Ibn Ḥumayd—Salamah—Muḥammad b. Isḥāq—Yazīd b. Muḥammad b. Khuthaym al-Muḥāribī—Muḥammad b. Kaʿb al-Quraẓī—Muḥammad b. Khuthaym, who is Abū Yazīd—ʿAmmār b. Yāsir: I and ʿAlī were companions . . . (and he gave a similar account).

A Variant Account

According to Muḥammad b. ʿUbayd al-Muḥāribī—ʿAbd al-ʿAzīz b. Abī Ḥāzim—his father: Someone said to Sahl b. Saʿd,[42] "A certain governor of Medina intends to send to you (ordering you to) abuse ʿAlī from the *minbar.*" He said, "What shall I say?" The man replied, "Say Abū Turāb." Saʿd said, "By God, nobody called him that but the Messenger of God." I said, "How was that, O Abū al-ʿAbbās?" Saʿd replied, "ʿAlī went to pay a visit to Fāṭimah, and then came out and lay down in the shadow of the mosque. When the Messenger of God went to pay a visit to Fāṭimah, he [1273]
asked her, 'Where is your cousin?' She replied, 'There he is, lying down in the mosque.' The Messenger of God went to him and found him with his cloak fallen off his back and the dust in direct contact with it. He began to wipe the dust off his back and to say, 'Sit up, Abū Turāb!' By God, nobody but the Messenger of God called him that, and, by God, he loved no name better than that."

---

41. The tribe of Thamūd is frequently mentioned in the Qur'ān as having been punished because they hamstrung a sacred camel. The perpetrator of the deed, Aḥmar (elsewhere Uḥaymir) is not named in the Qur'ān but is described as the "most wretched" (*ashqā*) of them (Qur.91.12).

42. Sahl b. Saʿd, with the *kunyah* Abū al-ʿAbbās, was a well-known Anṣārī, said to be aged fifteen in 632, who lived to be over ninety. The request to abuse ʿAlī was presumably made under the Umayyads to test whether he had Shīʿite sympathies.

ʿAlī Marries Fāṭimah

According to Abū Jaʿfar (al-Ṭabarī): In this year, a few days before the end of Ṣafar (which ended September 1, 623), ʿAlī b. Abī Ṭālib married Fāṭimah.[43] I have been told this on the authority of Muḥammad b. ʿAmr—Abū Bakr b. ʿAbd Allāh b. Abī Sabrah—Isḥāq b. ʿAbd Allāh b. Abī Farwah—Abū Jaʿfar.

Expedition of Nakhlah[44]

According to Abū Jaʿfar (al-Ṭabarī): When the Messenger of God returned to Medina from his pursuit of Kurz b. Jābir al-Fihrī in Jumādā al-Ākhirah (December 623), he sent out in Rajab (which began December 29, 623) ʿAbd Allāh b. Jaḥsh with eight men of the Emigrants without any Anṣārī among them. This was related to me by Ibn Ḥumayd—Salamah—Muḥammad b. Isḥāq—al-Zuhrī and Yazīd b. Rūmān—ʿUrwah b. al-Zubayr. As for al-Wāqidī, he asserts that the Messenger of God sent ʿAbd Allāh b. Jaḥsh (at the head of) a detachment of twelve Emigrants.

According to Ibn Isḥāq—al-Zuhrī and Yazīd b. Rūmān—
[1274] ʿUrwah: The Messenger of God wrote him (i.e., ʿAbd Allāh b. Jaḥsh) a letter, but ordered him not to look at it until he had travelled for two days. Then he was to look at it and to carry out what he was commanded in it but not to compel any of his companions to do anything against their will. When ʿAbd Allāh b. Jaḥsh had travelled two days, he opened the letter and looked at it, and it said, "When you look at my letter, march until you halt at Nakhlah, between Mecca and al-Ṭā'if. Observe Quraysh there, and find out for us what they are doing." When ʿAbd Allāh looked at the letter he said, "I heed and obey." Then he said to his companions, "The Messenger of God has commanded me to go to Nakhlah and observe Quraysh so that I can bring him news of them. He has for-

43. Different dates are given for this marriage in other sources; see *EI*², art. Fāṭimah.

44. For this expedition see IH, 423–7 and W, 13–19; also Watt, *Medina*, 5–8. The leader, ʿAbd Allāh b. Jaḥsh, was son of a maternal aunt of Muḥammad's. The reason for the sealed orders was doubtless to prevent enemy agents in Medina from learning the destination and passing on the information to Mecca. The precise location of this Nakhlah is uncertain; the road from Mecca to al-Ṭā'if runs eastwards.

bidden me to compel any of you against your will, so whoever of you wishes and desires martyrdom, let him come with me, and whoever does not, let him go back. As for myself, I am going to carry out the command of the Messenger of God." He went, and his companions went with him, and not one of them stayed behind. He made his way through Ḥijāz, until, when he was at a mine above al-Furʿ, called Buḥrān, Saʿd b. Abī Waqqāṣ and ʿUtbah b. Ghazwān lost a camel of theirs which they were taking turns to ride. They stayed behind to search for it, but ʿAbd Allāh b. Jaḥsh and the rest of his companions went on until he reached Nakhlah. A caravan of Quraysh went past him carrying raisins, leather, and other goods in which Quraysh traded. Among the Quraysh in it were ʿAmr b. al-Haḍramī, ʿUthmān b. ʿAbd Allāh b. al-Mughīrah and his brother Nawfal b. ʿAbd Allāh b. al-Mughīrah, both of the clan of Makhzūm, and al-Ḥakam b. Kaysān the *mawlā*[45] of Hishām b. al-Mughīrah (also of Makhzūm). When they saw (the Muslims) they were afraid of them, since they had halted very close to them. Then ʿUkkāshah b. Miḥṣan came into view and he had shaved his head, and when they saw him they felt safe [1275]
and said, "They are on their way to the ʿumrah (or lesser pilgrimage); there is nothing to fear from them." The (Muslims) consulted one another concerning them, this being the last day of Rajab, and said, "By God, if you leave these people alone today, they will get into the Ḥaram (the sacred territory of Mecca) and be out of your reach there; and if you kill them (today) you will have killed them in the sacred month." They hesitated and were afraid to advance upon them, but then they plucked up courage and agreed to kill as many of them as they could and to seize what they had with them. Wāqid b. ʿAbd Allāh al-Tamīmī shot an arrow at ʿAmr b. al-Ḥadramī and killed him, and ʿUthman b. ʿAbd Allāh and al-Ḥakam b. Kaysān surrendered, but Nawfal b. ʿAbd Allāh escaped and they were unable to catch him. Then ʿAbd Allāh b. Jaḥsh and his companions took the caravan and the two captives back to the Messenger of God in Medina.

---

45. At this period the *mawlā* or "client" was usually a slave, probably one captured in warfare, who had been set free. A man could also become a *mawlā* by exchanging oaths with a "patron" (also *mawlā*). Later a non-Arab convert to Islam was attached to an Arab tribe as a *mawlā*. See I. Goldziher, *Muslim Studies*, ed. S.M.Stern, London 1967, i.101–4.

Questions After the Return to Medina

Some of the family of ʿAbd Allāh b. Jaḥsh relate that he said to his companions, "The Messenger of God receives a fifth of the booty you have taken." This was before God made (surrendering) a fifth of booty taken a duty.[46] He set aside a fifth of the booty for the Messenger of God and divided the rest between his companions. When they reached the Messenger of God he said, "I did not order you to fight in the sacred month," and he impounded the caravan and the two captives and refused to take anything of it. When the Messenger of God said this they were aghast and thought that they were ruined, and the Muslims rebuked them severely for what they had done, saying to them, "You have done what you were not commanded to do, and have fought in the sacred month when you were not commanded to fight." Quraysh said, "Muḥammad and his companions have violated the sacred month and
[1276] shed blood in it, have seized property in it and taken men captive in it." Those Muslims who were (still) in Mecca refuted this, saying, "They seized what they seized in (the following month) Shaʿbān." The Jews, seeing in this (event) an omen unfavourable to the Messenger of God, said, "'ʿAmr b. al-Ḥaḍramī was killed by Wāqid b. ʿAbd Allāh. 'ʿAmr' means war is flourishing (ʿamarat); 'al-Ḥaḍramī' means war is at hand (*ḥaḍarat*); 'Wāqid b. ʿAbd Allāh' means war is set ablaze (*waqadat*)." However God turned this to their disadvantage, not their advantage, and when people began to say this frequently God revealed to His Messenger: "They question thee with regard to warfare in the sacred month. . . ."[47] When the Qur'ānic passage concerning this matter was revealed, and God relieved the Muslims from the fear in which they found themselves, the Messenger of God took possession of the caravan and the two prisoners. Quraysh sent to him to ransom

---

46. The fifth, *khums* or *khumus.* In pre-Islamic Arabia it had been customary for a tribal chief to receive a fourth of any booty taken in order to cover what he expended on behalf of the tribe. Qur. 8.41 prescribes that Muḥammad should receive a fifth and is said to have been revealed after Badr but first applied in the case of the Jewish clan of Qaynuqāʿ. See Watt. *Medina,* 232, 255. Muḥammad himself was probably not worried at the violation of a month whose sacredness was part of the pagan religion he was attacking, but he would be concerned because some of his followers had strong scruples. These scruples, however, probably got their strength from Muslim fears of Meccan reprisals.

47. Qur. 2.217.

ʿUthmān b. ʿAbd Allāh and al-Ḥakam b. Kaysān, but the Messenger of God said, "We will not release them to you on payment of ransom until our two companions (meaning Saʿd b. Abī Waqqāṣ and ʿUtbah b. Ghazwān) get back, for we are afraid that you may harm them. If you kill them, we will kill your companions." Saʿd and ʿUtbah came back, however, and the Messenger of God released the (prisoners) on payment of ransom. As for al-Ḥakam b. Kaysān, he became a Muslim, and an excellent one; he remained with the Messenger of God until he was killed as a martyr at the battle of Bi'r Maʿūnah.

Expedition of Nakhlah—Another Account

Abū Jaʿfar (al-Ṭabarī) says that al-Suddī[48] differs from both Muḥammad b. Isḥāq and al-Wāqidī on some points of this story.

According to Mūsā b. Hārūn—ʿAmr b. Ḥammād—Asbāṭ— [1277] al-Suddī: "They question thee with regard to warfare in the sacred month. Say: Warfare therein is a great (transgression), but to turn (man) from the path of Allah. . . ." This was revealed because the Messenger of God sent a detachment of seven men under the command of ʿAbd Allāh b. Jaḥsh al-Asadī, consisting of ʿAmmār b. Yāsir, Abū Ḥudhayfah b. ʿUtbah b. Rabīʿah, Saʿd b. Abī Waqqāṣ, ʿUtbah b. Ghazwān al-Sulamī the confederate of the Banū Nawfal, Suhayl b. Bayḍā', ʿĀmir b. Fuhayrah and Wāqid b. ʿAbd Allāh al-Yarbūʿī the confederate of ʿUmar b. al-Khaṭṭāb. He wrote a letter (which he gave) to Ibn Jaḥsh, ordering him not to read it until he halted at Baṭn Malal. When he halted at Baṭn Malal, he opened the letter, which read, "March until you halt at Baṭn Nakhlah." He said to his companions, "Whoever desires death, let him go on and make his will; I am making my will and acting on the orders of the Messenger of God." He went on, and Saʿd b. Abī Waqqāṣ and ʿUtbah b. Ghazwān, who had lost their riding-camel, stayed behind. They went to Buḥrān in search of it, while Ibn Jaḥsh went to Baṭn Nakhlah. Suddenly he encountered al-Ḥakam b. Kaysān, ʿAbd Allah b. Mughīrah, al-Mughīrah b. ʿUthmān, and ʿAmr b. al-Ḥaḍramī. They fought and took al-Ḥakam b. Kaysān and ʿAbd Allāh b. al-Mughīra captive, while al-

48. Well-known Qur'ān-commentator, d.128/745; see Sezgin, *GAS*, i.32f.

Mughīrah escaped and ʿAmr b. al-Ḥaḍramī was killed by Wāqid b. ʿAbd Allāh. This was the first booty taken by the companions of Muḥammad. When they returned to Medina with the two captives and the property they had taken, the people of Mecca
[1278] wanted to ransom the two captives. The Prophet said, "Let us see how our two companions fare." When Saʿd and his companion returned, he released the two captives on payment of a ransom. The polytheists spread lying slander concerning him, saying, "Muḥammad claims that he is following obedience to God, yet he is the first to violate the holy month and to kill our companion in Rajab." The Muslims said, "We killed him in (the previous month) Jumādā." Some say it was on the first night of Rajab, and some say it was on the last night of Jumādā and that the Muslims sheathed their swords when Rajab began. God revealed in rebuke of the Meccans, "They question thee with regard to warfare in the sacred month. Say: Warfare therein is a great (transgression). . . ."

Further Details About the Expedition of Nakhlah

According to Abū Jaʿfar (al-Ṭabarī): It is said that the Prophet had intended to ask Abū ʿUbaydah b. al-Jarrāḥ to lead this expedition but then thought it best to ask ʿAbd Allāh b. Jaḥsh.

According to Muḥammad b. ʿAbd al-Aʿlā—al-Muʿtamir b. Sulaymān—his father—a man—Abū al-Sawwār—Jundub b. ʿAbd Allāh: The Messenger of God sent a group of men with Abū ʿUbaydah b. al-Jarrāḥ in charge of them. When he was about to set off he wept in fervent love for the Messenger of God, so he sent another man in his place named ʿAbd Allāh b. Jaḥsh. He wrote him a letter, ordering him not to read it until he reached such-and-such a place, (and said) "Do not compel any of your companions to go with you against their will." When he read the letter he said, "Verily, we belong to God and to him we shall return," and also, "Heeding and obeying the command of God and his Messenger (is incumbent)." He told the (others) the news and read them
[1279] the letter. Two men went back and the rest went on. They met Ibn al-Ḥaḍramī and killed him, not knowing whether that day was in Rajab or Jumādā. The polytheists said to the Muslims, "You have done such-and-such in the sacred month." They came to the Prophet and told him the story, and God revealed, "They

question thee with regard to warfare in the sacred month . . ." up to ". . . for *fitnah* is worse than killing." The word *fitnah* here means polytheism.[49]

According to one of those whom I doubt: They were (several) in the expedition, and, by God, only one person killed him, and he said, "If it is a good deed, then I am responsible for it, and if it is a sin, then I do it knowingly."

---

49. *Fitnah* originally meant the assaying or testing of metals; it then came to have other meanings, such as trying to seduce. A civil war between Muslims is regularly called a *fitnah*. The phrase in the verse (Qur.2.217) probably means trying to lure men away from their religion rather than simply "polytheism."

Other Events of the Second Year of the Hijrah

The Change of Qiblah[50]

One of these is God's changing of the Muslims' Qiblah (the direction faced in prayer) from Syria (that is, Jerusalem) to the Kaʿbah. This was in the second year of the Prophet's residence in Medina, in Shaʿbān (which began January 28, 624). The early scholars disagree as to the date at which the Qiblah was changed in this year; the majority say that it was changed halfway through Shaʿbān, eighteen months after the arrival of the Messenger of God in Medina.

Those who say this.

According to Mūsā b. Hārūn al-Hamdānī—ʿAmr b. Ḥammād—Asbāṭ—al-Suddī—Abū Mālik and Abū Ṣāliḥ—Ibn
[1280] ʿAbbās and Murrah al-Hamdānī—Ibn Masʿūd and some companions of the Prophet: People used to pray towards

50. For the question of the Qiblah, the direction faced by the Muslims in prayer, cf. Watt, *Medina*, 198–202. The date, middle of Shaʿbān (about 11 February 624), is that given in most sources; but it is possible that the change followed a period of hesitation and was not made in a single day. This may explain the reports that the change took place two months earlier, presumably in Jumādā al-Ākhirah (December). The verse quoted is Qur.2.144, but the whole passage 2.142–52 deals with the question of the Qiblah, though it is difficult to relate it to the historical accounts. The change was apparently linked with Muḥammad's changing attitudes towards the Jews.

Jerusalem when the Prophet came to Medina, and for eighteen months after his Emigration. He used to raise his head to heaven when he prayed, to see what he would be commanded; he used to pray towards Jerusalem, and then this was abrogated in favour of the Ka'bah. The Prophet used to like to pray towards the Ka'bah, and God revealed the verse: "We have seen the turning of your face to Heaven . . ."

According to Ibn Ḥumayd—Salamah—Ibn Isḥāq: The Qiblah was changed in Sha'bān, eighteen months after the arrival of the Messenger of God in Medina.

Ibn Sa'd—al-Wāqidī offers a similar account, adding: The Qiblah was changed to the Ka'bah at midday on Tuesday, halfway through Sha'bān.

According to Abū Ja'far (al-Ṭabarī): Others say that the Qiblah was changed to the Ka'bah sixteen months after the beginning of the Hijrah era.

Those who have said this.

According to Al-Muthannā b. Ibrāhīm al-Āmulī—al-Ḥajjāj—Hammām b. Yaḥyā—Qatādah: They used to pray towards Jerusalem while the Messenger of God was in Mecca before the Hijrah. After the Messenger of God emigrated, he prayed towards Jerusalem for sixteen months and after that was turned towards the Ka'bah.

According to Yūnus b. 'Abd al-A'lā—Ibn Wahb—Ibn Zayd: The [1281] Prophet turned towards Jerusalem for sixteen months, and then it reached his ears that the Jews were saying, "By God, Muḥammad and his companions did not know where their Qiblah was until we directed them." This displeased the Prophet and he raised his face toward Heaven, and God said, "We have seen the turning of your face to Heaven."

Arrangements About Fasting[51]

According to Abū Ja'far (al-Ṭabarī): In this year, it is said, the fast of Ramaḍān was prescribed, and it is said that it was prescribed in

51. The Jewish fast of the 'Āshūrā' (Day of Atonement) had probably been observed by some Muslims in Medina before the Hijrah; cf. *EI*², art. 'Āshūrā' (A. J.

Sha'bān. When the Prophet came to Medina he saw the Jews fasting on the day of 'Āshūrā'. He questioned them, and they told him that it was the day upon which God drowned the people of Pharaoh and so saved Moses and those with him from them. He said, "We have a better right to Moses than they have," and he fasted and ordered people to fast with him. When the fast of Ramaḍān was prescribed, he did not order them to fast on 'Āshūrā', nor did he forbid them to do so.

In this year he commanded people to pay the *zakāt al-fiṭr*. It is said that the Prophet addressed the people one or two days before the *fiṭr* and commanded them to do this.

In this year he went out to al-Muṣallā and prayed the 'Īd prayer there.[52] This was the first occasion on which the people went out to al-Muṣallā for the 'Īd prayer.

In this year, it is said, the Staff was carried to al-Muṣallā for him and he prayed facing it. It belonged to al-Zubayr b. al-'Awwām and had been given to him by the Negus, and it was carried before him on festivals. I am informed that it is today in the custody of the muezzins in Medina.

The Battle of Badr—the Date

In this year the greater battle of Badr[53] took place between the Messenger of God and the Unbelievers of Quraysh. This was in the month of Ramaḍān. There is a difference of opinion as to the
[1282] day on which the fighting took place between them. Some say the Battle of Badr took place on 19 Ramaḍān (March 15, 624).

Those who have said this.

According to Ibn Ḥumayd—Hārūn b. al-Mughīrah—'Anbasah

Wensinck). The change to the fast of Ramaḍān is one aspect of the break with the Jews, but the precise details of the change are in dispute. The 'Āshūrā', observed on 10 Muḥarram, remains an optional feast for Muslims. The problems are discussed at length in K. Wagtendonk, *Fasting in the Koran*, Leiden 1968.

52. The *'Īd* prayer is that of *'īd al-fiṭr*, the festival of the breaking of the fast. The *zakāt al-fiṭr*, alms of the breaking of the fast, is a prescribed quantity of food to be given to needy persons not later than the day of the *'īd*. Both points imply that the fast of Ramaḍān was observed in year 2; but this is unlikely because of the expedition to Badr.

53. For the battle of Badr, see IH,427–539; W,19–174; also Watt, *Medina*, 10–13.

—Abū Isḥāq—ʿAbd al-Raḥmān b. al-Aswad—his father—Ibn Masʿūd: Make your requests (intended) for the Laylat al-Qadr[54] on the nineteenth night of Ramaḍān, for it is the night of Badr.

According to Muḥammad b. ʿUmārah al-Asadī—ʿUbayd Allāh b. Mūsā—Isrāʾīl—Abū Isḥāq—Ḥujayr al-Thaʿlabī—al-Aswad—ʿAbd Allāh: Make your requests (intended) for the Laylat al-Qadr on the nineteenth of Ramaḍān, for its morning was the morning of Badr.

According to Abū Kurayb—ʿUbayd b. Muḥammad al-Muḥāribī—Ibn Abī al-Zinād—his father—Khārijah b. Zayd—Zayd: He used not to celebrate any night of Ramaḍān like the nights of the nineteenth and twenty-third, and in the morning his face would be pale from the effects of sleeplessness. They asked him why, and he said, "On its morning, God distinguished between Truth and Falsehood."

According to others: (The battle of Badr) was on a Friday, on the morning of 17 Ramaḍān (March 13, 624).

Those who have said this.

According to Ibn al-Muthannā—Muḥammad b. Jaʿfar—Shuʿbah—Abū Isḥāq—Ḥujayr—al-Aswad and ʿAlqamah—ʿAbd Allāh b. [1283] Masʿūd: Make your requests (intended) for it (the Laylat al-Qadr) on the seventeenth, and he recited the verse: ". . . the day when the two armies met. . . ." that is, the day of Badr. Then he said, "Or on the nineteenth, or the twenty-first."

According to Al-Ḥārith—Ibn Saʿd—Muḥammad b. ʿUmar (al-Wāqidī) —al-Thawrī —al-Zubayr—ʿAdī —Ibrāhīm—al-Aswad—ʿAbd Allāh: Badr was on the morning of 19 Ramaḍān.

Al-Ḥārith—Ibn Saʿd—Muḥammad b. ʿUmar—al-Thawrī—Abū Isḥāq—al-Aswad—ʿAbd Allāh give a similar report.

According to Al-Ḥārith—Ibn Saʿd—al-Wāqidī: I mentioned this to Muḥammad b. Ṣāliḥ, and he said: "This is the most amazing thing! I never supposed that anyone in the world would doubt this! It was on the morning of 17 Ramaḍān, on Friday."

---

54. The Laylat al-Qadr (Night of Power or Decision) is spoken of in Surah L97, where it is said to be "better than a thousand months." It is popularly supposed that any prayer made on this night will be granted, but the precise date is not known. 19 Ramaḍān is only one suggestion. Cf. Wagtendonk, *Fasting,* 82–121, esp. 113.

Muḥammad b. Ṣāliḥ said to me (and I heard ʿĀṣim b. ʿUmar b. Qatādah and Yazīd b. Rūmān saying this), "O my nephew, what need have you to name authorities on this subject? This is too obvious for that. Even the women in their houses are not ignorant of this!"

Al-Wāqidī says: I mentioned it to ʿAbd al-Raḥmān b. Abī al-Zinād, and he said, "My father told me on the authority of Khārijah b. Zayd—Zayd b. Thābit: He used to celebrate the night of
[1284] 17 Ramaḍān, and in the morning the traces of sleeplessness would be on his face, and he would say, 'On this morning God distinguished between truth and falsehood, and on this morning he made Islam mighty, and on it he revealed the Qur'ān, and on it he humbled the leaders of unbelief; and the battle of Badr was on Friday.'"

According to Ibn Ḥumayd—Yaḥyā b. Wāḍiḥ—Yaḥyā b. Yaʿqūb, Abū Ṭālib—Abū ʿAwn Muḥammad b. ʿUbayd Allāh al-Thaqafī—Abū ʿAbd al-Raḥmān al-Sulamī ʿAbd Allāh b. Ḥabīb—al-Ḥasan b. ʿAlī b. Abī Ṭālib: The Laylat al-Furqān, the day when the two armies met, was on 17 Ramaḍān.[55] What provoked the Battle of Badr and the other fighting that took place between the Messenger of God and the polytheists of Quraysh, according to ʿUrwah b. al-Zubayr, was the killing of ʿAmr b. al-Ḥaḍramī by Wāqid b. ʿAbd Allāh al-Tamīmī.

The Account of the Greater Battle of Badr in the Letter of ʿUrwah[56]

According to ʿAlī b. Naṣr b. ʿAlī and ʿAbd al-Wārith b. ʿAbd al-Ṣamad b. ʿAbd al-Wārith—ʿAbd al-Ṣamad b. ʿAbd al-Wārith—his father—Abān al-ʿAṭṭār—Hishām b. ʿUrwah: ʿUrwah wrote to ʿAbd al-Malik b. Marwān as follows:

---

55. Part of Qur.8.41 is "on the day of the Furqān, the day the two armies met." The interpretation of the word *furqān* is difficult, but here it seems to mean something like "discrimination" or "deliverance"; God discriminated between believers and unbelievers, and delivered the believers. Laylat (night) has perhaps been introduced because of the relation to Laylat al-Qadr. For Furqān, see *EI*², art. Furḳān (R. Paret), and Watt, *Bell's Introduction to the Qur'ān*, Edinburgh 1970, 145–7.

56. This letter from ʿUrwah (cf.n.16) to the Umayyad caliph ʿAbd al-Malik is an important source apparently unknown to Ibn Isḥāq.

You have written to me asking about Abū Sufyān and the circumstances of his expedition. Abū Sufyān b. Ḥarb came from Syria at the head of nearly seventy horsemen from all [1285] the clans of Quraysh. They had been trading in Syria and they all came together with their money and their merchandise. The Messenger of God and his companions were informed about them. This was after fighting had broken out between them and people had been killed, including Ibn al-Ḥaḍramī at Nakhlah, and some of Quraysh had been taken captive, including one of the sons of al-Mughīrah and their *mawlā*, Ibn Kaysān. Those responsible were ʿAbd Allāh b. Jaḥsh and Wāqid, the confederate of the Banū ʿAdī b. Kaʿb, together with other companions of the Messenger of God whom he had sent out with ʿAbd Allāh b. Jaḥsh. This incident had provoked (a state of) war between the Messenger of God and Quraysh and was the beginning of the fighting in which they inflicted casualties upon one another; it took place before Abū Sufyān and his companions had set out for Syria.

Subsequently Abū Sufyān and the horsemen of Quraysh who were with him returned from Syria, following the coastal road. When the Messenger of God heard about them he called together his companions and told them of the wealth they had with them and the fewness of their numbers. The Muslims set out with no other object than Abū Sufyān and the horsemen with him. They did not think that these were anything but (easy) booty and did not suppose that there would be a great battle when they met them. It is concerning this that God revealed, "And ye longed that other than the armed one might be yours."[57]

When Abū Sufyān heard that the companions of the Messenger of God were on their way to intercept him, he sent to Quraysh (saying), "Muḥammad and his companions are going to intercept your caravan, so protect your merchandise." When Quraysh heard this, since all the clans of Kaʿb b. Lu'ayy[58] were represented in Abū Sufyān's caravan, the

57. Qur.8.7. The previous words are: "When God promised you one of the two bands (either the caravan or the armed body which came out to protect it). . . ."

58. Lu'ayy was the grandson of Quraysh (Fihr), and all the main clans of Quraysh except two were his descendants. Cf. the genealogical table, Watt, *Mecca*, 7.

[1286] people of Mecca hastened towards it. The body of men was drawn from the clans comprised in the Banū Kaʿb b. Luʾayy but did not contain any of the clan of ʿĀmir, except for some of the subclan of Mālik b. Ḥisl. Neither the Messenger of God nor his companions heard about this force from Mecca until the Prophet reached Badr, which was on the route of those horsemen of Quraysh who had taken the coastal road to Syria. Abū Sufyān then doubled back from Badr and kept to the coastal road, being afraid of an ambush at Badr.

The Prophet marched forward and spent the night near Badr. He sent al-Zubayr b. al-ʿAwwām at the head of a group of his companions to the water of Badr. They did not suppose that Quraysh had come out against them, but while the Prophet was standing in prayer some water-carriers of Quraysh suddenly came to draw water at the water of Badr. Among these water-carriers was a black slave of the Banū al-Ḥajjāj. The men whom the Messenger of God had sent with al-Zubayr to the water seized him, while some of the slave's companions escaped towards Quraysh. They brought him to the Messenger of God in his bivouac, and questioned him about Abū Sufyān and his companions, having no idea that he was not of that party. The slave began to tell them about (the protecting force of) Quraysh, which of them had set out and who their leaders were, and gave them a true account. This account, however, was the most unwelcome possible, for the only object of their expedition at the time was Abū Sufyān and his companions. Meanwhile the Prophet was praying, bowing and prostrating himself, (and also) seeing and hearing the treatment of the slave. When (the slave) told them that Quraysh had come to meet them, they began to beat him and call him a liar, saying, "You are trying to conceal the whereabouts of Abū Sufyān and his companions."
[1287] When they beat him severely and asked him about Abū Sufyān and his companions, although he had no knowledge about them and was only one of Quraysh's water-carriers he said, "Yes, this is Abū Sufyān." In fact the convoy was below them, as is referred to in the word of God: "When ye were on the near bank (of the valley) and they were on the

yonder bank, and the caravan was below you (on the coast plain). . . ." up to ". . . a thing that must be done."[59]

When the slave said to them, "This is Quraysh who have come out against you," they beat him, but when he said, "This is Abū Sufyān," they left him alone. When the Prophet saw what they were doing he left off his prayer, having heard the information which (the slave) had given them. They assert that the Messenger of God said, "By Him in Whose hand my soul rests, you beat him when he tells the truth and leave him alone when he lies." They said, "He is telling us that Quraysh have come." He replied, "He is telling the truth. Quraysh have come to protect their horsemen." He called the slave and questioned him, and the slave told him about Quraysh, and said, "I know nothing about Abū Sufyān." He asked him how many people there were, and the slave said, "By God, I do not know. There is a large number of them." They assert that the Prophet said, "Who fed them the day before yesterday?" and the slave named a man who had fed them. Then he said, "How many camels did he slaughter for them?" and the slave said, "Nine." Then he said, "Who fed them yesterday?" and the slave named a man. "How many camels did he slaughter for them?" he asked. "Ten," the slave said. They assert that the Prophet said, "There are between nine hundred and a thousand of them." The force of [1288]
Quraysh on that day was, in fact, nine hundred and fifty.

The Prophet set off and dismounted at the water. He filled up the cisterns and stationed his companions round them, waiting for the enemy to arrive. When the Messenger of God came to Badr, he said, "This is where you will fight." Thus Quraysh found that the Prophet had reached Badr before them and occupied it. When they came upon him, they assert that the Prophet said, "This is Quraysh, who have come with their hubbub and their boasting to oppose you and to show your Messenger to be a liar. O God, I ask you for what you

59. Qur.8.42. The verse asserts that the encounter between the Muslims and the armed party of Quraysh could not have happened in the normal course of events but was purposely brought about by God.

have promised me." When Quraysh advanced he met them and threw dust in their faces, and God put them to flight.[60]

Before the Prophet met the force from Mecca a horseman from Abū Sufyān and his convoy came to these and said, "Go back!"[61]—meaning that Quraysh was to withdraw while they were at al-Juḥfah. They said, "By God, we will not go back without halting at Badr and staying there for three nights so that the men of Ḥijāz who have come to us can see us, for none of the Arabs will see us and our army and dare to fight us." They are the people concerning whom God said, ". . . who came forth from their dwellings boastfully and to be seen of men."[62]

The Meccan force and the Prophet met and God gave victory to His Messenger, shamed the leaders of the unbelievers, and satisfied the Muslims' thirst for revenge on them.

Another Account

According to Hārūn b. Isḥāq—Muṣʿab b. al-Miqdām—Isrāʾīl—Abū Isḥāq[63]—Ḥārithah—ʿAlī: When we came to Medina we ate of its produce and became jaded with it and unwell from eating it.
[1289] The Messenger of God was making enquiries about Badr, and when we learnt that the polytheists had come the Messenger of God went to Badr (which is a well) and we got there before the polytheists. We found there two of them, a man of Quraysh and a *mawlā* of ʿUqbah b. Abī Muʿayṭ. As for the Qurashī, he escaped, and as for ʿUqba's *mawlā*, we took him and began to say, "How many men are there?" He said, "By God, they are many and formidable," and when he said that the Muslims began to beat him. Finally, they took him to the Messenger of God, and he said to him, "How many men are there?" He said, "By God, they are many and formidable." The Prophet tried to get him to tell him how many there were, but he refused. Then the Messenger of God

---

60. This is said to be evidence of a belief in magic, and it is claimed that Qur. 8.17 refers to it: "thou threwest not when thou didst throw but God threw"; but cf. Watt, *Medina*, 312f. (W,81 has the word *ramā* in the story.) Cf. 1322 below.

61. Omitting the words *wa-l-rakabu alladhīna* in De Goeje's text.

62. Qur. 8.47.

63. The historian Abū Isḥāq al-Sabīʿī (d. 127/745); cf. Sezgin, *GAS*, i.283.

asked him how many camels they slaughtered (for food) every day and he replied, "Ten each day." The Messenger of God said, "There are a thousand of them."

During the night there was a light drizzle, and we went under trees and leather shields to shelter from the rain there. The Messenger of God spent the night calling upon his Lord as follows: "O God, if this group perishes you will not be worshipped on earth." When dawn broke, he called out, "Come to prayer, servants of God!" and the people came from under the trees and the leather shields. The Messenger of God led us in prayer and urged us on to fight. Then he said, "The army of Quraysh is by that hillside." When they approached us and we drew ourselves up against them we suddenly saw a man on a red camel moving among them. The Messenger of God said, "ʿAlī, summon Ḥamzah to me (he was the closest to the unbelievers) and ask him who the man on the red camel is, and what he is saying to them." The Messenger of God said, "If there is anyone among them who will give them good advice, perhaps it will be the man on the red camel." Ḥamzah came [1290]
to him, and said, "It is ʿUtbah b. Rabīʿah, and he is telling them not to fight, and is saying to them, 'I see people who are determined to fight to the death. Your meeting them will not have any good outcome for yourselves. Wrap up my head, men, and say, "ʿUtbah b. Rabīʿah has turned coward"; yet you know that I am not the most cowardly of you.'"

Abū Jahl heard that and said, "Is this what you are saying? By God, if it were anyone else saying this, I would bite him! Your lungs and your belly are full of fear?" ʿUtbah replied, "Are you abusing me, you cowardly wretch? You will see today which of us is the greater coward!" Then ʿUtbah b. Rabīʿah, his brother Shaybah b. Rabīʿah, and his son al-Walīd went in front of the army in a fighting frenzy, and said, "Who will meet us in single combat?" Six young men of the Anṣār came forward, but ʿUtbah said, "We do not want these; we want some of our cousins from the sons of ʿAbd al-Muṭṭalib!"[64] The Messenger of God said, "ʿAlī, rise up! Ḥamzah, rise up! ʿUbaydah b. al-Ḥārith, rise up!" Then God killed ʿUtbah b. Rabīʿah, Shaybah b. Rabīʿah, and al-Walīd b. ʿUt-

64. Muḥammad's grandfather; but ʿUbaydah b. al-Ḥārith is from the clan of al-Muṭṭalib, which was closely associated with the clan of Hāshim.

bah, and ʿUbaydah b. al-Ḥārith was wounded, and then we killed seventy of them and took seventy of them captive.

A short man of the Anṣār brought al-ʿAbbās b. ʿAbd al-Muṭṭalib[65] captive, and the latter said, "O Messenger of God, it was not this man who took me captive, but a man with bald temples, one of the most handsome of men, on a piebald horse, whom I cannot see among your army." The Anṣārī said, "It was I who took him captive!" The Messenger of God replied, "God assisted you with a noble angel." ʿAlī said, "Of the sons of ʿAbd al-Muṭṭalib there were taken captive al-ʿAbbās, ʿAqīl, and Nawfal b. al-Ḥārith.

According to Jaʿfar b. Muḥammad al-Buzūrī—ʿUbayd Allāh b.
[1291] Mūsā—Isrā'īl—Abū Isḥāq—Ḥārithah—ʿAlī: When it was the day of Badr, and we were facing the enemy, we feared for the Messenger of God, for he was one of the most intrepid of men, and none of us was closer to the enemy than he.

According to ʿAmr b. ʿAlī—ʿAbd al-Raḥmān b. Mahdī—Shuʿbah—Abū Isḥāq—Ḥārithah b. Muḍarrib—ʿAlī: I heard him saying, "There was no horseman among us on the day of Badr except for Miqdād b. al-Aswad,[66] and I saw no one among us who was not sleeping except for the Messenger of God, who was standing by a tree praying and calling upon God until the morning."

Account of Badr by Ibn Isḥāq

According to Ibn Ḥumayd—Salamah—Muḥammad b. Isḥāq:[67] The Messenger of God heard that Abū Sufyān b. Ḥarb was coming from Syria in a great caravan belonging to Quraysh containing money and merchandise of theirs and including thirty or forty horsemen of Quraysh, among them Makhramah b. Nawfal b.

65. The Prophet's uncle. Because he was the ancestor of the ʿAbbāsid dynasty, the historians of that period tend to minimize the extent of his opposition to Muḥammad; but references such as this show that he fought with the Meccans at Badr and was taken prisoner. Cf. A. Guillaume, *The Life of Muhammad* (translation of Ibn Isḥāq), London 1955, xliv, 338n.; also 1323, 1339f., 1344, and n.101 below.

66. W, 27 says there were two horses and calls this man al-Miqdād b. ʿAmr, a confederate of the clan of Zuhrah.

67. From this point on, al-Ṭabarī gives Ibn Isḥāq's account of the battle of Badr (commencing IH, 428) with some slight additions and some omissions (cf. n. 101).

Uhayb b. ʿAbd Manāf b. Zuhrah and ʿAmr b. al-ʿĀṣ b. Wāʾil b. Hishām b. Suʿayd b. Sahm.[68]

According to Ibn Ḥumayd—Salamah—Muḥammad b. Isḥāq —Muḥammad b. Muslim al-Zuhrī and ʿĀṣim b. ʿUmar b. Qatādah and ʿAbd Allāh b. Abī Bakr and Yazīd b. Rūmān—ʿUrwah and other scholars—ʿAbd Allāh b. ʿAbbās: All of them have told me part of this narrative, and their narrative is combined in the narra- [1292]
tive I have given concerning Badr:[69] When the Messenger of God heard that Abū Sufyān was coming from Syria, he called the Muslims, both Emigrants and Anṣār, to go against them, saying, "This is the caravan of Quraysh, containing their wealth; so go out against it, and it is to be hoped that God will give it to you as booty." The people went out in answer to his urging, some eagerly and some reluctantly, as the latter did not suppose that the Messenger of God would take any booty. Abū Sufyān had been seeking information and questioning the riders whom he met as he approached Ḥijāz, being fearful for his people's wealth. Finally he received news from some riders; "Muḥammad has called his companions together to fight against you and your caravan." He was on his guard after that, and he engaged the services of Ḍamḍam b. ʿAmr al-Ghifārī and sent him to Mecca, telling him to go to Quraysh and summon them to come out to fight to protect their property, and to inform them that Muḥammad and his companions had set off to intercept the caravan. So Ḍamḍam b. ʿAmr set off swiftly to Mecca.

The Dream of ʿĀtikah, and the Relief Force

According to Ibn Ḥumayd—Salamah—Ibn Isḥāq—one whose veracity I do not doubt—ʿIkrimah the *mawlā* of Ibn ʿAbbās—Ibn ʿAbbās: also Yazīd b. Rūmān—ʿUrwah: Three days before Ḍamḍam got to Mecca, ʿĀtikah bt. ʿAbd al-Muṭṭalib had a dream which frightened her, so she sent for her brother al-ʿAbbās b. ʿAbd

---

68. Of these two men, the former became a Muslim after the capture of Mecca; the latter was converted before that event and played a prominent part in affairs as a Muslim; cf. *EI*², art. ʿAmr b. al-ʿĀṣ (A.J. Wensinck).

69. Ibn Isḥāq is speaking; he describes how he has used his sources.

al-Muṭṭalib and said to him, "Brother, last night I had a dream
[1293] which horrified me, and I am afraid that it may portend evil and affliction for your people, so keep what I am going to tell you to yourself." He said, "What did you dream?" She said, "I saw a rider coming up on his camel. He halted in the valley and shouted at the top of his voice, 'Hasten to your deaths, you people of treachery, in three days' time!' I saw the people gathering round him, then he went into the mosque with the people following him. While they were round him, his camel climbed on top of the Kaʿbah with him on its back. Then he shouted three times at the top of his voice as he had before, "Hasten to your deaths, you people of treachery, in three days' time!' Then his camel mounted to the summit of the mount of Abū Qubays with him on its back and he shouted the same thing. Then he picked up a boulder and sent it rolling down the mountain. When it reached the bottom it shattered into fragments, and a piece of it went into every house and settlement in Mecca."

Al-ʿAbbās said, "This is indeed a dream! As for you, keep it to yourself and do not mention it to anyone."

Then al-ʿAbbās went out and met al-Walīd b. ʿUtbah b. Rabīʿah, who was a friend of his. He mentioned the dream to him and asked him to keep it to himself. However al-Walīd told it to his father, ʿUtbah, and the story became public knowledge, and all Quraysh talked about it. Al-ʿAbbās said, "One morning I went to circumambulate the Kaʿbah and there was Abū Jahl b. Hishām[70] sitting with a group of Quraysh talking about ʿĀtikah's dream. When Abū Jahl saw me he said, "Abū al-Faḍl, when you have finished your circumambulation, come over to us." So when I had finished, I went over to him and sat down with them. Then Abū
[1294] Jahl said to me, "Sons of ʿAbd al-Muṭṭalib, when did this prophetess come among you?" I said, "What are you talking about?" He replied, "The dream which ʿĀtikah had." "What was that?" I asked. "Sons of ʿAbd al-Muṭṭalib," he replied, "are you not content with your men claiming to be prophets, that your women also claim to be prophets? ʿĀtikah claims that in her dream he

70. Abū Jahl of the clan of Makhzūm was about Muḥammad's age and a particularly bitter opponent; he led the force which went out to protect the caravan and was killed at Badr.

said, 'Hasten in three days' time!' We shall be watching over you for these three days, and if what she says comes true, then so be it; but if the three days go by and nothing of this comes about, we will put it in writing that your family are the greatest liars among the Arabs."

Al-ʿAbbās said, "By God, I did not make a great issue of it. I simply rebutted it and denied that she had dreamt anything." Then we separated, and by that evening there was not a woman of the family of ʿAbd al-Muṭṭalib who had not come to me and said, "Did you allow that vicious profligate to attack your men, and then go on to attack the women, while you listened to it without being outraged by what you heard?" I replied, "By God, that is what I did do—I did not make an issue of it. God's oath, I will confront him, and if he says it again, I will give you satisfaction against him." On the third day after ʿĀtikah's dream, I went out in the morning seething with rage, thinking I had missed the chance of paying him back for his words. I went into the mosque and saw him, and, by God, I went towards him to confront him and to give him the chance to repeat some of what he had said so that I could attack him—he was a slight man, with sharp fea- [1295] tures, a sharp tongue, and a sharp glance. Suddenly, however, he went out towards the gate of the mosque at a great pace. I said to myself, "What is the matter with him, God curse him! Is all of this because he is afraid that I will revile him?" In fact, however, he had heard something which I had not, the voice of Ḍamḍam b. ʿAmr al Ghifārī, who was shouting in the bottom of the wadi, standing on his camel. He had cut off his camel's nose, put his saddle on back to front, and torn his shirt, and he was saying, "O people of Quraysh, The caravan! The caravan! Your wealth is with Abū Sufyān, and Muḥammad and his companions have set off to intercept it, and I do not think you will reach it. Help! Help!"

This occurrence made me forget him and made him forget me. The people hastily equipped themselves, saying, "Do Muḥammad and his companions imagine that it will be like the caravan of Ibn al-Ḥaḍramī? No, by God; they will find otherwise!" They were divided into two groups, some setting out in person and others sending another man in their place. Quraysh went out in a body, and none of their nobles stayed behind except for Abū

Lahab b. ʿAbd al-Muṭṭalib,[71] who stayed behind and sent in his place al-ʿĀṣ b. Hishām b. al-Mughīrah. He induced the latter to do this because he owed Abū Lahab four thousand dirhams and was unable to pay him; so he hired al-ʿĀṣ for this sum to undertake the military duty in his place. Al-ʿĀṣ then went out on the expedition, while Abū Lahab stayed behind.

According to Ibn Ḥumayd—Salamah—Muḥammad b. Isḥāq—ʿAbd Allāh b. Abī Najīḥ: Umayyah b. Khalaf had decided to stay
[1296] at home, being a bulky and heavy old man. ʿUqbah b. Abī Muʿayṭ came to him while he was sitting in the mosque among his people carrying a brazier with fire and aloes-wood in it. He put it before him and said, "Scent yourself, Abū ʿAlī, for you are one of the women." He replied, "May God disgrace you and that which you have brought!" Then he equipped himself and went out with the others.

When they had finished equipping themselves and had decided to set out, they remembered the state of war which existed between them and the Banū Bakr b. ʿAbd Manāt b. Kinānah,[72] and said, "We are afraid that they may attack us from the rear."

According to Ibn Ḥumayd—Salamah—Muḥammad b. Isḥāq and Yazīd b. Rūmān—ʿUrwah b. al-Zubayr:[73] When Quraysh had decided to set out, they remembered the quarrel between them and the Banū Bakr. This almost caused them to go back, but Iblīs manifested himself to them in the form of Surāqah b. Juʿshum al-Mudlijī, who was one of the nobles of Kinānah. He said, "I will guarantee you security against any unwelcome attention from Kinānah." So they went off speedily.

The Number of Muslims at Badr

According to Abū Jaʿfar (al-Ṭabarī): The Messenger of God went out, as I have been informed by authorities other than Ibn Isḥāq, on 3 Ramaḍān (February 28, 624) at the head of over three hundred and ten of his companions. There is a difference of opinion as

71. The Prophet's uncle, who is denounced in Surah 111; cf. 1339 below.
72. An important section of the nomadic tribe of Kinānah with grounds to the west of Mecca; cf. Watt, *Medina*, 62f., 81–4.
73. This follows IH, 432.

to how many more than (three hundred and) ten there were. Some say there were three hundred and thirteen men.

Those who say this. [1297]

According to Abū Kurayb—Abū Bakr b. 'Ayyāsh—Abū Isḥāq—al-Barā': We used to relate that the people of Badr on the day of Badr were like the number of people of Saul,[74] three hundred men and thirteen men who crossed the river. The account ends at this point.

According to Muḥammad b. 'Ubayd al-Muḥāribī—Abū Mālik al-Janbī—al-Ḥajjāj—al-Ḥakam—Miqsam—a 'Abbās: The Emigrants on the day of Badr were seventy-seven men, and the Anṣār were two hundred and thirty-six men. The banner of the Messenger of God was carried by 'Alī b. Abī Ṭālib and the banner of the Anṣār was carried by Sa'd b. 'Ubādah.

According to Ibn Ḥumayd—Salamah—Ibn Isḥāq[76]: Those who were present, took part[75] in it, and reaped its reward were three hundred and fourteen men.

According to others: They were three hundred and eighteen.

Still others claim they were three hundred and seven. As for most of the early scholars, they (merely) say that there were over three hundred and ten men.

Those who say this.

According to Hārūn b. Isḥāq—Muṣ'ab b. al-Miqdām and Aḥmad b. Isḥāq al-Ahwāzī—Abū Aḥmad al-Zubayrī—Isrā'īl—Abū Isḥāq—al-Barā': We used to relate that the number of the people of Badr was the same as the number of the people of Saul who crossed the river with him; and nobody crossed with him but believers, over three hundred and ten of them. [1298]

According to Ibn Bashshār—Abū 'Āmir—Sufyān—Abū Isḥāq

---

74. Saul, king of Israel, is mentioned in the Qur'ān as Ṭālūt. The story to which reference is made here is to be found in al-Mas'ūdī, *Murūj al-dhahab*, ed. and tr. C. Barbier de Meynard and Pavet de Courteille, Paris 1861, i.102. Al-Mas'ūdī speaks of 313 men, but there seems to be some confusion with the story of Gideon and his 300 men in *Judges* 7.

75. Reading *ḍaraba* not *ḍaruba*.

76. IH, 506, after giving a complete list of names, concludes that there were 83 Emigrants and 231 of the Anṣār, or 314 in all.

—al-Barā': We used to relate that the companions of the Prophet on the day of Badr were over three hundred and ten, the same as the number of the people of Saul who crossed the river, and none but believers crossed with him.

Ibn Wakī'—his father—Sufyān—Abū Isḥāq—al-Barā' give a similar account.

According to Ismā'īl b. Isrā'īl al-Ramlī—'Abd Allāh b. Muḥammad b. al-Mughīrah—Mis'ar—Abū Isḥāq—al-Barā': The number of the people of Badr was the number of the people of Saul.

Aḥmad b. Isḥāq—Abū Aḥmad—Mis'ar—Abū Isḥāq—al-Barā' give a similar account.

According to Bishr b. Mu'ādh—Yazīd—Sa'īd—Qatādah: We were told that the Prophet of God said to his companions on the day of Badr: "You are the same number as the people of Saul on the day that he met Goliath." The companions of the Prophet of God on the day of Badr were over three hundred and ten men.

[1299] According to Mūsā b. Hārūn—'Amr b. Ḥammād—Asbāṭ—al-Suddī: Saul had over three hundred and ten men, the same number of people as the people of Badr.

According to Al-Ḥasan b. Yaḥyā—'Abd al-Razzāq—Ma'mar—Qatādah: There were with the Prophet on the day of Badr over three hundred and ten men.

The Advance of the Muslims to Badr

Resumption of the narrative of Ibn Isḥāq.[77]

When several days of Ramaḍān had passed, the Messenger of God went out at the head of his companions, putting Qays b. Abī Ṣa'ṣa'ah, the brother of the Banū Māzin b. al-Najjār, in charge of the rearguard. He himself went ahead, and when he was near al-Ṣafrā' he sent Basbas b. 'Amr al-Juhanī—the confederate of the Banū Sā'idah (of the Anṣār)—and 'Adī b. Abī al-Zaghbā' al-Juhanī—the confederate of the Banū al-Najjār (of the Anṣār)—to Badr, in order to glean information for him about Abū Sufyān b. Ḥarb and his caravan. Then the Messenger of God, having sent them on in advance, continued his march. When he got to al-Ṣafrā', which is

77. IH, 433f.

a village between two mountains, he asked the names of its two mountains. They said, "One of them is called Musliḥ and the other is called Mukhri'." He asked about the people who lived in them, and they said, "The Banū al-Nār and the Banū Ḥurāq, two clans of the Banū Ghifār." The Messenger of God took a dislike to these mountains and to passing between them, regarding their names and the names of their inhabitants as an evil omen,[78] so leaving them and al-Ṣafrā' to his left, he went to the right along a valley called Dhafirān. When he had gone part way along it, he came out of it and halted. Here he received news that Quraysh had marched to protect their caravan. The Prophet consulted the people and told them about Quraysh. Abū Bakr stood up and spoke well; then 'Umar b. al-Khaṭṭāb stood up and spoke well; then al-Miqdād b. 'Amr stood up and said, "O Messenger of God, carry on as God has commanded you, and we, by God, are with you; we will not say, as the Children of Israel said to Moses, 'Go thou and thy Lord and fight! We will sit here,'[79] but we will say, 'Go thou and thy Lord and fight! We will fight with thee.' By him who sent you with the truth, if you led us to Bark al-Ghimād[80] (meaning the town in Abyssinia), we would fight with you against those who stood in our way until you reached it." The Messenger of God replied, "Well said!"—and prayed for blessings for him. [1300]

According to Muḥammad b. 'Ubayd al-Muḥāribī—Ismā'īl b. Ibrāhīm Abū Yaḥyā—al-Mukhāriq—Ṭāriq—'Abd Allāh b. Mas'ūd: I saw something in al-Miqdād as a result of which I would rather be his companion than anything else in the world. He was a man who could read people's faces; when the Messenger of God was angry, his cheeks grew red, and so al-Miqdād came to him when he was in this condition and said, "Rejoice, O Messenger of God! We will not say to you, as the Children of Israel said to Moses, 'Go then and thy Lord and fight! We will sit here,' but, by him who sent you with the truth, we will be before you and behind [1301]

78. *Musliḥ* and *mukhri'* both mean "defecating"; *nār* is "fire" and *ḥurāq* "burning."

79. Qur.5.24.

80. This is said to be a place five nights' journey beyond Mecca towards the sea, or a town in the Yemen, or in the furthest part of the region of Hajar (eastern Arabia).

you, on your right hand and on your left hand, until God gives you victory!"

Resumption of the narrative of Ibn Isḥāq.[81]

Then the Messenger of God said, "Advise me, people," meaning by this the Anṣār, for they were the bulk of his force. The reason for this was that, when they had sworn allegiance to him at al-ʿAqabah,[82] they had said, "O Messenger of God, we are exempt from having to protect you until you reach our dwelling-place, but when you reach us, you will be under our protection, and we will protect you as we would our children and our womenfolk." The Messenger of God was afraid that the Anṣār might not consider themselves obliged to come to his aid except against those of his enemies who attacked him at Medina, nor might they consider themselves obliged to let him lead them out of their own territory against an enemy.

When the Messenger of God said this, Saʿd b. Muʿādh said to him, "By God, you seem to mean us, O Messenger of God." "Yes," he replied. "We have believed in you and accepted that what you say is true," Saʿd replied, "and we have testified that the message you have brought is the truth, and we have given you our word and covenant to that effect, to heed and to obey; so proceed
[1302] as you wish, O Messenger of God, and by him who sent you with the truth, if you lead us headlong to that sea and plunge into it, we will plunge into it with you and not a single man will lag behind. We are not unwilling for you to meet the enemy with us tomorrow; we are steadfast in war and true in battle. It may be that God means to show you something through us which will gladden your heart, so lead us with God's blessing."

The Messenger of God was gladdened by Saʿd's reply, and it filled him with vigour. Then he said, "March, with God's blessing, and rejoice, for God has promised me one of the two opposing parties. By God, I seem to be looking at the slaughtered enemy now!"

Then the Messenger of God set out from Dhafirān and went through the mountain passes called al-Aṣāfir. Then he descended

81. IH, 434–8.
82. Cf. IH, 296f.; Watt, *Mecca*, 144–9.

from them to a village called al-Dabbah, leaving al-Ḥannān (which is a huge sand dune as big as a mountain) to the right. Then he camped near Badr.

According to Ibn Ḥumayd—Salamah—Muḥammad b. Isḥāq—Muḥammad b. Yaḥyā b. Ḥibbān: The Messenger of God and one of his companions rode to an Arab shaykh and asked him what he had heard about Quraysh and about Muḥammad and his companions. The shaykh said, "I will not tell you until you tell me which side you are from." The Messenger of God replied, "If you tell us, [1303] we will tell you." "The one for the other?" he asked. "Yes," he said. The shaykh said, "I have heard that Muḥammad and his companions set out on such-and-such a date, and if the person who told me was telling the truth, he is today at such-and-such a place—naming the place where the Messenger of God in fact was—and I have heard that Quraysh set out on such-and-such a date, and if the person who told me was telling the truth, they are today at such-and-such a place—naming the place where Quraysh in fact were." When he had finished giving this information, he said, "Which side are you from?" The Messenger of God replied, "We are from water," and then left, while the shaykh was saying, "What do you mean, from water? From the water of Iraq?"

Then the Messenger of God went back to his companions, and the next morning he sent ʿAlī b. Abī Ṭālib, al-Zubayr b. al-ʿAwwām and Saʿd b. Abī Waqqāṣ and a few of his companions to the water of Badr to reconnoitre it for him, according to Ibn Ḥumayd—Salamah—Muḥammad b. Isḥāq—Yazīd b. Rūmān—ʿUrwah b. al-Zubayr. They came across a party of water-carriers from Quraysh there, including Aslam, a slave of the Banū al-Ḥajjāj, and ʿArīḍ Abū Yasār, a slave of the Banū al-ʿĀṣ b. Saʿīd, and took them to the Messenger of God. The Messenger of God was standing praying, so the companions questioned the slaves. They said, "We are water-carriers of Quraysh, who have sent us to get water for them from the water." This was unwelcome news to the companions, as they had hoped that the slaves belonged to [1304] Abū Sufyān; so they beat them, and when they had weakened them the slaves said, "We belong to Abū Sufyān," and were left alone.

The Messenger of God bowed and prostrated himself twice,

then greeted the companions and said, "When the slaves tell you the truth you beat them, and when they lie to you you leave them alone. By God, they are telling the truth, they belong to Quraysh. Tell me, where are Quraysh?" They replied, "They are behind that sand dune which you can see on the far bank." (The sand dune was al-ʿAqanqal.) The Messenger of God said to them, "How many men are there?" They replied, "A lot." He said, "How many?" "We do not know," they replied. "How many camels do they slaughter every day?" he asked. "Nine or ten a day," they replied. The Messenger of God said, "They are between nine hundred and a thousand." Then the Messenger of God said to them, "Which of the nobles of Quraysh are among them?" They replied, "ʿUtbah b. Rabīʿah, Shaybah b. Rabīʿah, Abū al-Bakhtarī b. Hishām, Ḥakīm b. Ḥizām, Nawfal b. Khuwaylid, al-Ḥārith b. ʿĀmir b. Nawfal, Ṭuʿaymah b. ʿAdī b. Nawfal, al-Naḍr b. al-Ḥārith b. Kaladah, Zamʿah b. al-Aswad, Abū Jahl b. Hishām, Umayyah b. Khalaf, Nubayh and Munabbih the sons of al-Ḥajjāj, Suhayl b.
[1305] ʿAmr, and ʿAmr b. ʿAbd Wudd." The Messenger of God turned to the people and said, "Here Mecca has flung its dearest flesh and blood to you!"[83]

Basbas b. ʿAmr and ʿAdī b. Abī al-Zaghbāʾ had gone ahead and stopped at Badr. They halted their camels by a hillock near the water and took an old water-skin to fetch water. Majdī b. ʿAmr al-Juhanī was at the water, and ʿAdī and Basbas heard two slave girls belonging to the settled inhabitants discussing a debt at the water. The first said to the second, "The caravan will come tomorrow or the day after. I will work for them, and then I will pay you what I owe." Majdī said, "That's right," and then separated them. ʿAdī and Basbas heard this, mounted their camels and left. They came to the Messenger of God and told him what they had heard.

Abū Sufyān Takes Evasive Action

Abū Sufyān came in advance of the caravan as a precaution and arrived at the water. He said to Majdī b. ʿAmr, "Have you noticed

83. The list includes most of the leading men of Mecca apart from the older generation. For details see Watt, *Mecca, Medina*, index.

anyone?" He replied, "I have not seen anyone I do not know, except that I saw two riders who halted their camels by that hillock, filled their water-skin with water, and left." Abū Sufyān went to the place where they had halted their camels, picked up some of the camels' droppings, and crumbled them; they contained datestones. "By God," he said, "This is the camel fodder of Yathrib!"[84] He went back hastily to his companions, turned his caravan away from that road, and took the coastal route, leaving Badr on his [1306] left. Then he set off with all speed.

The Advance of Quraysh

Meanwhile Quraysh were advancing. They halted at al-Juḥfah, where Juhaym b. al-Ṣalt b. Makhramah b. al-Muṭṭalib b. ʿAbd Manāf had a dream. He said, "I was between sleep and wakefulness when I had a dream. I saw a man coming on a horse. Then he stopped, and he had a camel with him. Then he said, 'ʿUtbah b. Rabīʿah, Shaybah b. Rabīʿah, Abū al-Ḥakam b. Hishām, Umayyah b. Khalaf, and so-and-so and so-and-so—enumerating nobles of Quraysh who were killed on that day—have been killed.' Then I saw him stab his camel's chest and send it off into the camp, and there was not a single tent in the camp which it did not sprinkle with its blood."

Abū Jahl heard of this dream, and said, "This is yet another prophet from the clan of al-Muṭṭalib. He will know tomorrow who is killed, if we meet in battle."

When Abū Sufyān saw that he had assured his caravan's safety, he sent to Quraysh saying, "You only came out to protect your caravan, your men, and your property. God has kept them safe, so [1307] go back." But Abū Jahl b. Hishām said, "By God! We will not go back until we have reached Badr—Badr was the location of one of the Arab festivals; every year a market was held there—spent three days there, slaughtered camels, given food to eat and wine to drink, and had our singing girls perform there, so that the Arabs may hear of what we have done and continue to hold us in

84. Since Yathrib (Medina) was an oasis, its camels could be fed on dates. The two scouts were actually nomads of the tribe of Juhaynah, as was also Abū Sufyān's scout, Majdī b. ʿAmr.

awe. Go ahead!" Al-Akhnas b. Sharīq b. ʿAmr b. Wahb al-Thaqafī,[85] who was a confederate of the Banū Zuhrah, who were at al-Juḥfah, said, "O Banū Zuhrah, God has saved your property and rescued your companion Makhramah b. Nawfal. You only came out to defend him and his property, so let any charge of cowardice rest on my shoulders and go back; for there is no need for you to take the field except in the defence of property. Ignore what this man is saying," meaning Abū Jahl. So they went back, and not one of the clan of Zuhrah took part in the battle, since his word was law among them.

There was not a clan of Quraysh from which some men did not go out (to Badr), except for the Banū ʿAdī b. Kaʿb, from whom not a single man had gone out. Since the Banū Zuhrah had gone back with al-Akhnas b. Sharīq, nobody from those two clans was present at Badr. The rest went on.

[1308] Words were exchanged between Ṭālib b. Abī Ṭālib,[86] who was with the army, and some of Quraysh, who said, "By God, Banū Hāshim, we know that your sympathies are with Muḥammad, even if you have come out with us," and so Ṭālib was among those who returned to Mecca.

According to Abū Jaʿfar (al-Ṭabarī): As for Ibn al-Kalbī,[87] among the narratives I was told on his authority is the following: Ṭālib b. Abī Ṭālib set out for Badr with the polytheists. He was sent out against his will, and he was not among the captives, nor the dead, and he did not return to his family. He was a poet, and he is the one who said:

> O Lord, if Ṭālib goes on an expedition in one of these defiles
> Let him be plundered, not the plunderer, conquered not the conqueror.

---

85. Although he was a confederate belonging to the tribe of Thaqīf in al-Ṭāʾif, he appears to have been the leading man in the clan of Zuhrah in Mecca at this time; he may have been related to them matrilineally. Cf. Watt, *Mecca*, index.

86. Muḥammad's cousin, son of his uncle and guardian Abū Ṭālib, who was now dead.

87. Hishām b. Muḥammad, known as Ibn al-Kalbī, was a well-known scholar of pre-Islamic and early Islamic affairs; cf. *EI*², art. (al-)Kalbī, II.

Resumption of the narrative of Ibn Isḥāq.[88]

Quraysh went on and halted on the further bank of the wadi behind al-ʿAqanqal. The bed of the wadi (which is called Yalyal) lies between Badr and al-ʿAqanqal, the sand dune behind which were Quraysh, and the wells at Badr are on the bank of the Yalyal which is nearer to Medina. God had sent rain, and the wadi-bed was soft; the effect of the rainfall as far as the Messenger of God and his companions were concerned was to compact the ground without impeding their movement, but its effect on Quraysh was that they were not able to set off because of it. So the Messenger of God set out to get to the water before them, and when he got to [1309]
the nearest well of Badr he halted.

According to Ibn Ḥumayd—Salamah—Muḥammad b. Isḥāq—some men of the Banū Salimah: Al-Ḥubāb b. al-Mundhir b. al-Jamūḥ[89] said, "O Messenger of God, do you consider that this is a position in which God has placed you, and that it is not for us to move it forward or back, or do you consider that it is a matter of judgement, tactics and stratagem?" He replied, "Certainly not; it is a matter of judgement, tactics and stratagem." Then al-Ḥubāb b. al-Mundhir b. al-Jamūḥ said, "O Messenger of God, this is not the proper position for you. Arise with your men and go to the nearest well to the enemy. Halt there and then fill in the other wells. Then build a cistern next to it and fill it with water. Then we will fight the enemy and have water to drink while they do not." The Messenger of God said, "You have given judicious advice." Then the Messenger of God and the men who were with him arose and went to the well nearest to the enemy and halted there. Then he gave orders to fill in the other wells, and to build a cistern next to the well at which he had halted. This was filled [1310]
with water and then they drew water from it in their drinking vessels.

According to Ibn Ḥumayd—Salamah—Muḥammad b. Isḥāq—ʿAbd Allāh b. Abī Bakr: Saʿd b. Muʿādh said, "O Messenger of God, let us build you a shelter of stripped palm branches, in which you

---

88. IH, 439–41.

89. This man, of the clan of Salimah, appears to have been the leader of the Khazraj at Badr but is not specially prominent in later events.

can remain, and we will keep your riding-camels ready by you. Then we will meet our enemy, and if God gives us strength and grants us victory over our enemy, that will be as we would wish; and if it turns out otherwise, you can mount on your riding-camels and join those of our people who are left behind us (in Medina), for there remain behind from your expedition, O Prophet of God, many people who love you just as greatly as we do, and would not have remained behind from your expedition if they had thought that you would become involved in fighting. God will defend you by means of them, and they will give you good advice and strive along with you."

The Messenger of God praised him greatly and prayed for God's blessings on him. Then a shelter was built for the Messenger of God and he stayed in it.

At dawn Quraysh had set out and advanced, and when the Messenger of God saw them moving down from al-ʿAqanqal, which is the sand dune from which they came, to the wadi, he said, "O God, here come Quraysh in their arrogance and their pride, opposing you and calling your Messenger a liar. O God, give me the aid which you have promised me. O God, destroy them this morning."

When the Messenger of God saw ʿUtbah b. Rabīʿah among the
[1311] enemy on his red camel he said, "If there is good in any of the enemy, it is in the man on the red camel. If they obey him, they will be rightly guided."

Preparations and Discussions of Quraysh

Khufāf b. Aymāʾ b. Raḥḍah al-Ghifārī, or his father Aymāʾ b. Raḥḍah[90] sent his son with a present of some slaughter-camels to Quraysh, as they passed by him, and added, "If you would like me to reinforce you with arms and fighting men, I will do so." They sent a message back to him by his son, saying, "You have discharged the duties of kinship and done what was incumbent upon you. By my life, if we are fighting against men, we are not too

90. The small nomadic tribe of Ghifār was reckoned a part of Bakr b. ʿAbd Manāt, but some members seem to have been friendly to Quraysh.

weak to deal with them, and if we are fighting God, as Muḥammad claims, nobody has any power against God."

When Quraysh halted, a number of them advanced until they reached the cistern of the Messenger of God; among them was Ḥakīm b. Ḥizām, riding his horse. The Messenger of God said, "Let them drink." Every man who drank was killed that day, with the exception of Ḥakīm b. Ḥizām. He escaped on his horse called al-Wajīh, and later became a Muslim, and a very good one. When he wanted to swear a very forcible oath, he would say, "No, [1312]
by him who saved me on the day of Badr."

According to Ibn Ḥumayd—Salamah—Muḥammad b. Isḥāq and Isḥāq b. Yasār and other scholars—some shaykhs of the Anṣār: When the enemy army had settled down, they sent ʿUmayr b. Wahb al-Jumaḥī, saying, "Estimate Muḥammad's numbers for us." So he circled the camp on his horse and then went back to them, saying, "Three hundred men, give or take a few, but give me a little more time so that I can see if they have any men lying in ambush or any reserves." He then rode about in the wadi for a considerable distance, but he could not see anything. He went back to them and said, "I could not see anything, but I saw, O people of Quraysh, saddlecloths carrying doom, the water-camels of Yathrib carrying certain death. The enemy are people who do not have any safe refuge or retreat except their swords. By God, I do not think a man of them will be killed until he has killed a man of you, and if they kill as many of you as there are of them, what will be the good of life after that? So decide as you think fit."

When Ḥakīm b. Ḥizām heard that, he went on foot among the [1313]
army to ʿUtbah b. Rabīʿah and said, "Abū al-Walīd, today you are a great man of Quraysh, their chief and obeyed among them. Would you like to continue to be remembered by them with gratitude to the end of time?" "How will I achieve that, Ḥakīm?" he asked. "Take the people back with you," he said, "and take upon yourself the responsibility for the blood of your confederate ʿAmr b. al-Ḥaḍramī." "I will do so," he replied. "You are my witness in this. He was my confederate, and it is for me to seek compensation for his killing and for the property of his which was taken. So go to Ibn al-Ḥanẓaliyyah (meaning Abū Jahl b. Hishām), for I do not fear that anyone else will dispute the matter."

According to Al-Zubayr b. Bakkār—ʿImāmah b. ʿAmr al-Sahmī—Musawwar b. ʿAbd al-Malik al-Yarbūʿī—his father—Saʿīd b. al-Musayyab: While we were with Marwān b. al-Ḥakam[91] his chamberlain came in and said, "Abū Khālid Ḥakīm b. Ḥizām is here." "Admit him," he said. When Ḥakīm b. Ḥizām came in he said, "Welcome, Abū Khālid! Come close." Then Marwān left his place at the head of the *majlis* until he was halfway between him and the cushion. Then Marwān welcomed him and said, "Tell us the story of Badr." He said, "We went out and halted at al-Juḥfah. Then one of the clans of Quraysh left in their entirety, and not
[1314] one of their polytheists was present at Badr. Then we went on and halted on the bank which is mentioned by God.[92] I went to ʿUtbah b. Rabīʿah and said, 'Abū al-Walīd, would you like to win the honour of this day as long as you live?' 'What must I do?' he asked. 'You want nothing from Muḥammad but restitution for the blood of Ibn al-Ḥaḍramī' I said, 'for he was your confederate; so take upon yourself the responsibility for his blood-money, and take the people back to Mecca with you.' 'I will do as you say,' he said. 'I will take upon myself the responsibility for his blood-money. Go to Ibn al-Ḥanẓaliyyah (meaning Abū Jahl) and say, "Would you and those with you be prepared to retreat from your cousin today?"'

"So I went to him, and saw him in a group of people in front of him and behind him. Suddenly I beheld Ibn al-Ḥaḍramī[93] standing at his head and saying, 'I take the responsibility for avenging me away from the clan of ʿAbd Shams and give it to the clan of Makhzūm.' So I said to him, 'ʿUtbah b. Rabīʿah says to you, "Would you and those with you be prepared to retreat from your cousin today?"' Abū Jahl said to me, 'Could he find no other emissary but you?' I replied, 'No, and I have no intention of being an emissary for anybody except him.' I went out hastily to ʿUtbah (Ḥakīm continued) in order not to miss any of the story. ʿUtbah was leaning on Aymāʾ b. Raḥḍah al-Ghifārī, who had given ten slaughter-camels to the polytheists, when Abū Jahl appeared with malice

91. A prominent member of the clan of Umayyah, probably governor of Medina at the time of this incident. He became caliph in 64/684 but died about ten months later and was succeeded by his son ʿAbd-al-Malik.
92. Qur. 8.42, "when ye were on the near bank (of the valley). . . ."
93. ʿĀmir b. al-Ḥaḍramī, brother of the man killed at Nakhlah.

all over his face, and said to ʿUtbah, 'Your lungs are inflated with fear.' 'You will soon find out,' retorted ʿUtbah. Abū Jahl drew his sword and slapped his horse's back with it, and Aymāʾ b. Raḥḍah said 'This is an evil omen.' Thereupon the battle began." [1315]

Resumption of the narrative of Ibn Isḥāq.[94]

Then ʿUtbah b. Rabīʿah rose up to give a speech. "O people of Quraysh," he said, "you will achieve nothing by meeting Muḥammad and his companions in battle. By God, if you defeat him you will not be able to look one another in the face without loathing, for you will see someone who has killed the son of your paternal or maternal uncle, or a man from your clan. Go back, and leave Muḥammad to the rest of the Arabs. If they kill him, that will be what you want, and if not he will find that you have not done to him what you would have liked to do (and will respect you for it)."

"I left," said Ḥakīm, "to go to Abū Jahl, and I found him preparing his coat of mail which he had removed from its bag. 'Abū al-Ḥakam,' I said to him, "ʿUtbah has sent me to you to tell you such-and-such (repeating what he had said).' 'By God!' he replied, 'his lungs were inflated with fear when he saw Muḥammad and his companions. No, by God, we will not go back until God gives the decision either for us or for Muḥammad and his companions. What is really troubling ʿUtbah is not what he says, but the fact [1316]
that he sees Muḥammad and his companions so few in number that one slaughtered camel would suffice them. His son is among them, and he is afraid of you for his sake.'

"Then he sent to ʿĀmir b. al-Ḥaḍramī and said to him, 'This confederate of yours wants to take the army back at a time when you see your revenge before your eyes; so rise and remind them of your covenant and your brother's murder.' So ʿĀmir b. al-Ḥaḍramī rose and uncovered himself; then he shouted out, 'Alas for ʿAmr! Alas for ʿAmr!' Then the zeal for battle grew intense, and they were ruined. They agreed upon the evil course on which they were set, and the counsel which ʿUtbah b. Rabīʿah had urged upon them was wasted on them.

"When ʿUtbah b. Rabīʿah heard that Abū Jahl had said, 'His

94. IH, 441–4.

lungs are inflated with fear,' he said, 'That cowardly wretch will find out whose lungs are inflated with fear, mine or his!' Then he asked for a helmet to put on his head, but he could not find a helmet in the army to fit him because his head was so big. When he saw this, he wrapped a striped cloth he had round his head."

The Fighting Begins

In the expedition was al-Aswad b. ʿAbd al-Asad al-Makhzūmī, who was a quarrelsome and bad-natured man. He now said, "I make a covenant with God that I will drink from their cistern and will destroy it, or will die in the attempt." When he took the field, Ḥamzah b. ʿAbd al-Muṭṭalib came out to meet him, and in the encounter Ḥamzah struck him and cut off his foot together with half his leg before he had reached the cistern. He fell on his back with blood gushing from his leg toward his companions.
[1317] Then he crawled toward the cistern and flung himself into it, intending[95] to fulfil his oath; but Ḥamzah followed him and struck him a blow which killed him in the cistern.

After this, ʿUtbah b. Rabīʿah took the field, between his brother Shaybah b. Rabīʿah and his son al-Walīd b. ʿUtbah. When he had drawn clear of the battle line, he issued a challenge to single combat. Three young men of the Anṣār came forward to meet him, ʿAwf and Muʿawwidh, sons of al-Ḥārith with ʿAfrāʾ for their mother,[96] and another man called ʿAbd Allāh b. Rawāḥah. The Meccans said, "Who are you?" and the three young men replied, "A group of the Anṣār." "We have no business with you," the Meccans said. Then their herald called out, "Muḥammad, send out people of our rank from our tribe!" The Messenger of God said, "Ḥamzah b. ʿAbd al-Muṭṭalib, rise; ʿUbaydah b. al-Ḥārith, rise; ʿAlī b. Abī Ṭālib, rise." When they arose and approached the three Meccans, the latter said, "Who are you?" ʿUbaydah said "ʿUbaydah," Ḥamzah said, "Ḥamzah," and ʿAlī said "ʿAlī." The Meccans said, "Yes, these are noble equals." ʿUbaydah b. al-

95. Omitting *zaʿama*.
96. Each of these two (and a third brother) was commonly known as "Ibn ʿAfrāʾ," perhaps a relic of the former matrilineal kinship system. See Watt, *Medina*, 166, 378, etc.

Ḥārith, who was the oldest of the Muslims, engaged ʿUtbah b. Rabīʿah in single combat, Ḥamzah engaged Shaybah b. Rabīʿah, and ʿAlī engaged al-Walīd b. ʿUtbah. It was no time before Ḥamzah had killed Shaybah, and ʿAlī had killed al-Walīd. ʿUbaydah and ʿUtbah, however, each inflicted a blow upon his adversary which disabled him. Ḥamzah and ʿAli then turned upon ʿUtbah [1318] with their swords and finished him off, and lifted up their companion ʿUbaydah and brought him to his companions. His foot had been cut off and the marrow was flowing out. When they brought ʿUbaydah to the Messenger of God he said, "Am I not a martyr, O Messenger of God?" "Yes indeed," Muḥammad replied. "If Abū Ṭālib were alive," said ʿUbaydah, "he would know that I am more worthy than he of his line of verse when he says:

> We keep him safe until we are struck down around him,
> and forget our sons and our wives."

According to Ibn Ḥumayd—Salamah—Muḥammad b. Isḥāq—ʿĀṣim b. ʿUmar b. Qatādah: ʿUtbah b. Rabīʿah said to the young men of the Anṣār when they gave their lineages, "Noble equals! But we only want men of our own tribe!"

The armies then advanced and drew near to one another. The Messenger of God had ordered his companions not to attack until he gave the command, and he had said, "If they approach you, keep them at a distance from you with a hail of arrows." The Messenger of God remained in the shelter with Abū Bakr.

According to Abū Jaʿfar (al-Ṭabarī)—Ibn Ḥumayd—Salamah—Muḥammad b. Isḥāq—Abū Jaʿfar Muḥammad b. ʿAlī b. al-Ḥusayn: The Battle of Badr was on Friday morning, 17 Ramaḍān (March 13, 624).

According to Ibn Ḥumayd—Salamah—Muḥammad b. Isḥāq [1319] —Ḥibbān b. Wāsiʿ b. Ḥibbān b. Wāsiʿ—some shaykhs of his people: The Messenger of God straightened the ranks of his companions on the day of Badr with an arrow which he had in his hand. As he passed by Sawād b. Ghaziyyah, the confederate of the Banū ʿAdī b. al-Najjār, who was standing forward from the line in his eagerness to fight, the Messenger of God poked him in the stomach with the arrow and said, "Get into line, Sawād b. Ghaziyya." "O Messenger of God," he said, "you have hurt me! God has sent

you with the truth, so allow me to retaliate!" The Messenger of God uncovered his stomach and said, "Take your retaliation!" Sawād embraced him and kissed his stomach. "What induced you to do that, Sawād?" he asked. "O Messenger of God," he replied, "you see the situation we are in. I was not sure that I would not be killed, and I wanted my last recollection of you to be that my skin had touched yours." The Messenger of God prayed for his welfare and encouraged him. After straightening the ranks, the Messenger of God went back to the shelter and entered it. Abū Bakr was there with him but nobody else. The Messenger of God was calling on his Lord to grant him the aid which he had promised him, saying, among other things, "O God, if this band of people perishes today (meaning the Muslims), you will not be worshipped after today." Abū Bakr was saying, "O Prophet of
[1320] God, do not call upon your Lord so much; for God will assuredly fulfil what he has promised you."

According to Muḥammad b. ʿUbayd al-Muḥāribī—ʿAbd Allāh b. al-Mubārak—ʿIkrimah b. ʿAmmār—Simāk al-Ḥanafī—Ibn ʿAbbās—ʿUmar b. al-Khaṭṭāb: When it was the day of Badr, and the Messenger of God looked at the polytheists and their number, and then looked at his companions, who were something over three hundred, he turned toward the Qiblah and began to pray, saying, "O God, fulfil what you have promised me. O God, if this band of Muslims perishes, you will not be worshipped on the earth." He continued to say this until his cloak fell off. Abū Bakr picked it up and put it back on him, then grasped him from behind and said, "O Prophet of God, whom I value more than my father and mother, this is enough of calling upon your Lord. He will assuredly fulfil what he has promised you." Then God revealed, "When ye sought help of your Lord and he answered you (saying): I will help you with a thousand of the angels, rank on rank."[97]

According to Ibn Wakīʿ—al-Thaqafī (meaning ʿAbd al-Wahhāb) —Khālid—ʿIkrimah—Ibn ʿAbbās: The prophet said when he was in his awning on the day of Badr, "O God, I ask you to keep your contract and your promise. O God, if you so wish, you will not be worshipped after today." Abū Bakr took his hand and said, "This is enough, O Prophet of God. You have tired your Lord with your

97. Qur. 8.9.

importuning." He was in his coat of mail, and he went out saying, "The hosts will all be routed and will turn and flee. Nay, but the Hour (of doom) is their appointed tryst, and the Hour will be more wretched and more bitter (than this earthly failure)."[98]

Resumption of the narrative of Ibn Isḥāq.[99]

The Messenger of God slept a light sleep in the shelter for a while; then he awoke and said, "Abū Bakr, God's aid has come to you. Here is Gabriel, taking hold of the reins of his horse and leading it, and there is dust on its front teeth." [1321]

Mihja', the *mawlā* of 'Umar b. al-Khaṭṭāb, was struck by an arrow and killed. He was the first Muslim to be killed. Then Ḥārithah b. Surāqah, one of the Banū 'Adī b. al-Najjār, was struck by an arrow as he was drinking at the cistern and was killed. Then the Messenger of God went out to his men and urged them to battle. He promised every man that he could keep all the booty he took, and then said, "By him in whose hands Muḥammad's soul rests, if any man fights them today and is killed, fighting steadfastly and with resignation, going forward and not turning back, then God will cause him to enter Paradise." 'Umayr b. al-Ḥumām, the brother of the Banū Salimah, who was holding some dates in his hand and eating them, said, "Excellent! All that stands between me and entering Paradise is being killed by these people!" Then he threw down the dates, took his sword, and fought the enemy until he was killed, reciting the following lines:

> I hasten to God without provision except fear of God
> and working for the Hereafter
> And patience in God in the struggle, for every other
> provision is liable to be exhausted
> Except for fear of God, piety and right guidance.

According to Ibn Ḥumayd—Salamah—Muḥammad b. Isḥāq —'Āṣim b. 'Umar b. Qatādah: 'Awf b. al-Ḥārith, known as Ibn 'Afrā', said, "O Messenger of God, what makes the Lord laugh [1322]

98. Qur. 54.45f.

99. IH, 444–64. In this, al-Ṭabarī follows Ibn Isḥāq closely, though he has a short passage from another source on p.1328. He has also retained from Ibn Isḥāq passages about the capture of al-'Abbās (1340, 1344) which are omitted from Ibn Hishām's recension of Ibn Isḥāq in the form in which we have it; see n.65.

with joy at his servant?" He replied, "Plunging his hand into the enemy without armour." So he took off a coat of mail he was wearing and threw it away; then he took his sword and fought the enemy until he was killed.

According to Ibn Ḥumayd—Salamah—Muḥammad b. Isḥāq—Muḥammad b. Muslim b. Shihāb al-Zuhrī—ʿAbd Allāh b. Thaʿlabah b. Ṣuʿayr al-ʿUdhrī the confederate of the Banū Zuhrah: When the armies met and drew close to one another, Abū Jahl said, "O God, whichever of us has severed the ties of kinship more, and has committed more unacceptable acts, destroy him today." He was thus asking God to give the victory against himself.

Then the Messenger of God picked up a handful of gravel and faced Quraysh with the words, "May their faces be deformed!"[100] Then he threw it at them, and ordered his companions to attack. A rout followed, in which God killed many chiefs of Quraysh and caused many of their nobles to be taken captive. While the Muslims were taking captives, the Messenger of God was in his shelter. Saʿd b. Muʿādh was standing at the door, girt with his sword, along with a few of the Anṣār, guarding the Messenger of God, since they were afraid that the enemy would wheel round and attack him. The Messenger of God, I have been told, saw in the face
[1323] of Saʿd b. Muʿādh disapproval of what the people were doing, and said, "It seems, Saʿd, that you disapprove of what the people are doing." "Yes, by God, O Messenger of God," he replied. "This was the first defeat inflicted by God on the polytheists, and killing the prisoners would have been more pleasing to me than sparing them."

According to Ibn Ḥumayd—Salamah—Muḥammad b. Isḥāq—al-ʿAbbās b. ʿAbd Allāh b. Maʿbad—a member of his family—Ibn ʿAbbās: The Messenger of God said to his companions that day, "I know that some of the Banū Hāshim and others have been forced to march against us against their will, having no desire to fight us. Whoever of you meets one of the Banū Hāshim, let him not kill him; whoever meets Abū al-Bakhtarī b. Hishām b. al-Ḥārith b. Asad, let him not kill him; whoever meets al-ʿAbbās b.

100. See 1288 above and n.60.

ʿAbd al-Muṭṭalib, the uncle of the Messenger of God,[101] let him not kill him, for he has been forced to march against us against his will."

Abū Ḥudhayfah b. ʿUtbah b. Rabīʿah[102] said, "Are we to kill our fathers, our sons, our brothers, and our clansmen, and leave al-ʿAbbās alone? By God, if I meet him I will hack him with my sword!" These words reached the Messenger of God, and he said to ʿUmar b. al-Khaṭṭāb, "Abū Ḥafṣ, have you heard what Abū Ḥudhayfah says? He says, 'I will strike the face of the uncle of the Messenger of God with my sword!'" ʿUmar said, "O Messenger of God, give me permission and I will cut off his head with my sword. By God, he is a Hypocrite!" In later times ʿUmar used to say, "By God, that was the first day on which the Messenger of [1324]
God addressed me by the name Abū Ḥafṣ."

Abū Ḥudhayfah used to say, "I never felt safe afterwards on account of those words which I spoke that day, and I continued to be afraid because of them, but hoped that martyrdom might expiate them." He was killed as a martyr on the day of al-Yamāmah.[103]

The Messenger of God forbade the killing of Abū al-Bakhtarī because he used to restrain the people from harming the Messenger of God while he was still in Mecca. He himself neither injured him nor caused him any unpleasantness; and he was one of those who were active in cancelling the document[104] which Quraysh drew up against the Banū Hāshim and the Banū al-Muṭṭalib.

He was met by al-Mujadhdhar b. Dhiyād al-Balawī, the confederate of the Banū ʿAdī of the Anṣār.[105] Al-Mujadhdhar b. Dhiyād said to Abū al-Bakhtarī, "The Messenger of God has forbidden us to kill you." Abū al-Bakhtarī had a fellow rider with him, who had come with him from Mecca, whose name was Junādah b. Mulayḥah bt. Zuhayr b. al-Ḥārith b. Asad. Junādah was a member of the Banū Layth, and Abū al-Bakhtarī's full name was al-ʿĀṣ b.

---

101. See 1290 above and n.65.

102. Abū Ḥudhayfah was of the clan of ʿAbd Shams, and his father and several other kinsmen were among those killed at Badr.

103. The fierce battle in 12/633 in which the false prophet Musaylimah was defeated.

104. The so-called "boycott" of the clans of Hāshim and al-Muṭṭalib; cf. Watt, *Mecca*, 120–2.

105. Of the tribe of Balī; IH, 446, says he was a confederate of the clan of Sālim b. ʿAwf.

Hishām b. al-Ḥārith b. Asad. He replied, "And my fellow rider?" Al-Mujadhdhar said, "No, by God. We will not spare your fellow rider. The Messenger of God only gave us orders about you." "No, by God," he replied. "Then he and I will die together. The women of Quraysh in Mecca will not relate of me that I abandoned my fellow rider in my greed for life." As he was engaged by al-Mujadhdhar and insisted on fighting, Abū al-Bakhtarī recited the following lines of *rajaz*:

[1325] The son of a noble woman will not surrender the man who shares his food
Until he dies or sees his (friend's) way (clear).

In the combat between the two he was killed by al-Mujadhdhar b. Dhiyād.

Then al-Mujadhdhar b. Dhiyād went to the Messenger of God and said, "By him who sent you with the truth, I tried to make him give himself up so that I could bring him to you, but he insisted on fighting, and I fought him and killed him."

According to Ibn Ḥumayd—Salamah—Muḥammad b. Isḥāq—Yaḥyā b. 'Abbād b. 'Abd Allāh b. al-Zubayr—his father: also 'Abd Allāh b. Abī Bakr and others (than he and Yaḥyā)—'Abd al-Raḥmān b. 'Awf: Umayyah b. Khalaf was a friend of mine in Mecca. My name was 'Abd 'Amr, but when I became a Muslim I was called 'Abd al-Raḥmān.[106] Umayyah used to meet me when we were in Mecca and would say, "'Abd 'Amr, do you dislike the name your father gave you?" I would reply, "Yes." He would then say, "I do not recognise al-Raḥmān, so find some name that I can call you by when we meet. You do not answer to your old name, and I will not call you by something I do not recognise." When he called me 'Abd 'Amr, I would refuse to answer him. At length I said to him, "You suggest whatever name you like for our use, Abū 'Alī." He said, "Well then, you are 'Abd al-Ilāh."[107] I agreed.

106. Omitting the words *wa-naḥnu bi-Makkah*.

107. The form 'Abd 'Amr, "servant (or slave) or 'Amr," implies that 'Amr was a pagan deity, and for this reason this name and several others were changed by Muḥammad. Nothing has been recorded, however, of any such deity; but it might conceivably be a secondary name or epithet of a deity known by some other name. The pagan Umayyah rejects Raḥmān as a name of the one God. 'Abd al-Ilāh means "servant of the god," and could be understood as either polytheistic or monotheistic. Cf. J. Wellhausen, *Reste arabischen Heidentums*^{2}, Berlin 1897, 1–9.

After that when I passed him, he would say "'Abd al-Ilāh!"—and I would answer him and talk with him. On the day of Badr I passed him as he was standing with his son 'Alī b. Umayyah, holding his hand. I had with me some coats of mail which I had taken as plunder, which I was carrying, and when he saw me he said, [1326]
"'Abd 'Amr!"—so I did not answer him. Then he said, "'Abd al-Ilāh!"—and I said, "Yes." "Would you like to take me (as prisoner)?" he asked. "I will be more use to you than those coats of mail which you are carrying." I said, "Yes! Come here then." I flung away the coats of mail and took his hand and his son 'Alī's hand while he said, "I have never seen a day like this. Have you no need for milk?"[108] Then I left, taking the two of them with me.

According to Ibn Ḥumayd—Salamah—Muḥammad b. Isḥāq—'Abd al-Wāḥid b. Abī 'Awn—Sa'd b. Ibrāhīm b. 'Abd al-Raḥmān b. 'Awf—his father—'Abd al-Raḥmān b. 'Awf: Umayyah b. Khalaf said to me, while I was between him and his son, holding them by the hands, "'Abd al-Ilāh, who is that man in your army wearing an ostrich feather on his chest as a mark of identification?" I said, "That is Ḥamzah b. 'Abd al-Muṭṭalib." He said, "He is the one who wrought such havoc on us." 'Abd al-Raḥmān continued: And, by God, while I was leading them, Bilāl[109] saw him with me. It was Umayyah who used to torture Bilāl in Mecca in an attempt to make him abandon Islam. He used to take him out to the sun-baked ground of Mecca when it was scorching hot and make him lie down on his back. Then he would order a huge boulder to be placed on his chest, and then he would say, "You will stay like this until you leave the faith of Muḥammad." Bilāl would say, "God is one, God is one." When he saw Umayyah [1327]
Bilāl said, "The head of disbelief, Umayyah b. Khalaf! May I not be spared, if they are spared!" I said, "Bilāl, would you harm my captives?" "May I not be spared, if they are spared!" he replied. "Do you hear what I am saying, son of the black woman?" I asked. "May I not be spared if they are spared!" he said. Then he shouted at the top of his voice, "O Helpers of God, the head of disbelief, Umayyah b. Khalaf! May I not be spared if he is spared!"

108. He is referring to the fact that the ransom will be paid in milch-camels.

109. Bilāl was an Abyssinian slave, tortured to make him renounce Islam (IH, 205), and ransomed by Abū Bakr. He was the first muezzin.

People surrounded us and placed us under a kind of restraint, while I was trying to protect Umayyah. One man struck his son, who fell down. Umayyah gave a scream the like of which I have never heard. I said, "Save yourself, for there is no escape (for him).[110] By God, I cannot do anything for you." Then they hacked at them with their swords until they had finished with them. ʿAbd al-Raḥmān used to say, "May God have mercy on Bilāl! I lost my coats of mail, and he deprived me of my captives."

According to Ibn Ḥumayd—Salamah—Muḥammad b. Isḥāq—ʿAbd Allāh b. Abī Bakr—Ibn ʿAbbās—a man from the Banū Ghifār: I and a cousin of mine went and mounted a hill from which we could overlook Badr (we were polytheists then) to await the outcome of the battle and see who would be defeated, so that we could join in the plundering afterwards. While we were on the
[1328] hill a cloud approached us. We heard the neighing of horses in it, and I heard a voice saying, "Forward, Ḥayzūm!"[111] As for my cousin, the covering of his heart split open, and he died on the spot; as for myself, I almost perished, but then pulled myself together."

According to Ibn Ḥumayd—Salamah—Muḥammad b. Isḥāq—his father Isḥāq b. Yasār—some men of the Banū Māzin b. al-Najjār—Abū Dā'ūd al-Māzinī, who was present at Badr: I was pursuing one of the polytheists on the day of Badr in order to strike him, when his head suddenly fell off before my sword touched him. Then I knew that someone other than I had killed him.

According to ʿAbd al-Raḥmān b. ʿAbd Allāh b. ʿAbd al-Ḥakam al-Miṣrī—Yaḥyā b. Bukayr—Muḥammad b. Yaḥyā al-Iskandarānī—al-ʿAlā' b. Kathīr—Abū Bakr b. ʿAbd al-Raḥmān b. al-Miswar b. Makhramah—Abū Umāmah b. Sahl b. Ḥunayf: My father said to me, "My son, I saw us Muslims on the day of Badr, and saw that one of us would wave his sword at a polytheist, and the man's head would fall from his body before the sword touched him."

According to Ibn Ḥumayd—Salamah—Muḥammad b. Isḥāq—al-Ḥasan b. ʿUmārah—al-Ḥakam b. ʿUtaybah—Miqsam the

110. Adding *bi-hi* with IH.
111. The angel Gabriel's horse; for angelic help cf. Qur. 8.9,12.

mawlā of ʿAbd Allāh b. al-Ḥārith—ʿAbd Allāh b. ʿAbbās: The sign of the angels on the day of Badr was white turbans which trailed down their backs, and on the day of Ḥunayn it was red turbans. The angels did not fight on any day except the day of Badr; on the [1329] other days they were assistants and helpers, but they struck no blows.

Abū Jahl and Other Meccan Dead

According to Ibn Ḥumayd—Salamah—Muḥammad (ibn Isḥāq) —Thawr b. Zayd the *mawlā* of the Banū al-Dīl—ʿIkrimah the *mawlā* of Ibn ʿAbbās—Ibn ʿAbbās: also ʿAbd Allāh b. Abī Bakr: Muʿādh b. ʿAmr b. al-Jamūḥ the brother of the Banū Salimah used to say, "When the Messenger of God had finished with his enemy, he gave orders that Abū Jahl should be searched for among the dead, and said, 'O God, let him not have escaped you!'" The first man who encountered Abū Jahl was Muʿādh b. ʿAmr b. al-Jamūḥ, who said, "Abū Jahl was in a sort of thicket and I heard the people saying, 'We cannot get at Abū al-Ḥakam.' When I heard this, I made him my mark, and I made my way toward him. When he was within my reach, I attacked him and struck him a blow which severed his foot and half his leg. By God, when it flew [1330] off I could only compare it to a date-stone which flies out of a date-stone crusher when it is struck.

"Then his son ʿIkrimah struck me on the shoulder and struck off my arm, which dangled at my side from a piece of skin. The fighting prevented me from reaching him after that. I fought the whole day, dragging my arm behind me. When it began to hurt me, I put my foot on it and stood on it until I pulled it off." Muʿādh survived this wound and lived until the caliphate of ʿUthmān b. ʿAffān.

Then Muʿawwidh b. ʿAfrāʾ passed by Abū Jahl, who was now crippled, and struck him until he could no longer move, leaving him at his last gasp. Then Muʿawwidh fought until he was killed. ʿAbd Allāh b. Masʿūd[112] passed by Abū Jahl when the Messenger of God ordered that he should be searched for among the slain; the

112. One of the earliest Muslims and a client of the Meccan clan of Zuhrah; he later became an authority on the Qurʾān. Cf. *EI*², art. Ibn Masʿūd (J. Vadet).

Messenger of God had said to them, I have been told, "If you cannot identify him among the dead, look for the mark of a wound on his knee, for I jostled against him at a feast given by ʿAbd Allāh b. Judʿān[113] when we were boys. I was a little thinner than he was, and I pushed him, so that he fell on his knees and got a scratch on one of them, the mark of which never went away." ʿAbd Allāh b. Masʿūd said, "I found Abū Jahl at his last gasp and recognised him, and put my foot on his neck. He had grabbed hold of me once at Mecca and had hurt me and punched me. Then I said,
[1331] 'Has God disgraced you, O enemy of God?' 'In what way has he disgraced me?' he replied. 'Am I anything more important than a man whom you have killed? Tell me, to whom is the victory?' I said, 'To God and his Messenger.'"

According to Ibn Ḥumayd—Salamah—Muḥammad b. Isḥāq: Some men of the Banū Makhzūm assert that Ibn Masʿūd used to say, "Abū Jahl said to me, 'You have ascended a difficult ascent, you little shepherd.' Then I cut off his head and brought it to the Messenger of God, and I said, 'O Messenger of God, this is the head of the enemy of God, Abū Jahl.' Then the Messenger of God said, 'Is this so, by God, than whom there is no other deity?' This was the oath of the Messenger of God. I said, 'Yes, by God, than whom there is no other deity.' Then I threw down his head in front of the Messenger of God. He said, 'Praise be to God!'"

According to Ibn Ḥumayd—Salamah—Muḥammad b. Isḥāq and Yazīd b. Rūmān—ʿUrwah b. al-Zubayr—ʿĀ'isha: When the Messenger of God ordered the dead to be thrown into the well, all were thrown into it, except Umayyah b. Khalaf. He had swollen up in his coat of mail and filled it. They went to move him, but he fell apart, so they left him where he was and flung upon him enough earth and stones to cover him. When he threw the dead into the well, the Messenger of God stood over them and said, "O people of the well, have you found what your Lord promised you to be true? For I have found what my lord promised me to be
[1332] true." His companions said to him, "O Messenger of God, are you speaking to dead people?" He replied, "They know (*laqad ʿalimū*) that what I promised them is the truth." ʿĀ'ishah said, "Other

113. A prominent man in Mecca at an earlier period; cf. Watt, *Mecca*, index.

people report this saying with the words *laqad samiʿū* (they hear), but the Messenger of God said *'laqad ʿalimū.'"*

According to Ibn Ḥumayd—Salamah—Muḥammad b. Isḥāq—Ḥumayd al-Ṭawīl—Anas b. Mālik: The companions of the Messenger of God heard the Messenger of God saying in the depths of the night, "O people of the well, O ʿUtbah b. Rabīʿah, O Shaybah b. Rabīʿah, O Umayyah b. Khalaf, O Abū Jahl b. Hishām—and he enumerated those who were with them in the well—have you found what your Lord promised you to be true? For I have found what my Lord promised me to be true." The Muslims said, "O Messenger of God, are you addressing people who have putrefied?" He replied, "You hear what I say no better than they, but they cannot answer me."

According to Ibn Ḥumayd—Salamah—Muḥammad b. Isḥāq—certain scholars: The Messenger of God, on the day on which he uttered these words, also said, "O people of the well, you were evil fellow tribesmen to your prophet! You disbelieved me, when other people believed me. You drove me out, when other people gave me shelter. You fought me, when other people came to my aid." Then he added, "Have you found what your Lord promised you to be true?" . . . and the rest.

When the Messenger of God ordered the dead to be thrown into [1333]
the well, ʿUtbah b. Rabīʿah was taken and dragged to the well. As I have been informed, the Messenger of God looked into the face of his son Abū Ḥudhayfah b. ʿUtbah, which was dejected and altered, and said, "Abū Ḥudhayfah, perhaps some sadness has entered you on account of your father," or words to that effect. "No, by God, O Messenger of God," he replied. "I had no doubts about my father, nor about his death. But I knew my father to be a judicious, forbearing, and virtuous man, and I used to hope that these qualities would lead him to Islam. When I saw what had happened to him and remembered the state of unbelief in which he died, after the hopes which I had had for him, it saddened me." The Messenger of God prayed for his welfare and encouraged him.

The Division of the Booty

Then the Messenger of God gave orders concerning the contents of the camp which the people had collected, and it was all brought together. Among the Muslims, however, there was a difference of opinion concerning it. Those who had collected it said, "It is ours. The Messenger of God promised every man that he could keep the booty he took." Those who were fighting and pursuing the enemy said, "If it had not been for us, you would not have taken it. We distracted the enemy from you so that you could take what you took." Those who were guarding the Messenger of God for fear that the enemy would attack him said, "By God, you have no better right to it than we have. We wanted to kill the enemy when God gave us the opportunity and made them turn their backs, and we wanted to take property when there was no one to protect it; but we were afraid that the enemy might wheel round and attack the Messenger of God, so we remained standing before him; you have no better right to booty than we have."

According to Ibn Ḥumayd—Salamah—Muḥammad b. Isḥāq
[1334] —ʿAbd al-Raḥmān b. al-Ḥārith and other companions of ours—Sulaymān b. Mūsā al-Ashdaq—Makḥūl—Abū Umāmah al-Bāhilī: I asked ʿUbādah b. al-Ṣāmit about (*Sūrat*) *al-Anfāl* (8). He replied, "It was revealed concerning us, the participants in the battle of Badr, when we disagreed about the booty and became very bad-tempered about it. God removed it from our hands and handed it over to his Messenger, and the Messenger of God divided it equally among the Muslims. In this matter there can be seen fear of God, obedience to his Messenger, and the settling of differences."

The Return of the Muslims to Medina

After the victory, the Messenger of God sent ʿAbd Allāh b. Rawāḥah to take the good news that God had given the victory to his Messenger and the Muslims to the people of the upper part (of Medina), and he sent Zayd b. Ḥārithah to the people of the lower part. Usāmah b. Zayd said,[114] "The news came to us when we had buried Ruqayyah, the daughter of the Messenger of God, who was married to ʿUthmān b. ʿAffān. The Messenger of God had left me to look after her together with ʿUthmān. Then Zayd b. Ḥārithah

114. Usāmah, the son of Muḥammad's adopted son, Zayd b. Ḥārithah, was possibly only about eleven at this time.

arrived so I went to him. He was standing in al-Muṣallā surrounded by people, and he was saying, "ʿUtbah b. Rabīʿah has been killed, and Shaybah b. Rabīʿah, Abū Jahl b. Hishām, Zamʿah b. al-Aswad, Abū al-Bakhtarī b. Hishām, Umayyah b. Khalaf, and Munabbih and Nubayh, the sons of al-Ḥajjāj.' I said, 'Father, is this true?' 'Yes, by God, my son,' he replied."

Then the Messenger of God came back to Medina, bringing with him the booty which had been taken from the polytheists. In charge of the booty he put ʿAbd Allāh b. Kaʿb b. Zayd b. ʿAwf b. Mabdhūl b. ʿAmr b. Māzin b. al-Najjār. Then he himself ad- [1335] vanced, halting when he had emerged from the defile of al-Ṣafrā' at a sand dune called Sayar between the defile and al-Nāziyah beside a *sarḥ* tree. There he divided equally the booty which God had bestowed upon the Muslims from the polytheists. After water had been brought to him from the spring there called al-Arwāq, he travelled on. When he was at al-Rawḥā', the Muslims met him, congratulating him and the Muslims with him on the victory which God had given them.

According to Ibn Ḥumayd—Salamah—Muḥammad b. Isḥāq—ʿĀṣim b. ʿUmar b. Qatādah and Yazīd b. Rūmān: Salamah b. Salāmah b. Waqsh said, "What are they congratulating us on? By God, we met nothing but bald old women like hobbled sacrificial camels, so we slaughtered them." The Messenger of God smiled and said, "My nephew, those were the *mala'*."[115]

The polytheist captives were with the Messenger of God, and there were forty-four of them. There was a similar number of dead.[116] Among the captives were ʿUqbah b. Abī Muʿayṭ and al-Naḍr b. al-Ḥārith b. Kaladah,[117] but when the Messenger of God was at al-Ṣafrā' he had al-Naḍr b. al-Ḥārith killed by ʿAlī b. Abī Ṭālib.

According to Ibn Ḥumayd—Salamah—Muḥammad b. Isḥāq—one of the scholars of the people of Mecca: Then the Messenger [1336] of God went on, and when he was at ʿIrq al-Ẓabyah he killed ʿUq-

115. The council or senate of Mecca; cf. Watt, *Mecca*, 8f.

116. Ibn Isḥāq has lists which give the numbers as 50 dead and 43 prisoners (IH, 511, 515); but Ibn Hishām adds further names which bring the totals to 70 dead and 70 prisoners.

117. Of the Meccan clan of ʿAbd al-Dār; he had produced Persian stories which he claimed were as good as those in the Qur'ān

bah b. Abī Muʿayṭ. When the Messenger of God ordered him to be killed, ʿUqbah said, "Who will look after my children, Muḥammad?" 'Hellfire," Muḥammad replied. He was killed by ʿĀṣim b. Thābit b. Abī al-Aqlaḥ al-Anṣārī, a member of the Banū ʿAmr b. ʿAwf. As I was informed by Abū ʿUbaydah b. Muḥammad b. ʿAmmār b. Yāsir, when the Messenger of God reached ʿIrq al-Ẓabyah and killed ʿUqbah b. Abī Muʿayṭ, he was met by Abū Hind, the *mawlā* of Farwah b. ʿAmr al-Bayāḍī with a butter-skin full of *ḥays* (ground dates mixed with butter). He had stayed away from Badr, but afterwards he was present at all the other battles with the Messenger of God; he was the Messenger of God's cupper.[118] The Messenger of God said, "Abū Hind is truly a man of the Anṣār, so relate yourselves to him by marriage," and they did so. Then the Messenger of God went on, reaching Medina a day before the captives.

According to Ibn Ḥumayd—Salamah—Muḥammad b. Isḥāq —ʿAbd Allāh b. Abī Bakr—Yaḥyā b. ʿAbd Allāh b. ʿAbd al-Ra-
[1337] ḥmān b. Asʿad[119] b. Zurārah: When the captives were brought in, Sawdah bt. Zamʿah, the wife of the Prophet, was with the family of ʿAfrāʾ participating in their mourning for her sons ʿAwf and Muʿawwidh. This was before the veil had been imposed on women. Sawdah used to say, "By God, I was with them when someone came to us and said, 'Here are the captives who have been brought.' I went to my house," she said, "and the Messenger of God was there, and there was Abū Yazīd Suhayl b. ʿAmr[120] at one side of the room with his hands tied to his neck with a rope. By God," she said, "I could not restrain myself, when I saw Abū Yazīd like that, from saying, 'Abū Yazīd, did you surrender yourself? Why did you not choose an honourable death?' By God, it was only the voice of the Messenger of God coming from the house saying, 'Sawdah, (are you saying) this against God and to his Messenger?' which brought me back to myself. 'O Messenger

---

118. Cupping as a medical treatment to draw blood was popular with the Arabs.

119. IH, 459, reads Asʿad, the well-known brother of Saʿd; but the editor of al-Ṭabarī says that Asʿad had no sons.

120. Of the Meccan clan of ʿĀmir (to which Sawdah belonged), and brother of her former husband. He was prominent in the resistance to Muḥammad in the years preceding the conquest of Mecca, but afterwards became a good Muslim; cf. Watt, *Medina*, index.

of God,' I said, 'by him who sent you with the truth, when I saw Abū Yazīd with his hands tied to his neck with a rope I could not restrain myself from saying what I said.'"

According to Ibn Ḥumayd—Salamah b. al-Faḍl—Muḥammad b. Isḥāq—Nubayh b. Wahb, the brother of the Banū 'Abd al-Dār: When the Messenger of God came with the captives he divided them up among his companions, saying, "Look after the captives well." Abū 'Azīz b. 'Umayr b. Hāshim, the brother of Muṣ'ab b. 'Umayr by his father and his mother, was among the captives. Abū 'Azīz said, "My brother Muṣ'ab b. 'Umayr passed by me while a man of the Anṣār had me captive, and said, 'Hold on to him tight, for his mother has property and she may ransom him from you.' I was in a group of the Anṣār when they brought me [1338] from Badr. When they took their lunch and their supper, they gave me bread in preference to themselves while they ate dates, because the Messenger of God had enjoined them concerning us, 'No crust of bread will fall into the hands of any one of them, but that he will reward me for it.' I would feel ashamed and give it back to one of them, but he would return it to me without touching it."

News of Defeat Reaches Mecca

According to Ibn Ḥumayd—Salamah—Muḥammad b. Isḥāq: The first person to reach Mecca with news of the defeat of Quraysh was al-Ḥaysumān b. 'Abd Allāh b. Iyās b. Ḍubay'ah b. Māzin b. Ka'b b. 'Amr al-Khuzā'ī. (According to Abū Ja'far (al-Ṭabarī), Al-Wāqidī says his name was al-Ḥaysumān b. Ḥābis al-Khuzā'ī.) "What has happened?" they asked. He said, "'Utbah b. Rabī'ah has been killed, and also Shaybah b. Rabī'ah, Abū al-Ḥakam b. Hishām, Umayyah b. Khalaf, Zam'ah b. al-Aswad, Abū al-Bakhtarī b. Hishām, and Nubayh and Munabbih, the sons of al-Ḥajjāj." When he started to enumerate the nobles of Quraysh, Ṣafwān b. Umayyah, who was sitting in the Ḥijr, said, "By God, if this man is in his right mind, question him about me." "What happened to Ṣafwān b. Umayyah?" they asked. "There he is sitting in the Ḥijr," he said, "and by God, I saw his father and his brother when they were killed."

According to Ibn Ḥumayd—Salamah—Muḥammad b. Isḥāq

[1339] —Ḥusayn b. ʿAbd Allāh b. ʿUbayd Allāh b. ʿAbbās—ʿIkrimah the *mawlā* of Ibn ʿAbbās: Abū Rāfiʿ, the *mawlā* of the Messenger of God, said, "I was a slave of al-ʿAbbās b. ʿAbd al-Muṭṭalib, and Islam had entered us, the *Ahl al-Bayt* ("the people of the house," that is, Muḥammad's extended family). Umm al-Faḍl[121] became a Muslim, and I became a Muslim. Al-ʿAbbās was afraid of his people and was unwilling to oppose them, and he concealed the fact that he had become a Muslim. He had much property which was dispersed among his people. Abū Lahab, the enemy of God, had not gone to Badr and had sent in his place al-ʿĀṣ b. Hishām b. al-Mughīrah; this is what they did—no man stayed away without sending another man in his place. When the news of the disaster which befell Quraysh at Badr came, God humbled and disgraced Abū Lahab, while we felt strength and might in our souls.

"I was a weak man, and I used to make arrows, which I would smooth in the enclosure of Zamzam.[122] By God, I was sitting there smoothing arrows, and Umm al-Faḍl was sitting there with me, both of us overjoyed by the news we had received, when the evildoer Abū Lahab approached, dragging his feet in malice. He sat down by the guy rope of the enclosure, so that his back was to my back. While he was sitting there the people said, 'Here is Abū Sufyān b. al-Ḥārith b. ʿAbd al-Muṭṭalib who has just arrived.' Abū Lahab said, 'Come over here, my nephew, for you have news.' He sat down next to him while the others stood around him. Then Abū Lahab said, 'My nephew, tell me, what happened to our people?' 'Nothing, by God,' he replied, 'except that we met them and
[1340] turned our backs, while they killed us and took us captive as they saw fit. Even so, I swear by God, I do not blame our people. We met white-robed men on piebald horses, between heaven and earth, for which we were no match and which nothing could resist."

"I lifted the guy rope of the enclosure with my hand and said, 'Those were the angels.' Abū Lahab raised his hand and gave me a violent blow on the face. I rushed at him but he picked me up and threw me to the ground and then knelt on me and beat me, for I was a weak man. Umm al-Faḍl went to one of the tent poles of

121. The wife of al-ʿAbbās.
122. A well near the Kaʿbah.

the enclosure, picked it up and gave him a blow which split his scalp open and made an unpleasant wound. Then she said, 'You treat him arrogantly when his master is absent!' He got up and turned away humiliated. By God, he only lived for seven days before God afflicted him with pustules from which he died.[123] His two sons left him for two or three days without burying him until he began to stink in his house, for Quraysh were as afraid of pustules and their infectiousness as people are afraid of the plague. Finally, a man of Quraysh said to them, 'Woe to you! Are you not ashamed that your father is stinking in his house and you do not bury him?' 'We are afraid of those ulcers,' they said. 'Go, and I will come with you,' he said. They did not wash his corpse except by throwing water over it from a distance without touching it. Then they lifted it up and buried it in the highest part of Mecca [1341] next to a wall, and then threw stones over it until they covered it."

The Treatment of the Captives

According to Ibn Ḥumayd—Salamah b. al-Faḍl—Muḥammad b. Isḥāq—al-ʿAbbās b. ʿAbd Allāh b. Maʿbad—a member of his family—ʿAbd Allāh b.ʿAbbās: On the evening after the day of Badr, when the captives were confined in fetters, the Messenger of God could not sleep in the first part of the night. His companions said, "O Messenger of God, why do you not sleep?" He said, "I can hear al-ʿAbbās writhing in his fetters." So they went to al-ʿAbbās and released him from his fetters, and the Messenger of God went to sleep.

According to Ibn Ḥumayd—Salamah b. al-Faḍl—Muḥammad b. Isḥāq—al-Ḥasan b. ʿUmārah—al-Ḥakam b. ʿUtaybah—Miqsam—Ibn ʿAbbās: The man who took al-ʿAbbās captive was Abū al-Yasar Kaʿb b. ʿAmr, the brother of the Banū Salimah. Abū al-Yasar was a slightly-built man, and al-ʿAbbās was a big man, and the Messenger of God said to Abū al-Yasar, "How did you take al-ʿAbbās captive, Abū al-Yasar?" "O Messenger of God," he replied, "a man whom I have never seen before or after helped me against

123. From here to the foot of p. 1341 is not in Ibn Hishām's text of Ibn Isḥāq, though al-Ṭabarī gives the latter as his source.

him. His appearance was so-and-so." The Messenger of God said, "A noble angel helped you against him."

[1342] According to Ibn Ḥumayd—Salamah b. al-Faḍl—Muḥammad b. Isḥāq: and Yaḥyā b. 'Abbād—his father 'Abbād: Quraysh bewailed their dead, and then said, "Do not act thus, in case Muḥammad and his companions get to hear of it and rejoice at your misfortune; and do not send any messages concerning the ransom of your captives, but keep Muḥammad and his companions waiting, so that they do not make excessive demands for ransoms."

Al-Aswad b. al-Muṭṭalib had lost three sons, Zam'ah b. al-Aswad, 'Aqīl b. al-Aswad, and al-Ḥārith b. al-Aswad, and he wanted to weep for them.[124] While he was in this condition, he suddenly heard a woman wailing in the night. He said to his slave, as he himself had lost his sight, "See if wailing has been made lawful and whether Quraysh are weeping for their dead, so that perhaps I can weep for Abū Ḥakīmah (meaning Zam'ah), for my belly is on fire." When the slave came back he said, "It is only a woman weeping for a camel of hers which she has lost." It was on that occasion that he composed the following verses:

Does she weep because a camel of hers is lost,
    and does sleeplessness prevent her from sleeping?
[1343 Do not weep for a young camel, but for Badr where our
    good fortune deserted us
For Badr and the chiefs of the Banū Ḥusayṣ, and
    Makhzūm and the clan of Abū al-Walīd.[125]
And weep, if you must weep, for 'Aqīl, and weep for
    al-Ḥārith, the lion of lions
Weep for them all without tiring, and there is no
    equal to Abū Ḥakīmah.

---

124. Al-Ṭabarī appears to have made a mistake here and to have confused al-Aswad b. 'Abd Yaghūth (of the clan of Zuhrah) with al-Aswad b. al-Muṭṭalib (of the clan of Asad). The former had no son called Zam'ah (al-Zubayrī, *Nasab Quraysh*, ed. E. Lévi-Provençal, Cairo 1953, 262), but the latter had a son Zam'ah and his *kunyah* was Abū Zam'ah. Al-Ṭabarī is also mistaken in speaking of al-Ḥārith b. al-Aswad; the man who died was his grandson al-Ḥārith b. Zam'ah b. al-Aswad. Below (1374) one should read Abū Zam'ah al-Aswad, since Zam'ah b. al-Aswad was killed at Badr.

125. Banū Ḥuṣayṣ means the clans of Sahm and Jumaḥ, Ḥuṣayṣ being nominally their grandfather. Abū al-Walīd is presumably 'Utbah b. Rabī'ah of 'Abd Shams.

Indeed, men have become chiefs after them who would
never have become chiefs if not for Badr.

Among the captives was Abū Wadāʿah b. Ḍubayrah al-Sahmī. The Messenger of God said, "He has a son who is a shrewd merchant with much money. It is as though he had already come to you about his father's ransom." When Quraysh said, "Do not hurry in ransoming your captives, so that Muḥammad and his companions do not make excessive demands on you," al-Muṭṭalib b. Abī Wadāʿah, who was the man the Messenger of God meant, said, "You are right! Do not hurry in ransoming your captives." Then he slipped away at night, went to Medina, ransomed his father for four thousand dirhams, and departed with him. After that, Quraysh sent to discuss ransoming the captives. Mikraz b. Ḥafṣ b. al-Akhyaf came to ransom Suhayl b. ʿAmr, who had been taken captive by Mālik b. al-Dukhshum, the brother of the Banū Sālim b. ʿAwf; Suhayl b. ʿAmr had a split lower lip.

According to Ibn Ḥumayd—Salamah—Muḥammad b. Isḥāq —Muḥammad b. ʿAmr b. ʿAṭāʾ b. ʿAyyāsh b. ʿAlqamah, the [1344] brother of the Meccan clan of Banū ʿĀmir b. Luʾayy: ʿUmar b. al-Khaṭṭāb said to the Messenger of God, "O Messenger of God, pull out Suhayl b. ʿAmr's two lower front teeth so that his tongue will loll out and he will never be able to stand up and make speeches against you anywhere." The Messenger of God said, "I will not mutilate him, or God will mutilate me even if I am a prophet." I have heard that the Messenger of God said to ʿUmar in this ḥadīth, "Perhaps he will play a role which you will not find blameworthy." When Mikraz bargained with them over his ransom and finally reached an agreement with them, they said, "Give us what is due to us." He replied, "Fetter my foot instead of his and let him go, so that he can send you his ransom." So they let Suhayl go, and imprisoned Mikraz in his place.

According to Ibn Ḥumayd—Salamah—Muḥammad b. Isḥāq—al-Kalbī—Abū Ṣāliḥ—Ibn ʿAbbās: The Messenger of God said to al-ʿAbbās b. ʿAbd al-Muṭṭalib when he reached Medina with him, "Al-ʿAbbās, you must ransom yourself, your two nephews, ʿAqīl b. Abī Ṭālib and Nawfal b. al-Ḥārith, and your confederate, ʿUtbah b. ʿAmr b. Jaḥdam, the brother of the Banū al-Ḥārith b. Fihr, for you are a wealthy man." "O Messenger of God," he

replied, "I was a Muslim, but the people forced me (to fight) against my will." "God knows best concerning your Islam," he said. "If what you say is true, God will reward you for it. As for your external acts, they were against us; so ransom yourself." The Messenger of God had taken twenty ounces (*ūqiyyah*) of gold from him after Badr, and al-ʿAbbās said, "O Messenger of God, credit me with this amount towards my ransom." "No," he said, "that was something which God gave to us from you." "I have no
[1345] money," al-ʿAbbās then said. "Well," was the reply, "Where is the money which you deposited with Umm al-Faḍl bt. al-Ḥārith in Mecca when you were setting out? You were by yourselves, and you said to her, 'If I am killed on my journey, so much is for al-Faḍl, so much is for ʿAbd Allāh, so much is for Qutham, and so much is for ʿUbayd Allāh'?" "By him who sent you with the Truth," he said, "nobody knows this except myself and her, and I know that you are the Messenger of God." So al-ʿAbbās ransomed himself, his two nephews, and his confederate.

According to Ibn Ḥumayd—Salamah b. al-Faḍl—Muḥammad (Ibn Isḥāq)—ʿAbd Allāh b. Abī Bakr b. Muḥammad b. ʿAmr b. Ḥazm: ʿAmr b. Abī Sufyān b. Ḥarb, who was married to the daughter of ʿUqbah b. Abī Muʿayṭ, was a captive in the hands of the Messenger of God, one of the captives of Badr. They said to Abū Sufyān, "Ransom ʿAmr." "Shall I lose both my blood and my wealth?" he asked. "They have killed Ḥanẓalah and I am to ransom ʿAmr? Leave him in their hands and they can hold on to him as long as they like." While he was imprisoned in this way in the custody of the Messenger of God, Saʿd b. al-Nuʿmān b. Akkāl, the brother of the clan of ʿAmr b. ʿAwf, from the subclan of Muʿāwiyah,[126] went to Mecca to perform the ʿumrah accompanied by a young wife. He was a very old man, a Muslim, who had flocks in al-Naqīʿ. From there he went to perform the ʿumrah, not fearing what was to befall him and not imagining that he would be held captive in Mecca. He came simply to perform the ʿumrah, for Quraysh had undertaken not to interfere in any way with anyone
[1346] who came to perform the ḥajj or the ʿumrah, apart from helping them. Abū Sufyān wrongfully imprisoned him at Mecca in ex-

126. Cf. genealogical table in Watt, *Medina*, 154.

change for his son 'Amr b. Abī Sufyān. Then Abū Sufyān composed the following lines of verse:

> O clan of Ibn Akkāl, answer his prayer; may you lose
> one another! Do not forsake your mature chief.
> The Banū ʿAmr are base and lowly if they do not
> remove the fetters from their captive.

The Banū ʿAmr b. ʿAwf went to the Messenger of God, told him about this, and asked him to give them ʿAmr b. Abī Sufyān so that they could obtain the release of their shaykh. The Messenger of God did so, and they sent ʿAmr to Abū Sufyān, who allowed Saʿd to go.

The Release of Zaynab's Husband

Among the captives was Abū al-ʿĀṣ b. al-Rabīʿ b. ʿAbd al-ʿUzzā b. ʿAbd Shams, the son-in-law of the Messenger of God, being the husband of his daughter Zaynab. Abū al-ʿĀṣ was one of the esteemed men of Mecca in respect of wealth, trustworthiness, and commerce. He was the son of Hālah bt. Khuwaylid (sister of Muḥammad's wife Khadījah) so that Khadījah was his maternal aunt. Khadījah asked the Messenger of God to marry him (to Zaynab) and he did not oppose this; this was before he had received any revelations. He married him (to her) and (Khadījah) used to regard Abū al-ʿĀṣ as her son. When God honoured his Messenger with his Prophethood Khadījah and his daughters believed in him, testified that the message which he brought was the truth, and followed his religion, but Abū al-ʿĀṣ held fast to his polytheism. The Messenger of God had married one of his daughters, either Ruqayyah or Umm Kulthūm, to ʿUtbah b. Abī Lahab,[127] and when he openly proclaimed the command of God to Quraysh and they shunned it, they said to one another, "You had relieved Muḥammad of the worry of providing for his daughters; but now return his daughters to him and let him have responsibil-

127. As becomes clear later, this was not an actual marriage but only a betrothal. It is sometimes said that two daughters of Muḥammad had been betrothed to two sons of Abū Lahab. It was apparently Ruqayyah who, on being rejected by ʿUtbah, was married to ʿUthmān.

ity for them." When they went to Abū al-ʿĀṣ b. al-Rabīʿ and said
[1347] to him, "Leave your wife, and we will marry you to any woman you wish from Quraysh," he replied, "By God, I will do no such thing! I will not leave my wife, and I do not want any woman from Quraysh in exchange for my wife." I have been told that the Messenger of God used to praise him for being a good son-in-law.

Then they went to the evildoer, the son of the evildoer, ʿUtbah b. Abī Lahab, and said to him, "Divorce Muḥammad's daughter and we will marry you to any woman you want from Quraysh." He said, "If you will marry me to the daughter of Abān b. Saʿīd b. al-ʿĀṣ or the daughter of Saʿīd b. al-ʿĀṣ, I will leave her." So they married him to the daughter of Saʿīd b. al-ʿĀṣ, and he left Muḥammad's daughter. The enemy of God had not yet consummated the marriage, and God rescued Muḥammad's daughter from his enemy's clutches, to her honour and his shame. ʿUthman b. ʿAffān (the later caliph) succeeded ʿUtbah as her husband. The Messenger of God could not permit or forbid such marriages while in Mecca, since he was not in a position of authority.[128] Although Islam had in a sense separated Zaynab, the daughter of the Messenger of God, from Abū al-ʿĀṣ b. Rabīʿ when she became a Muslim, the Messenger of God was not able actually to separate them, and she continued to live with him until the Hijrah of the Messenger of God to Medina, despite the fact that she was a Muslim and he a polytheist. When Quraysh marched to Badr, Abū al-ʿĀṣ b. Rabīʿ marched with them, was taken captive on the day of Badr, and held in custody by the Messenger of God in Medina.

According to Ibn Ḥumayd—Salamah—Muḥammad b. Isḥāq—Yaḥyā b. ʿAbbād b. ʿAbd Allāh b. al-Zubayr—his father, ʿAbbād[129]—ʿĀʾishah the wife of the Messenger of God: When the people of Mecca sent to negotiate about ransoming their captives, Zaynab, the daughter of the Messenger of God, sent money for
[1348] the ransom of Abū al-ʿĀṣ b. al-Rabīʿ and included with it a necklace which Khadījah had presented to her when Abū al-ʿĀṣ married her. When the Messenger of God saw it, his heart softened greatly, and he said to the Muslims, "If you see fit to set free

128. The marriage of a Muslim woman to a non-Muslim, whether pagan or from the People of the Book, was later forbidden.

129. Cf. n.16; ʿĀʾishah was also maternal aunt of ʿAbbād.

Zaynab's captive for her and to return her property to her, do so." They said, "Yes, O Messenger of God," and set Abū al-ʿĀṣ free and returned Zaynab's property. Either the Messenger of God extracted an undertaking from Abū al-ʿĀṣ, or he promised the Messenger of God that he would let Zaynab go to him, or else this was one of the conditions of his release which was not made public either by him or the Messenger of God so that we might know what it was. Whatever the truth of this, however, after Abū al-ʿĀṣ had been allowed to go and had reached Mecca, the Messenger of God sent Zayd b. Ḥārithah and a man of the Anṣār, saying, "Be in the Baṭn Ya'jaj until Zaynab passes by you, and then accompany her back to me." The two went there, a month or so after Badr. When Abū al-ʿĀṣ reached Mecca, he told Zaynab to go to her father, and she proceeded to get ready to travel.

Zaynab's Journey to Medina

According to Ibn Ḥumayd—Salamah—Muḥammad b. Isḥāq—ʿAbd Allāh b. Abī Bakr b. Muḥammad b. ʿAmr b. Ḥazm: I have been told that Zaynab said, "While I was getting ready to travel in Mecca in order to join my father, Hind bt. ʿUtbah[130] met me and said, 'Daughter of Muḥammad, have I not heard that you wish to join your father?' I said, 'I do not want to do so.' She said, 'Cousin, do not deny it. If you need anything which will make your journey more comfortable or any money to help you reach your father, I have whatever you need, so do not be ashamed to ask; for [1349] men's quarrels have nothing to do with the women.' And, by God, I am sure that she meant what she said, but I was afraid of her, and denied that I wanted to go. Nevertheless, I got ready to travel."

When the daughter of the Messenger of God had completed her preparations, her brother-in-law, Kinānah b. al-Rabīʿ, her husband's brother, brought her a camel, which she mounted. Then, taking his bow and quiver, he went out with her in broad day-

---

130. Hind was the wife of Abū Sufyān, who was of the same clan as Zaynab's husband, and this may be why Hind was friendly here; but she thirsted for vengeance on Muḥammad's uncle Ḥamzah because he had killed her father and uncle at Badr.

light, leading the camel with her in the camel litter. The men of Quraysh discussed this, and went out in pursuit of her, catching up with her at Dhū Ṭawā. The first men to reach her were Habbār b. al-Aswad b. al-Muṭṭalib b. Asad b. ʿAbd al-ʿUzzā and Nāfiʿ b. ʿAbd al-Qays al-Fihrī. Habbār threatened her with a spear while she was in the camel litter; it is said that she was pregnant, and that when she went back again to Mecca, she had a miscarriage. After Habbār's threat, her brother-in-law knelt down, spread out the contents of his quiver, and said, "By God, if any man comes near me I will put an arrow into him." At this, they drew back from him until Abū Sufyān and the main body of Quraysh arrived. Abū Sufyān said, "Man, lower your bow so that we can talk to you." He lowered his bow, and Abū Sufyān came up and stood by him, and said, "You did the wrong thing in taking the woman away in public under everyone's noses. You know the affliction and disaster which have befallen us as a result of Muḥammad's actions. If his daughter is taken away from among us publicly, under their noses, people will think that this shows the humiliation which has befallen us as a result of the disaster we suffered, and
[1350] that it is weakness and feebleness on our part. By my life, we have no need to keep her away from her father, and we have no intention of exacting vengeance in that way. But take the woman back, and when the clamour has died down and people are saying that we have brought her back, slip out secretly with her, and reunite her with her father." Kinānah did so, and when the clamour had died down he took Zaynab out by night and handed her over to Zayd b. Ḥārithah and his companion, and they took her to the Messenger of God.

The Conversion of Abū al-ʿĀṣ

Abū al-ʿĀṣ remained in Mecca, and Zaynab remained with the Messenger of God in Medina, separated by Islam. Just before the conquest of Mecca, however, Abū al-ʿĀṣ went on a trading expedition to Syria. He was regarded as a trustworthy man, and he had with him, besides his own merchandise, goods belonging to other men of Quraysh which they had entrusted to him to trade with. When he had concluded his business and was on his return journey, he encountered a detachment of the Messenger of God's men. They seized the goods he had with him, but he himself managed to elude them by flight. After the detachment reached Medina with his property which they had seized, Abū al-ʿĀṣ came under cover of night, entered the house of Zaynab, the daughter of the Messenger of God, and sought her protection, which she gave. He did this, seeking the recovery of his property.

According to Ibn Ḥumayd—Salamah—Muḥammad b. Isḥāq—Yazīd b. Rūmān: When the Messenger of God came for the morning prayer, he said, "Allāh Akbar" and the people responded. Then Zaynab cried out from the women's bench, "O people, I have taken Abū al-ʿĀṣ b. al-Rabīʿ under my protection."

When the Messenger of God had completed his prayer, he turned round to the people and said, "O people, did you hear what I heard?" They said, "Yes." He said, "By him in whose hand Muḥammad's soul rests, I knew nothing of this until I heard the words you heard from Zaynab. It is the case, however, that the humblest of the Muslims has the right to extend protection (to someone) on their behalf."[131] Then the Messenger of God left and went to visit his daughter, and said, "Look after him well, but do not let him come near you, for you are not lawful for him (as a [1351] wife)."

According to Ibn Ḥumayd—Salamah—Muḥammad b. Isḥāq ʿAbd Allāh b. Abī Bakr: The Messenger of God sent to the detachment who had seized Abū al-ʿĀṣ's property and said, "You know this man's relationship to us, and you have seized his property. If you would do him a kindness and return his property to him, we would like that, but if you do not wish to, then it is God's booty which he has bestowed upon you, and you have a better right to it." They replied, "O Messenger of God, we will return it to him."

So they returned his property to him; one man even brought rope, another brought old water-skins and leather bottles, and somebody even brought pegs for fastening sacks, until they had returned his property in its entirety, and nothing was missing. Abū al-ʿĀṣ then went to Mecca, and to every member of Quraysh who had entrusted him with merchandise handed over what be-

131. This is the practice of *ijārah*, that is, the granting of protection as a "neighbour" (*jār*). Muḥammad emphasizes that the protection given by Zaynab is to be binding on all Muslims.

longed to him. Finally, he said, "Men of Quraysh, has any of you property remaining with me which he has not received back?" They said, "No, may God reward you well. We have found you to be faithful to your promise and generous." "Indeed then," he said, "I testify that there is no deity but God, and that Muḥammad is his servant and his Messenger. By God, nothing prevented me from accepting Islam when I was with him except the fear that you might think that I only wanted to help myself to your merchandise. Now that God has delivered it to you and I have no more to do with it, I accept Islam." Then he left Mecca and went to the Messenger of God.

According to Ibn Ḥumayd—Salamah—Muḥammad b. Isḥāq—Dā'ūd b. al-Ḥuṣayn—'Ikrimah the *mawlā* of Ibn 'Abbās—'Abd Allāh b. 'Abbās: The Messenger of God returned Zaynab to him on the terms of his previous marriage six years earlier, and did not make any new conditions.

The Conversion of 'Umayr b. Wahb

[1352] According to Ibn Ḥumayd—Salamah b. al-Faḍl—Muḥammad b. Isḥāq—Muḥammad b. Ja'far b. al-Zubayr—'Urwah b. al-Zubayr: 'Umayr b. Wahb al-Jumaḥī was sitting in the Ḥijr with Ṣafwān b. Umayyah, a little after the disaster suffered by Quraysh at Badr. 'Umayr b. Wahb was one of the evil men of Quraysh, those who used to torment the Messenger of God and his companions, and cause them distress so long as they remained in Mecca. His son Wahb b. 'Umayr was among the captives of Badr. While 'Umayr was discussing the People of the Well and what had happened to them, Ṣafwān said, "By God, there is nothing good in life after their death." "You are right, by God," replied 'Umayr. "If I did not have a debt which I cannot discharge, and a family who I fear might perish when I am gone, I would ride to Muḥammad and kill him. I have cause against his followers, for my son is captive in their hands." Ṣafwān b. Umayyah seized this opportunity and said, "I will accept your debt and will discharge it for you, and I will look after your family in exactly the same way as my own, as long as they live. They will lack nothing that is within my means." "Keep this agreement between us a secret, then," 'Umayr said. "I will do so," Ṣafwān replied.

Then ʿUmayr called for his sword, had it sharpened and poisoned, and set out and came to Medina. While ʿUmar b. al-Khaṭṭāb and a number of Muslims were in the Mosque talking about [1353] the day of Badr and discussing the way God had honoured them by it, and what he had taught them by the fate of their enemy, ʿUmar suddenly noticed ʿUmayr b. Wahb making his camel kneel at the door of the Mosque, and girt with his sword. "This is the dog, the enemy of God, ʿUmayr b. Wahb," he said. "He has certainly come for some evil purpose. He is the one who set us against one another and estimated our numbers for the enemy on the day of Badr." ʿUmar then went in to the Messenger of God and said, "O Messenger of God, here is the enemy of God ʿUmayr b. Wahb, who has come wearing his sword." "Bring him in to me, then," he said. ʿUmar went up to him, took hold of the shoulder-belt from which his sword was hanging, and seized him round the neck with it. Then he said to some men of the Anṣār who were with him, "Go in to the Messenger of God and sit near him, and watch out for this villain, for he is not to be trusted." ʿUmar then took ʿUmayr in to the Messenger of God, and when the Messenger of God saw him with ʿUmar grasping his sword-belt he said, "Let him go, ʿUmar. Approach, ʿUmayr." He approached and said, "*Anʿimū ṣabāḥan*" (good morning). This was the greeting of the people of the Jāhiliyyah among themselves. The Messenger of God replied, "God has honoured us with a greeting better than your greeting, ʿUmayr, which is "*al-salām*" (peace), the greeting of the people of Paradise." "By God, Muḥammad," he said, "You have not been using this expression for long." "What brings you here, ʿUmayr?" he asked. "I have come for this captive who is in your hands," he said, "so treat me well over him." "What is that sword round your neck for?" he asked. "God curse the swords," ʿUmayr said. "Have they been of any use to us?" "Tell me the truth," he replied, "about what you have come for." "I have come for nothing but this," ʿUmayr insisted. "No," the Messenger of God replied. "While you and Ṣafwān b. Umayyah were sitting in the Ḥijr and discussing the People of the Well of Quraysh, you happened to say, 'If it were not for a debt which I owe and for my family, I would go and kill Muḥammad.' Ṣafwān then said he would be responsible for your debt and your family on condition that you would kill me for him. God has intervened, however, be- [1354]

tween you and me." Then ʿUmayr said, "I testify that you are the Messenger of God. We used to disbelieve the tidings of Heaven which you brought us and the revelations which came down to you. This is a meeting at which only Ṣafwān and I were present. By God, I know that nobody but God can have informed you of it. Praise be to God who has guided me to Islam and led me along this path." Then he pronounced the *Shahādah*,[132] and the Messenger of God said to the Muslims present, "Instruct your brother in his faith, teach him to recite and understand the Qur'ān, and release his captive for him," and they did so.

Later ʿUmayr said, "O Messenger of God, I used to strive to put out the light of God and to persecute those who were in God's religion. I would like you to give me permission to go to Mecca and call the people there to God and to Islam. Perhaps God will guide them rightly; but, if not, I will make difficulties for them in their religion as I used to make difficulties for your companions in theirs."

The Messenger of God gave him permission and he went to Mecca. After ʿUmayr b.Wahb had left Mecca, Ṣafwān used to say to Quraysh, "Rejoice, good news will come to you, in a few days from now, of an event which will make you forget what happened at Badr." Ṣafwān used to ask riders about ʿUmayr, until one arrived who told him that he had become a Muslim. Ṣafwān swore that he would never again speak to ʿUmayr and never again confer any benefit on him. ʿUmayr, on arriving in Mecca, remained there calling people to Islam and making great difficulties for those who opposed him; many people accepted Islam at his hands.

Discussions About the Lawfulness of Taking Captives

When the events of Badr were over, God revealed *al-Anfāl* (Surah 8) in its entirety concerning it.

According to Aḥmad b. Manṣūr—ʿĀṣim b. ʿAlī—ʿIkrimah b. ʿAmmār—Abū Zumayl—ʿAbd Allāh b. ʿAbbās—ʿUmar b. al-Khaṭṭāb: On the day of Badr, the two armies met, and God de-

132. The *shahādah* is the profession of faith: "I bear witness there is no deity but God, Muḥammad is the Messenger of God." Pronouncing this made a man a Muslim.

feated the polytheists. Seventy of them were killed and seventy were taken captive. On that day the Messenger of God consulted Abū Bakr, ʿAlī and ʿUmar. Abū Bakr said, "O Prophet of God, [1355] these people are cousins, fellow clansmen and nephews. I think that you should accept ransoms for them so that what we take from them will strengthen us, and perhaps God will guide them aright so that they may be an assistance for us." The Messenger of God said, "What do you think, Ibn al-Khaṭṭāb?" I said, "I say no, by God! I am not of the same opinion as Abū Bakr. I think that you should hand so-and-so over to me so that I can cut off his head, and that you should hand Ḥamzah's brother over to him so that he can cut off his head, and that you should hand over ʿAqīl to ʿAlī (his brother) so that he can cut off his head. Thus God will know that there is no leniency in our hearts towards the unbelievers. These are their chiefs, their leaders, and their foremost men."

The Messenger of God liked what Abū Bakr said and did not like what I said, and accepted ransoms for the captives. The next day I went to the Prophet in the morning. He was sitting with Abū Bakr, and they were weeping. I said, "O Messenger of God, tell me, what has made you and your companion weep? If I find cause to weep, I will weep with you, and if not, I will pretend to weep because you are weeping." The Messenger of God said, "It is because of the taking of ransoms which has been laid before your companions. It was laid before me that I should punish them, more nearly than this tree (and he pointed to a nearby tree)." God revealed: "It is not for any Prophet to have captives until he hath made slaughter in the land . . ." to the words, "(Had it not been for an ordinance of Allah which had gone before) . . . an awful doom had come upon you on account of what ye took."[133] After that, God made the booty lawful for them. In the following year, at Uḥud, they were punished for what they had done. Seventy men of the companions of the Messenger of God were killed, and seventy were taken captive. (Muḥammad's) lateral incisor was bro-

133. Qur. 8.67f. The verses are interpreted to mean that Muḥammad should not have taken captives at Badr and that the Muslims should not have been so anxious to gain the ransom money. The next verse, however, says that they may keep and enjoy what they have taken (69).

ken, his helmet was shattered on his head, and the blood flowed over his face; the Prophet's companions fled and took to the mountain. (Then) God revealed: "And was it so, when a disaster smote you, though ye had smitten (them with a disaster) twice (as
[1356] great), that ye said, How is this? Say (unto them, O Muḥammad): It is from yourselves. 'Lo! Allah is able to do all things.'"[134] And this other verse was revealed: "When ye climbed (the hill) and paid no heed to anyone, while the messenger in your rear was calling you (to fight). Therefore, he rewarded you grief for (his) grief that (he might teach) you not to sorrow either for that which ye missed or for that which befell you. . . . Then after grief he sent down security for you."[135]

According to Salm b. Junādah—Abū Muʿāwiyah—al-Aʿmash—ʿAmr b. Murrah—Abū ʿUbaydah—ʿAbd Allāh: When it was the day of Badr and the captives were brought, the Messenger of God asked, "What do you say concerning these captives?" Abū Bakr replied, "O Messenger of God, they are your people and your family. Spare them and give them time. Perhaps God will relent against them." ʿUmar said, "O Messenger of God, they have called you a liar and driven you out. Bring them forward and cut off their heads." ʿAbd Allāh b. Rawāḥah said, "O Messenger of God, look for a wadi with a lot of firewood in it, put them in it and set fire to it around them." Al-ʿAbbās said to him, "Your own kin have severed the bonds of kinship."

The Messenger of God was silent and did not answer them. Then he went indoors, and some people said, "He will take Abū Bakr's advice," some said, "He will take ʿUmar's advice," and other people said, "He will take the advice of ʿAbd Allāh b. Rawāḥah." When the Messenger of God came out again, he said, "God softens the hearts of men in each, so that they become softer than milk, and God hardens the hearts of men in each so that they become harder than stones. Abū Bakr, you are like Abraham, who said, 'Whoso followeth me, he verily is of me. And whoso disobeyeth me—Still thou art Forgiving, Merciful.'[136] And Abū Bakr, you are (also) like Jesus, who said, 'If thou punish them, lo! they are thy slaves, and if thou forgive them (lo! they are

134. Qur. 3.165.
135. Qur. 3.153f.

thy slaves). Lo! Thou, only Thou art the Mighty, the Wise.'[137] You, 'Umar, are like Noah, who said, 'My Lord! Leave not one of the disbelievers in the land.'[138] And you are like Moses, who said, 'Our Lord! Destroy their riches and harden their hearts so that they believe not till they see the painful doom.' "[139] [1357]

Then the Messenger of God said, "You today are a single household. Let not one of them escape without paying a ransom or losing his head." 'Abd Allāh b. Mas'ūd said, "Except for Suhayl b. Bayḍā', for I heard him professing Islam." The Messenger of God was silent, and I do not think that I have ever been more fearful that stones would fall on me from Heaven than I was that day; but at last the Messenger of God repeated, "Except for Suhayl b. Bayḍā'." In respect of this matter God revealed, "It is not for any Prophet to have captives until he hath made slaughter in the land . . ." to the end of the three verses.

According to Ibn Ḥumayd—Salamah—Muḥammad b. Isḥāq: When it was revealed, "It is not for any Prophet to have captives . . ." the Messenger of God said, "If punishment were to descend from Heaven, none would escape from it but Sa'd b. Mu'ādh, because he said, 'O Prophet of God, extensive killing is dearer to me than sparing men's lives.' "

Abū Ja'far (al-Ṭabarī) says: The total number of the Emigrants who were present at Badr and who were given a share and a reward from it by the Messenger of God was eighty-three, according to Ibn Isḥāq (Ibn Ḥumayd—Salamah). The total number of al-Aws who were present and received a share was sixty-one, and the total number of al-Khazraj who were present was one hundred and seventy, according to Ibn Isḥāq. The total number of Muslims [1358] martyred on that day was fourteen men, six from the Emigrants and eight from the Anṣār.

The polytheists, so al-Wāqidī asserts, consisted of nine hundred and fifty fighters, and their cavalry consisted of a hundred horse.

On that day the Messenger of God sent back a number of people whom he considered to be too young, according to al-Wāqidī.

136. Qur. 14.36.
137. Qur. 5.118.
138. Qur. 71.26.
139. Qur. 10.88.

Among them, he claims, were ʿAbd Allāh b. ʿUmar, Rāfiʿ b. Khadīj, al-Barāʾ b. ʿĀzib, Zayd b. Thābit, Usayd b. Ẓuhayr and ʿUmayr b. Abī Waqqāṣ. Then he allowed ʿUmayr to take part after sending him back, and he was killed on that day.[140]

Before setting out from Medina the Messenger of God had sent Ṭalḥah b.ʿUbayd Allāh and Saʿīd b. Zayd b. ʿAmr b. Nufayl along the road to Syria to gather information about the caravan. Their return to Medina did not take place until the actual day of the battle of Badr. They met the Messenger of God at Turbān, which is the descent from Badr, as he was making for Medina.

Al-Wāqidī says:[141] The Messenger of God set out from Medina with three hundred and five men. The Emigrants numbered seventy-four, and the rest were Anṣār. Eight (other) men got their rewards and shares; three of the Emigrants, ʿUthmān b. ʿAffān who stayed behind to look after (his wife) the daughter of the Messenger of God, until she died, together with Ṭalḥah b. ʿUbayd Allāh and Saʿīd b. Zayd, whom he sent to gather information about the caravan; and five of the Anṣār, Abū Lubābah Bashīr b. ʿAbd al-Mundhir, whom he left in charge of Medina, ʿAṣim b. ʿAdī b. al-ʿAjlān, whom he left in charge of the ʿĀliyah, al-Ḥārith b.
[1359] Ḥāṭib, whom he sent back from al-Rawḥāʾ to the Banū ʿAmr b. ʿAwf on account of some news he had about them, al-Ḥārith b. al-Ṣimmah, who broke his leg at al-Rawḥāʾ (he belonged to the Banū Mālik b. al-Najjār), and Khawwāt b. Jubayr, who was from the Banū Amr b. ʿAwf, who also broke his leg. There were seventy camels and two horses, one belonging to al-Miqdād b. ʿAmr and one to Marthad b. Abī Marthad.[142]

According to Abū Jaʿfar (al-Ṭabarī)—Ibn Saʿd—Muḥammad b. ʿUmar—Muḥammad b. Hilāl—his father—Abū Hurayrah: The Messenger of God was seen in pursuit of the polytheists on the day of Badr with drawn sword reciting, "The hosts will all be routed and will turn and flee."[143] On the Badr expedition, the Messenger of God took his sword Dhū al-Faqār as booty. It had belonged to Munabbih b. al-Ḥajjāj. On that day he also took Abū

140. W, 21.
141. W, 101; W. says that ʿĀṣim b. ʿAdī was left in charge of Qubāʾ and of Ahl al-ʿĀliyah, "the people of the upper districts."
142. W, 102.
143. Qur. 55.45.

Jahl's camel as booty. It was a Mahrī dromedary on which he used to go on raids and which he used to put to stud with his milch camels.

The Campaign Against the Banū Qaynuqāʿ

Abū Jaʿfar (al-Ṭabarī) says: The Messenger of God remained in Medina after his return from Badr. When he first came to Medina he had made a compact with its Jews that they would not aid anyone against him and that if any enemy attacked him there they would come to his aid. After the Messenger of God killed many polytheists of Quraysh at Badr, (the Jews) were envious and behaved badly towards him, saying, "Muḥammad has not met anyone who is good at fighting. Had he met us, he would have had a battle which would be unlike a battle with anyone else." They also infringed the contract in various ways.

According to Ibn Ḥumayd—Salamah—Muḥammad b. Isḥāq:[144] What happened with regard to the Banū Qaynuqāʿ was that the [1360] Messenger of God assembled them in the Market of the Banū Qaynuqāʿ and said, "O Jews, beware lest God bring on you the like of the retribution which he brought on Quraysh. Accept Islam, for you know that I am a prophet sent by God. You will find this in your scriptures and in God's covenant with you." They replied, "Muḥammad, do you think that we are like your people? Do not be deluded by the fact that you met a people with no knowledge of war and that you made good use of your opportunity. By God, if you fight us you will know that we are real men!"

According to Ibn Ḥumayd—Salamah—Muḥammad b. Isḥāq —ʿĀṣim b. ʿUmar b.Qatādah: The Banū Qaynuqāʿ were the first Jews to infringe the agreement between them and the Messenger of God; they took to arms between Badr and Uḥud.

According to Al-Ḥārith—Ibn Saʿd—Muḥammad b. ʿUmar—Muḥammad b. ʿAbd Allāh—al-Zuhrī: The campaign of the Messenger of God against the Banū Qaynuqāʿ was in Shawwāl (which began March 27, 624) in the second year of the Hijrah.

144. IH, 545. The Jewish clan had a settlement near the middle of the oasis of Medina; they worked as goldsmiths and armourers but did not engage in agriculture.

According to Al-Zuhrī—ʿUrwah: Gabriel brought the following verse down to the Messenger of God: "And if thou fearest treachery from any folk, then throw back to them their treaty fairly."[145] When Gabriel had finished delivering this verse, the Messenger of God said, "I fear the Banū Qaynuqāʿ."

ʿUrwah says: It was on the basis of this verse that the Messenger of God advanced upon them.

According to Al-Wāqidī—Muḥammad b. Ṣāliḥ—ʿĀṣim b.ʿUmar b. Qatādah: The Messenger of God besieged them for fifteen days and prevented any of them from getting out. They then surrendered at the discretion of the Messenger of God. They were fettered, and he wanted to kill them, but ʿAbd Allāh b. Ubayy spoke to him on their behalf.[146]

[1361] Resumption of the narrative of Ibn Isḥāq—ʿĀṣim b. ʿUmar b. Qatādah.

The Messenger of God besieged them until they surrendered at his discretion. ʿAbd Allāh b. Ubayy b. Salūl rose up when God had put them in his power, and said, "Muḥammad, treat my *mawālī* well"; for they were the confederates of al-Khazraj. The Prophet delayed his answer, so ʿAbd Allāh repeated, "Muhammad, treat my *mawālī* well." The Prophet turned away from him, and he put his hand into (the Messenger's) collar. The Messenger of God said, "Let me go!"—he was so angry that they could see shadows in his face (that is, his face coloured). Then he said, "Damn you, let me go!" He replied, "No, by God, I will not let you go until you treat my *mawālī* well. Four hundred men without armour and three hundred with coats of mail, who defended me from the Arab and the non-Arab alike, and you would mow them down in a single morning? By God, I do not feel safe and am afraid of what the future may have in store." So the Messenger of God said, "They are yours."

According to Abū Jaʿfar (al-Ṭabarī)—Muḥammad b. ʿUmar—Muḥammad b. Ṣāliḥ—ʿĀṣim b. ʿUmar b. Qatādah: The Prophet said, "Let them go; may God curse them, and may he curse (ʿAbd Allāh b. Ubayy) with them." So the Muslims let them go. Then

145. Qur. 8.58.
146. W, 177, summarized.

the Messenger gave orders to expel them, and God gave their property as booty to his Messenger and the Muslims. The Banū Qaynuqāʿ did not have any land, as they were goldsmiths. The Messenger of God took many weapons belonging to them and the tools of their trade. The person who took charge of their expulsion from Medina along with their children was ʿUbādah b. al-Ṣāmit. He accompanied them as far as Dhubāb, saying "The most distant and furthest honour is the furthest." On this occasion [1362] the Messenger of God left Abū Lubābah b. ʿAbd al-Mundhir in charge of Medina.

Abū Jaʿfar (al-Ṭabarī) says: In this year, the first *khums* (fifth) to be levied by the Messenger of God in Islam took place. The Messenger of God took his *ṣafī*, the *khums* and his share, and distributed the other four fifths among his companions. This was the first *khums* to be taken by the Messenger of God.[147]

The banner of the Messenger of God in the battle against the Banū Qaynuqāʿ was a white banner, carried by Ḥamzah b. ʿAbd al-Muṭṭalib. There were no flags (*rāyāt*) on that day.

Celebration of the First ʿĪd al-Aḍḥā

Then the Messenger of God returned to Medina, and (the festival of) al-Aḍḥā came.[148] It is related that the Messenger of God made his sacrifice together with those of his companions who had the means to do so on the tenth of Dhū al-Ḥijjah (June 3, 624). He took the people to al-Muṣallā and led them in prayer. This was the first prayer which the Messenger of God led at al-Muṣallā on a festival. On this festival, he slaughtered two sheep there with his own hands, or according to some people, one sheep.

According to Al-Wāqidī—Muḥammad b. Faḍl, one of the descendants of Rāfiʿ b. Khadīj—Abū Mubashshir: I heard Jābir b. ʿAbd Allāh saying, "When we came back from fighting the Banū

147. The *khums* or "fifth" has already been mentioned (1275; n.45). The *ṣafī* or "first pick" was a special privilege of the Messenger (as of tribal chiefs). The "share" was what was due to him as one of the participants.

148. The *ʿīd al-aḍḥā* or "festival of the sacrifice" is primarily part of the Ḥajj or pilgrimage to Mecca. On the 10th of the pilgrimage month (Dhū al-Ḥijjah), the pilgrims immolate sacrificial victims (sheep, camels, etc.) at Mina. The festival is also celebrated by all Muslims everywhere. See *EI*², art. ʿĪd al-aḍḥā.

Qaynuqāʿ, we sacrificed on the morning of the tenth of Dhū al-Ḥijjah. This was the first Aḍḥā which the Muslims witnessed. We sacrificed in the territory of the Banū Salimah, and seventeen sacrificial victims were counted there."[149]

Minor Expeditions—Dating[150]

Abū Jaʿfar (al-Ṭabarī) says: As for Ibn Isḥāq, he does not specify any date for the campaign of the Messenger of God against the Banū Qaynuqāʿ, except for saying that it was between the expedition of al-Sawīq and the expedition of the Messenger of God from Medina against Quraysh, in which he went as far as the Banū Sulaym and Buḥrān, a mine in Ḥijāz in the direction of al-Furʿ.
[1363] Others say that there were three expeditions led by the Messenger of God himself and one raiding party which he dispatched between his first expedition to Badr and the campaign against the Banū Qaynuqāʿ. They claim that the Prophet attacked the latter on 7 Ṣafar (July 30, 624) in the third year of the Hijrah, and that the Messenger of God led this attack after coming back from Badr, his return to Medina being on a Wednesday, eight days before the end of Ramaḍān (which ended March 26, 624). After spending the rest of Ramaḍān there, he led an expedition to Qarqarat al-Kudr[151] when he heard that the Banū Sulaym and Ghaṭafān were gathering. He set out from Medina on a Friday, when the sun was high in the sky, on the first day of Shawwāl in the second year of the Hijrah (March 27, 624).

According to Ibn Ḥumayd—Salamah—Ibn Isḥāq: When the Messenger of God came to Medina from Badr, having finished with Badr at the end of Ramaḍān or the beginning of Shawwāl, he spent only seven days in Medina before leading an expedition in person against the Banū Sulaym. He got as far as one of their watering places, called al-Kudr, stayed there for three days, and then went back to Medina without any fighting. He remained there for

149. This paragraph seems to be from a source other than the *Maghāzī* of al-Wāqidī.

150. There is much uncertainty about the order and dating of these minor expeditions between the battles of Badr and Uḥud; they are described in IH, 539–55 and W, 181–98.

151. W, 182, has Qarārat al-Kudr.

the rest of Shawwāl and Dhū al-Qa'dah (which ended May 24, 624), and during this period most of the captives of Quraysh were ransomed.

As for al-Wāqidī, he asserts that the Prophet's expedition to al-Kudr was in Muḥarram in the third year of the Hijrah (which began June 24, 624), that on this expedition his banner was carried by 'Alī b. Abī Ṭālib, and that he left Ibn Umm Maktūm al-Ma'īṣī in charge of Medina.[152]

Some authorities say that the Prophet returned to Medina from the expedition to al-Kudr, having driven off livestock without any fighting, on 10 Shawwāl (April 5, 624). He then sent Ghālib b. [1364] 'Abd Allāh al-Laythī, on Sunday, 10 Shawwāl, as leader of a raid against the Banū Sulaym and Ghaṭafān. The Muslims killed some of the enemy, took their livestock, and returned to Medina with their booty, on Saturday, fourteen days before the end of Shawwāl (April 11, 624). Three of the Muslims were martyred. The Messenger of God stayed in Medina until Dhū al-Ḥijjah (May 25—June 23, 624) and led the expedition of al-Sawīq on Sunday, seven days before the end of Dhū al-Ḥijjah.

The Expedition of al-Sawīq (the Barley-Meal)[153]

Abū Ja'far (al-Ṭabarī)—Ibn Ḥumayd—Salamah—Ibn Isḥāq: When the Messenger of God returned to Medina from the expedition to al-Kudr, he remained there for the rest of Shawwāl of the second year of the Hijrah and Dhū al-Qa'da (which ended May 24, 624). Then Abū Sufyān b. Ḥarb went on the expedition of al-Sawīq in Dhū al-Ḥijjah. In this year the polytheists led the pilgrimage.

According to Ibn Ḥumayd—Salamah—Muḥammad b. Isḥāq—Muḥammad b. Ja'far b. al-Zubayr, and Yazīd b. Rūmān and one whose authority I do not doubt—'Ubayd Allāh b. Ka'b b. Mālik, who was one of the best-informed of the Anṣār: After the battle of Badr, when Abū Sufyān b. Ḥarb returned to Mecca, along with the routed remnants of Quraysh, he swore that no water would touch his head to purify him from ritual impurity until he had led an ex- [1365]

---

152. Ibn Umm Maktūm is said to have been the blind man in respect of whom Sūrah 80 was revealed. Ma'īṣ is a subclan of the Meccan clan of 'Āmir.

153. IH, 543f.; W, 181f. *Sawīq* is barley-meal, which was usually consumed in the form of gruel. The reason for the name is explained by al-Wāqidī below.

pedition against Muḥammad. In order to fulfil his vow, he set out at the head of two hundred horsemen of Quraysh and took the Najdī route, halting in the upper part of Qanāt by a mountain called Tayt (variant Thayb), a stage or so from Medina. Then he set out by night and came, while it was still night, to the Banū al-Naḍīr. He went to Ḥuyayy b. Akhṭab and knocked at his door, but Ḥuyayy refused to open up, being afraid of him. Then he went to Sallām b. Mishkam, who was the chief of al-Naḍīr at that time and their treasurer, and asked to be allowed to enter. Sallām did so, provided him with food and drink, and gave him confidential information about the Muslims. Towards the end of the night, Abū Sufyān left and returned to his companions, then sent some men of Quraysh into Medina. These went to a district called al-ʿUrayḍ, set fire to date gardens there, and killed a man of the Anṣār and his confederate whom they found in arable ground belonging to the man. After that, they left and went back. The Muslims caught sight of them, however, and the Messenger of God set out in pursuit. He went as far as Qarqarat al-Kudr but then turned back, because Abū Sufyān and his companions had eluded them. The Muslims saw the provisions which these had discarded in the fields in order to lighten their load and escape. When the Messenger of God returned, the Muslims said to him, "Do you hope that this will be counted in our favour as an expedition?" He replied, "Yes."

As Abū Sufyān was equipping himself to go from Mecca to Medina, he had recited the following lines of verse to spur on Quraysh:

[1366] Wheel round and attack Yathrib and its population,
for what they have gathered together is booty for you.
Even though the day of the Well may have gone in their favour,
what comes after it will turn out in your favour.
I have sworn that I will not approach women
and that the water of ablution will not touch my head and skin
Until you destroy the tribes of al-Aws
and al-Khazraj; indeed my heart is on fire.

Ka'b b. Mālik replied to him in these words:

The mother of those who praise God sighs
for Ibn Ḥarb's army which was so futile in the *Ḥarrah*
When the Muslims threw aside the bodies of those upon whom
the birds had gorged their fill, flying to the top of the mountains.
They came with an army the kneeling-place of whose camels,
if it were measured,
would be no more than the hollow left by a jackal,
Denuded of victory and wealth, and denuded
of the heroes of the Valley, and of spears.

As for al-Wāqidī, he asserts that the expedition of al-Sawīq was in Dhū al-Qa'dah in the second year of the Hijrah (which began April 25, 624), and says, "The Messenger of God set out at the head of two hundred of his companions, of the Emigrants and the Anṣār." Then he gives an account of the journey of Abū Sufyān which is similar to that given by Ibn Isḥāq, except that he says, "He (meaning Abū Sufyān) passed by a man called Ma'bad b. 'Amr, who had a hired worker with him, at al-'Urayḍ, killed them both and set fire to some houses and straw there. He then consid- [1367]
ered that he was released from his vow. The clamour came to the ears of the Prophet, and the people assembled for fighting and set out on his track, but they were unable to catch him."

He goes on, "Abū Sufyān and his companions were throwing down sacks of barley-meal in order to lighten themselves, this being the main part of their provisions. For this reason it was called the *ghazwat al-sawīq* (the barley-meal expedition).

Al-Wāqidī says: The Messenger of God left Abū Lubābah b. 'Abd al-Mundhir in charge of Medina.

Other Events of the Year

Abū Ja'far (al-Ṭabarī says): In this year, that is the second year of the Hijrah, there died, in Dhū al-Ḥijjah, 'Uthmān b. Maẓ'ūn. The Messenger of God buried him in al-Naqī', and set a stone at his head to mark his grave. It is said that al-Ḥasan b. 'Alī b. Abī Ṭālib was born in this year.

According to Abū Ja'far (al-Ṭabarī)—al-Wāqidī—Ibn Abī Sabrah—Isḥāq b. 'Abd Allāh—Abū Ja'far: 'Alī b. Abī Ṭālib married Fāṭimah in Dhū al-Ḥijjah, at the beginning of the twenty-second month.

Abū Ja'far (al-Ṭabarī) says: If this account is correct, then the previous report is erroneous.[154]

It is said that in this year the Messenger of God wrote the *Ma'āqil*, which was suspended from his sword.[155]

---

154. See 1273 above and n.43.

155. *Ma'āqil*, plural of *ma'qūlah*, which like *diyah* means "blood-money." Muḥammad is said to have drawn up regulations about this; Aḥmad b. Ḥanbal, *Musnad*, i.271; ii.204. Cf. also *EI*², arts 'Āḳila (R.Brunschwig), Diya (E. Tyan).

The Events of the Year 3

(June 24, 624–June 12, 625)

According to Ibn Ḥumayd—Salamah—Muḥammad b. Isḥāq: When the Messenger of God returned from the "barley-meal expedition" he remained in Medina for the rest of Dhū al-Ḥijjah (which began May 25, 624) and for Muḥarram (which began June 24, 624), or nearly all of it, and then mounted an expedition to Najd against Ghaṭafān, which is known as the expedition of Dhū Amarr.[156] He spent the whole of Ṣafar (which began July 24, 624), or almost all of it, in Najd and then returned to Medina without [1368] any fighting. He spent all but a small part of Rabīʿ al-Awwal (which began August 22, 624) there, and then went on an expedition against Quraysh and the Banū Sulaym. He went as far as Buḥrān, a mine in Ḥijāz in the region of al-Furʿ, spent Rabīʿ al-Ākhir and Jumādā al-Ūlā (September 21–November 18, 624) there, and then returned to Medina without any fighting.

156. IH, 544. IH omits "Muḥarram," but it is implied by what follows.

The Story of Ka'b b. al-Ashraf[157]

Abu Ja'far (al-Ṭabarī) says: In this year the Prophet sent a party against Ka'b b. al-Ashraf. Al-Wāqidī asserts that the Prophet sent this party in Rabī' al-Awwal of this year. Ibn Ḥumayd—Salamah—Ibn Isḥāq says: When the Meccans suffered disaster at Badr, Zayd b. Ḥārithah went to the people of the Sāfilah and 'Abd Allāh b. Rawāḥah went to the people of the 'Āliyah, both sent by the Messenger of God to the Muslims in Medina to bring the good news of the victory granted to him by God and the killing of a number of polytheists.

According to Ibn Ḥumayd—Salamah—Muḥammad b. Isḥāq —'Abd Allāh b. Mughīth b. Abī Burdah b. Asīr al-Ẓafarī, and 'Abd Allāh b. Abī Bakr b. Muḥammad b. 'Amr b. Ḥazm, and 'Āṣim b. 'Umar b. Qatādah and Ṣāliḥ b. Abī Umāmah b. Sahl; all of them, (Ibn Isḥāq) said, related a part of his story to me: Ka'b b. al-Ashraf, was a man of (the tribe of) Ṭayyi', one of the Banū Nabhān, and his mother was from the (Jewish clan of) Banū al-Naḍīr. When the news reached him, he said, "Alas! Is this true? Can Muḥammad have killed these people whom these two men (meaning Zayd b.
[1369] Ḥārithah and 'Abd Allāh b. Rawāḥah) have named? These are the nobles of the Arabs and the kings of men! By God, if Muḥammad has killed these people, then the belly of the earth is a better place for us than its surface!" When the enemy of God became convinced of the truth of the report, he set out and went to Mecca to stay with al-Muṭṭalib b. Abī Wadā'ah b. Ḍubayrah al-Sahmī, who was married to 'Ātikah bt. Asīd b. Abī al-'Īṣ b. Umayyah b. 'Abd Shams. She received him and offered him hospitality, and he began to arouse people against the Messenger of God, to recite verses, and to weep for the People of the Well from Quraysh who were killed at Badr. Then Ka'b b. al-Ashraf went back to Medina and composed the following amatory poem on Umm al-Faḍl bt. al-Ḥārith:[158]

Are you leaving without stopping in a valley,
and abandoning Umm al-Faḍl in the Ḥaram?

---

157. IH, 548–55; W, 184–93.

158. Umm al-Faḍl bt. al-Ḥārith was the wife of al-'Abbās, but it is not clear why Ka'b should have praised her. She was from the important nomadic tribe of 'Āmir b. Ṣa'ṣa'ah.

Pale-skinned she is, and scented with saffron; if she
were squeezed, she would exude scent, henna and hair-dye.
When she makes to rise, but then does not, what
lies between her ankles and her elbows quivers.
Like Umm Ḥakīm when she was close to us,
the bonds that link us are firm and unsevered
One of the Banū ʿĀmir by whom my heart is driven
to madness; but if she wished, she could cure Kaʿb of
his sickness.
The chief of women; and her father is the chief of
his tribe, a people of high repute, who live up to their
obligations.
Never before her have I seen a sun rising at
night, appearing to us when there is no moon.

Then he composed love poetry on some of the women of the Muslims, causing them offence.

According to Ibn Ḥumayd—Salamah—Muḥammad b. Isḥāq—ʿAbd Allāb b. al-Mughīth b. Abī Burdah: The Prophet said, "Who will rid me of Ibn al-Ashraf?" Muḥammad b. Maslamah, the brother of the Banū ʿAbd al-Ashhal, said, "I will rid you of him, O Messenger of God. I will kill him." "Do it then," he said, [1370] "if you can." Muḥammad b. Maslamah went back and remained for three days, neither eating nor drinking more than would keep him alive. The Messenger of God got to hear of this, so he summoned him and said to him, "Why have you left off food and drink?" "O Messenger of God," he said, "I said something, and I do not know whether or not I can fulfil it." "All that you are obliged to do is try," he replied. "O Messenger of God," he said, "we shall have to tell lies." "Say what you like," he replied. "You are absolved in the matter." Then Muḥammad b. Maslamah, Silkān b. Salāmah b. Waqsh, otherwise known as Abū Nā'ilah, one of the Banū ʿAbd al-Ashhal, and the foster brother of Kaʿb, ʿAbbād b. Bishr b. Waqsh, one of the Banū ʿAbd al-Ashhal, al-Ḥārith b. Aws b. Muʿādh, one of the Banū ʿAbd al-Ashhal, and Abū ʿAbs b. Jabr, one of the Banū Hārithah, made a plan to kill him. Before they all went to Ibn al-Ashraf, they sent ahead Silkān b. Salāmah Abū Nā'ilah. He went to him, and they spoke together for a while, and recited verses to one another, for Abū Nā'ilah was

something of a poet. Then he said, "Ibn al-Ashraf, I have come to you about a matter of which I should like to speak to you, but keep it to yourself." "Go ahead," he replied. "The arrival of this man has been an affliction for us," he said. "The Beduin are hostile to us, and all of them attack us. We cannot travel along the roads, and the result is that our families are facing ruin and suffering. We are all suffering and our families are suffering." Kaʿb replied, "By God, I, Ibn al-Ashraf, warned you, Ibn Salāmah, that things would turn out like this." Silkān said, "I would like you to sell us some food. We will give you a surety and make a firm contract; please treat us generously." "Give me your sons as a surety," he said. "Do you want to disgrace us?" he asked. "I have
[1371] some companions with me who think the same way that I do. I would like to bring them to you so that you can sell to them; please treat us generously. We will deposit with you sufficient coats of mail to guarantee payment of the debt." Silkān wanted him not to be suspicious about the weapons when they came bearing them. He replied, "Coats of mail will be a satisfactory guarantee." Silkān went back to his companions, informed them of what had happened, and told them to take their weapons, set off, and join him. They came together at the house of the Messenger of God.

According to Ibn Ḥumayd—Salamah—Muḥammad b. Isḥāq —Thawr b. Zayd al-Dīlī—ʿIkrimah, the *mawlā* of Ibn ʿAbbās —Ibn ʿAbbās: The Messenger of God went with them to Baqīʿ al-Gharqad and then sent them off, saying, "Go in the name of God; O God, aid them!" Then the Messenger of God went back to his house. It was a moonlit night, and they went forward until they reached Kaʿb's stronghold.[159] Then Abū Nā'ilah called out to him. He had recently married, and he leapt up in his blanket. His wife took hold of one end of it, and said, "You are a fighting man; a man of war does not leave his house at an hour like this." He replied, "It is Abū Nā'ilah. If he had found me sleeping, he would not have wakened me." "By God," she said, "I sense evil in his voice!" Then Kaʿb said to her, "Even if a brave man is summoned

159. One of the features of Medina was the existence of many "strongholds" (*āṭām*, sing. *uṭum*), that is, small forts or fortified houses where those inside were secure from hostile attack.

to a sword thrust, he responds." He went down and spoke with them for a while, and they spoke with him. Then they said to him, "Would you like to walk with us, Ibn al-Ashraf, to Shiʿb al-ʿAjūz, so that we can talk there for the rest of the night?" "If you like," he said. So they set out together and walked for a while. Then Abū Nā'ilah thrust his hand into the hair of his temple, smelt it, and said, "I have never known perfume to smell so good as it does tonight." Then he walked on for a while, and did the [1372] same thing again, so that Ka'b relaxed his guard. Then he walked on for a while, and did it again, taking hold of the hair of both temples. Then he said, "Strike the enemy of God!" Their swords rained blows upon him, but to no avail. Muḥammad b. Maslamah said later, "When I saw that our swords were of no avail, I remembered a long, thin dagger which I had in my scabbard, and took hold of it. By this time the enemy of God had shouted so loudly that lamps had been lit in all the strongholds around us. I plunged the dagger into his breast and pressed upon it so heavily that it reached his pubic region, and the enemy of God fell. Al-Ḥārith b. Aws b. Muʿādh had been wounded in the head or the leg, struck by one of our swords. We left, passing through the quarters of the Banū Umayyah b. Zayd and the Banū Qurayẓah, and then through Buʿāth, until we climbed up the *ḥarrah* of al-ʿUrayḍ. Our companion al-Ḥārith b. Aws was lagging behind us, bleeding heavily, so we waited for him for a while, and then he came to us, having followed in our footsteps.

We lifted him up and carried him to the Messenger of God at the end of the night. He was standing in prayer, so we greeted him, and he came out to meet us. We told him that the enemy of God had been killed, he spat upon the wound of our companion, and we returned to our families. The next morning, the Jews were in a state of fear on account of our attack upon the enemy of God, and there was not a Jew there but feared for his life.

The Messenger of God said, "Whoever of the Jews falls into your hands, kill him." So Muḥayyiṣah b. Masʿūd fell upon Ibn Sunaynah, one of the Jewish merchants who was on close terms with them and used to trade with them, and killed him. Ḥuway- [1373] yiṣah b. Masʿūd (his brother) at that time had not accepted Islam; he was older than Muḥayyiṣah, and when (the latter) killed (the Jew), he began beating him and saying, "O enemy of God, have you killed him? By God, you have much fat in your belly from his wealth." Muḥayyiṣah said, "I said to him, 'By God, if he who commanded me to kill him had commanded me to kill you, I would have cut off your head.'" And, by God, that was the beginning of Ḥuwayyiṣah's acceptance of Islam. He said, "If Muḥammad had ordered you to kill me, you would have killed me?" and I replied, "Yes, by God, if he had ordered me to kill you I would have cut off your head." "By God," he said, "a faith which has brought you to this is indeed a marvel." Then Ḥuwayyiṣah accepted Islam.

According to Ibn Ḥumayd—Salamah—Muḥammad b. Isḥāq: This report was related to me by a *mawlā* of the Banū Ḥārithah—the daughter of Muḥayyiṣah—her father.

Abū Ja'far (al-Ṭabarī) says: Al-Wāqidī asserts that they brought Ibn al-Ashraf's head to the Messenger of God. Al-Wāqidī also asserts that in Rabī' al-Awwal of this year (which began August 22, 624) 'Uthmān b. 'Affān married Umm Kulthūm, the daughter of the Messenger of God, and that she was brought to his house in Jumādā al-Ākhirah (which began November 19, 624). He further asserts that in Rabī' al-Awwal of this year the Messenger of God led the expedition of Anmār, known as Dhū Amarr. We have mentioned Ibn Isḥāq's opinion about this previously.

Al-Wāqidī says: In this month was born al-Sā'ib b. Yazīd b. Ukht al-Namir.

The Expedition to al-Qaradah[160]

Al-Wāqidī says: in Jumādā al-Ākhirah (which began November
[1374] 19, 624) of this year the expedition to al-Qaradah took place. Its leader is said to have been Zayd b. Ḥārithah. This is the first expedition led by Zayd b. Ḥārithah.

According to Abū Ja'far (al-Ṭabarī)—Ibn Ḥumayd—Salamah—Ibn Isḥāq: The Messenger of God sent Zayd b. Ḥārithah on an expedition in which he captured the caravan of Quraysh led by Abū Sufyān b. Ḥarb at Qaradah, a watering place in Najd. After what happened at the battle of Badr, Quraysh were afraid to take the road which they used to follow to Syria and instead took the

160. IH, 547f.; W, 197f.

Iraq route. A number of their merchants set out, and among them was Abū Sufyān b. Ḥarb with a large amount of silver, since this was the main part of their merchandise. They hired a man of Bakr b. Wā'il named Furāt b. Ḥayyān to guide them along this route. The Messenger of God sent out Zayd b. Ḥārithah, who met them at that watering place and captured the caravan and its goods, but was unable to take the men. He then brought the caravan to the Messenger of God.

Abū Jaʿfar (al-Ṭabarī) says: As for al-Wāqidī, he asserts that the reason for this expedition was that Quraysh said, "Muḥammad has damaged our trade, and sits astride our road." Abū Sufyān and Ṣafwān b. Umayyah then argued, "If we stay in Mecca we will consume our capital." Abu Zamʿah al-Aswad said, "I will show you a man who will guide you along the Najdī route; he would find his way if he followed it with his eyes shut." Ṣafwān said, "Who is he? Our need for water is small, for winter is upon us." He said, "Furāt b. Ḥayyān." They summoned him and hired him. He led them out, it being winter, and took them by Dhāt ʿIrq and then by Ghamrah. The news of the caravan reached the Prophet, [1375] as also the information that it contained much wealth and silver vessels which were being carried by Ṣafwān b. Umayyah. Zayd b. Ḥārithah therefore set out, intercepted the caravan, and made himself master of it, although the leading men escaped. The fifth (*khums*) was twenty thousand (dirhams); the Messenger of God took it and divided the other four fifths among the members of the expedition. Furāt b. Ḥayyān al-ʿIjlī was taken captive. They said to him, "If you accept Islam, the Messenger of God will not kill you." When the Messenger of God summoned him to Islam, he accepted it, and was allowed to go free.

The Killing of Abū Rāfiʿ the Jew[161]

Abū Jaʿfar (al-Ṭabarī) says: In this year, it is said, the killing of Abū Rāfiʿ the Jew took place. The reason for his being killed was, it is said, that he used to take the part of Kaʿb b. al-Ashraf against the Messenger of God. The Messenger of God is said to have sent

161. IH, 714–6, 981; W, 391–5; Watt, *Medina*, 212f.

ʿAbd Allāh b.ʿAtīk against him in the middle of Jumādā al-Ākhirah of this year (which began November 19, 624).

According to Hārūn b. Isḥāq al-Hamdānī—Muṣʿab b. Miqdām—Isrāʾīl—Abū Isḥāq—al-Barāʾ: The Messenger of God sent some of the Anṣār under the command of ʿAbd Allāh b. ʿUqbah or ʿAbd Allah b. ʿAtīk against Abū Rāfiʿ the Jew, who was in the Ḥijāz. Abū Rāfiʿ used to injure and wrong the Messenger of God. He lived in his stronghold in the Ḥijāz. When the Muslim party drew
[1376] close to it, as the sun was setting and the people were bringing their flocks back, ʿAbd Allāh b. ʿUqbah or ʿAbd Allāh b. ʿAtīk said to the others, "Stay where you are, and I will go and ingratiate myself with the doorkeeper, in the hope of gaining entrance." He went forward, and when he was close to the door, he wrapped himself up in his cloak as though he were relieving himself. Everybody else had gone in, and the doorkeeper called to him, "You there, if you want to come in, come in, because I want to shut the door." "I went in," he said, "and hid myself in a donkey pen. When everybody had come in, the man shut the door and hung up the keys on a wooden peg. I went to the keys, took them, and opened the door. Abū Rāfiʿ had company that evening in some upper rooms, and when his guests left I went up to him. Every time I opened a door, I shut it again behind me from inside, saying to myself, 'If they become aware of me, they will not be able to reach me before I kill him.' When I reached him, he was in a dark room along with his family. As I did not know where he was in the room, I said, 'Abū Rāfiʿ!' and he said, 'Who is that?' I rushed toward the sound and gave him a blow with my sword, but I was in a state of confusion and did not achieve anything. He gave a shout, and I left the room but remained close at hand. I then went in again and said, 'What was that noise, Abū Rafiʿ?' 'God damn it,' he said, 'there is a man in the house who has just struck me with
[1377] his sword.' Then I hit him and covered him with wounds, but I could not kill him, so I thrust the point of my sword into his stomach until it came out through his back. At that, I knew that I had killed him, and I opened the doors one by one until I reached a flight of stairs. Thinking that I had reached the ground, I put my foot out but fell into a moonlit night and broke my leg. I bound it up with my turban and moved on. Finally, finding myself sitting by the door, I said to myself, 'By God, I will not leave tonight un-

til I know whether I have killed him or not.' When the cock crowed, the announcer of his death stood upon the wall and said, 'I announce the death of Abū Rāfiʿ, the profit-maker of the people of Ḥijāz.' I went to my companions and said, 'Deliverance! God has killed Abū Rāfiʿ.' Then I went to the Prophet and told him, and he said, 'Stretch out your leg!' When I stretched it out, he stroked it, and it was as though I had never had anything wrong with it."

Abū Jaʿfar (al-Ṭabarī) says: As for al-Wāqidī, he asserts that this expedition sent by the Messenger of God against Abū Rāfiʿ Sallām b. Abī al-Ḥuqayq was sent in the fourth year of the Hijrah in Dhū al-Ḥijjah (which began May 4, 626) and that those who went to him and killed him were Abū Qatādah, ʿAbd Allāh b. ʿAtīk, Masʿūd b. Sinān, al-Aswad b. Khuzāʿī, and ʿAbd Allāh b. Unays. [1378]

According to Ibn Ḥumayd—Salamah—Ibn Isḥāq: Sallām b. Abī al-Ḥuqayq, who was Abū Rāfiʿ, was one of those who had mustered the *aḥzāb* against the Messenger of God. Al-Aws had killed Kaʿb b. al-Ashraf before Uḥud on account of his enmity to the Messenger of God and his inciting people against him, and so al-Khazraj asked permission of the Messenger of God to kill Sallām b. Abī al-Ḥuqayq, who was in Khaybar, and was granted this.

According to Ibn Ḥumayd—Salamah—Muḥammad b. Isḥāq—Muḥammad b. Muslim b. ʿUbayd Allāh b. Shihāb al-Zuhrī—ʿAbd Allah b. Kaʿb b. Mālik: One of the favours which God conferred upon his Prophet was that these two tribes of the Anṣār, al-Aws and al-Khazraj, used to vie with one another like stallions as regards the Messenger of God; al-Aws did not do anything which benefited the Messenger of God without al-Khazraj saying, "By God, they will not gain superiority over us in Islam in the eyes of the Messenger of God by doing this," and they would not cease until they had done something similar. When al-Khazraj did something, al-Aws said the same. Thus, when al-Aws killed Kaʿb b. al-Ashraf on account of his hostility to the Messenger of God, al-Khazraj said, "They will never take superiority from us by doing that." They conferred together to find a man comparable to Ibn al-Ashraf in hostility to the Messenger of God and called to mind Ibn Abī al-Ḥuqayq, who was in Khaybar. They then asked the Messenger of God for permission to kill him, and this he gave. Five men of al-Khazraj, of the clan of Banu Salimah, [1379] set out, ʿAbd Allāh b. ʿAtīk, Masʿūd b. Sinān, ʿAbd Allah b. Unays, Abū Qatādah al-Ḥārith b. Ribʿī, and Khuzāʿī b. al-Aswad, a confederate of theirs from (the tribe of) Aslam. The Messenger of God put ʿAbd Allāh b. ʿAtīk in command of them and forbade them to kill women or children. Setting out, they reached Khaybar and entered Ibn Abī al-Ḥuqayq's house by night. As they went, they shut the door of every room in the house upon its occupants. Ibn Abī al-Ḥuqayq was in an upper room reached by a spiral stairway. They climbed up this, went to the door, and asked permission to enter. A woman came out to them and said, "Who are you?" They replied, "We are some beduin seeking provisions of grain." She said, "The man you want is over there; go in and see him." "When we went in," (they said), "we shut the door behind her, ourselves, and him, being afraid that a patrol might prevent us from getting at him. His wife gave a shout to warn him of our presence, and we rushed upon him with our swords as he was in his bed. By God, the only thing which guided us to him in the blackness of the night was his whiteness, as though he were a piece of Egyptian linen thrown down there.

"When his wife shouted that we were there, one of us would raise his sword against her; then he would remember the Prophet's prohibition and withdraw his hand. If it had not been for that, we would have dispatched him that night. After we had struck him with our swords, ʿAbd Allāh b. Unays thrust his sword into his stomach and transfixed him while he was shouting, 'Enough! Enough!' At once we went out. ʿAbd Allāh b. ʿAtīk had bad eye-
[1380] sight, and he fell off the stairway, bruising his leg severely. We lifted him up, took him to one of their water channels, and entered it. They lit lamps, and searched for us in every nook and cranny, but finally they gave up hope and went back to their master, crowding round him as he lay dying. We said to ourselves, 'How shall we know that the enemy of God is dead?' One of us said, 'I will go and look for you.' He set off and mingled with the people. He said later, 'I found him with the men of the Jews, and with his wife, who had a lamp in her hand and was looking into his face. Then she said, speaking to them, "By God, I recognised the voice of Ibn ʿAtīk, but then I thought I must be wrong, and said to myself, 'How could Ibn ʿAtīk be in this country?'" Then she turned to him to look in his face, and said, "By the God of the

Jews, he is dead." 'I never heard any words more pleasing to me,' said our companion.

"He then came back to us and told us the news. We lifted up our injured companion, went to the Messenger of God, and told him that we had killed the enemy of God. We disagreed in his presence about the killing of Ibn Abī al-Ḥuqayq, each of us claiming to have done it. The Messenger of God then said, 'Bring your swords,' and when we did so he looked at them and said, 'This sword of ʿAbd Allāh b. Unays killed him. I can see the marks left by bones on it.'"

Speaking of the killing of Kaʿb b. al-Ashraf and Sallām b. Abī al-Ḥuqayq, Ḥassān b.Thābit[162] said:

How excellent are the people whom we met, Ibn (Abī)
al-Ḥuqayq and you, Ibn al-Ashraf!
Travelling by night towards you with nimble swords, [1381]
as proud as lions in a wooded den
Until they came to you in your country, and made you
taste death with sweeping swords,
Vigilant for the victory of the faith of their Prophet,
and setting at naught every calamity.

According to Mūsā b.ʿAbd al-Raḥmān al-Masrūqī and ʿAbbās b. ʿAbd al-ʿAẓīm al-ʿAnbarī—Jaʿfar b. ʿAwn—Ibrāhīm b. Ismāʿīl—Ibrāhīm b. ʿAbd al-Raḥmān b. Kaʿb b. Mālik—his father—his mother, the daughter of ʿAbd Allāh b. Unays—ʿAbd Allāh b. Unays: The company whom the Messenger of God sent to Ibn Abī al-Ḥuqayq to kill him comprised ʿAbd Allāh b. ʿAtīk, ʿAbd Allāh b. Unays, Abū Qatādah, one of their confederates, and a man of the Anṣār. They reached Khaybar at night. ʿAbd Allāh b. Unays said, "We went to their doors, shut them from the outside, and took the keys, so that they were locked in. Then we threw the keys into an irrigation ditch and went to the upper room where [1382]
Ibn Abī al-Ḥuqayq was lying. ʿAbd Allāh b.ʿAtīk and I went up there while our companions sat down by the wall. ʿAbd Allāh b.ʿAtīk asked permission to enter, and Ibn Abī al-Ḥuqayq's wife

162. Ḥassān b. Thābit of the tribe of al-Khazraj in Medina was the most prominent of the poets supporting Muḥammad; cf. *EI*², art. Ḥassān b. Thābit (W. Arafat). This poem is to be found in his *Dīwān*, ed. Arafat, London 1971, i.211f.

said, 'That is 'Abd Allāh b. 'Atīk's voice.' Ibn Abī al-Ḥuqayq said, 'May your mother be bereaved of you! 'Abd Allāh b. 'Atīk is in Yathrib. How could he be with you at this hour? Open the door! No honourable man turns visitors from his door at such an hour.' So she got up and opened the door, and I and 'Abd Allāh went in to Ibn Abī al-Ḥuqayq. 'Abd Allāh b. 'Atīq said, 'You take care of her!' So I unsheathed my sword against her, and I was going to strike her with it, but I remembered that the Messenger of God had forbidden the killing of women and children, and I desisted. 'Abd Allāh b. 'Atīk went up to Ibn Abī al-Ḥuqayq. 'I looked at him,' he said, 'at the extreme whiteness of his skin in a dark upper room, and when he saw me and saw the sword, he took the pillow and tried to fend me off with it. I made to strike him, but was unable to do so, and instead pierced him with it.' Then 'Abd Allāh b. Unays came out to join me, and said, 'Shall I kill him?' I said, 'Yes,' so he went in and finished him off.

"Then (said 'Abd Allāh b. Unays) I went out to 'Abd Allāh b. 'Atīk and we left, and the woman shouted, 'A night raid! A night raid!' Then 'Abd Allāh b. 'Atīk fell down the staircase and said, 'My leg! My leg!' I carried him until I was able to lay him down on the ground and said, 'Go! There is nothing wrong with your leg.' So we left. We came to our companions and set off. Then I remembered my bow, which I had left in the staircase. I returned for my bow, and there were the people of Khaybar, surging against
[1383] one another and saying nothing but, 'Who has killed Ibn Abī al-Ḥuqayq? Who has killed Ibn Abī al-Ḥuqayq?" I did not look anybody in the face, while nobody looked me in the face, but I merely said, "Who has killed Ibn Abī al-Ḥuqayq?" I then went up the staircase, while people were going up and down, took my bow from where it was and left. When I reached my companions, we hid during the day and travelled by night; when we were hiding we posted one of our number as a sentry to keep watch for us, and if he saw anything he would signal to us, and we would move on. When we were at al-Bayḍā', I (Mūsā said, 'I was their sentinel,' and 'Abbās said, 'I was their sentry,') gave the signal, and they moved off at a brisk pace. I followed in their footsteps until we were close to Medina, and then caught up with them. They said, "What is the matter? Have you seen something?" "No," I said,

"But I knew that you were exhausted and ill, and I wanted fear to spur you on."'"

The Prophet Marries Ḥafṣah

Abū Ja'far (al-Ṭabarī) says: In this year the Prophet married Ḥafṣah bt. 'Umar, in Sha'bān (which began January 17, 625).[163] She had previously been married to Khunays b. Ḥudhāfah al-Sahmī in the Jāhiliyyah, and he had left her a widow.

The Expedition to Uḥud[164]

In this year also there took place the expedition of the Messenger of God to Uḥud. This is said to have been on Saturday, 7 Shawwāl, in Year Three of the Hijrah (March 23, 625).

Abū Ja'far (al-Ṭabarī) says: What provoked the expedition to Uḥud by the polytheists of Quraysh against the Messenger of God was the battle of Badr and the killing of those nobles and chiefs of Quraysh who were killed there.

According to Ibn Ḥumayd—Salamah—Muḥammad b. Isḥāq:
(Ibn Isḥāq said) Muḥammad b. Muslim b. 'Ubayd Allāh b. Shihāb [1384]
al-Zuhrī and Muḥammad b. Yaḥyā b. Ḥibbān and 'Āṣim b. 'Umar b. Qatāda b and al-Ḥuṣayn b. 'Abd al-Raḥmān b. 'Amr b. Sa'd b.Mu'ādh and others of our scholars have all related a part of this narrative concerning the day of Uḥud, and their narrative is combined in the account which I have given of the day of Uḥud. They say that when Quraysh—or, according to some versions, when the People of the Well of the unbelievers of Quraysh on the day of Badr—were overtaken by disaster, and their defeated remnants reached Mecca, and when Abū Sufyān b. Ḥarb returned with his caravan, 'Abd Allāh b. Abī Rabī'ah, 'Ikrimah b. Abī Jahl, and Ṣafwān b. Umayyah went at the head of a number of men of Quraysh whose fathers, sons, and brothers had been killed at Badr

163. There were reasons of state for Muḥammad's marriage with Ḥafṣah, as with virtually all his other marriages. She was the daughter of one of his chief supporters, 'Umar, later second caliph. Her first husband was a Muslim from Mecca killed at Badr.

164. IH, 555–638; W, 199–334; Watt, *Medina*, 21–9.

and addressed Abū Sufyān b. Ḥarb and those members of Quraysh who had goods in that caravan, saying, "Men of Quraysh, Muḥammad has bereaved you and killed the best of you; aid us with this wealth to wage war against him and perhaps we will obtain vengeance upon him for those of us who have been killed." They agreed to do so. When Abū Sufyān and the owners of the caravan agreed to this, Quraysh assembled to wage war against the Messenger of God, together with their Aḥābīsh[165] and those of the tribes of Kinānah and the people of Tihāmah who obeyed them.
[1385] All of these people raised a clamour to wage war against the Messenger of God.

Abū ʿAzzah ʿAmr b. ʿAbd Allāh al-Jumaḥī had been treated kindly by the Messenger of God on the day of Badr, being a poor man with daughters. He was among the captives, and he said, "O Messenger of God, I am a poor man with a family and with needs which you are aware of; so treat me kindly, may God bless you!" The Messenger of God then treated him kindly.

Ṣafwān b. Umayyah now said, "Abū ʿAzzah, you are a poet, so aid us with your tongue, and join our expedition." "Muḥammad has treated me kindly," he replied, "and I do not wish to help against him." "No," he urged, "aid us in person, and I swear before God that if you return I will make you a rich man and that if you are killed I will treat your daughters as I treat my own daughters; whatever hardship or prosperity comes my daughters' way will come their way." With this assurance, Abū ʿAzzah joined the expedition, travelling through Tihāmah and calling upon the Banū Kinānah. Similarly, Musāfiʿ b. ʿAbd Manāf b. Wahb b. Hudhāfah b. Jumaḥ went to the Banū Mālik b. Kinānah to rouse them and call upon them to fight the Messenger of God.

Jubayr b.Muṭʿim called a slave of his called Waḥshī, who was an Abyssinian who threw his javelin in the Abyssinian manner and rarely missed with it, and said to him, "Go with the army, and if you kill Muḥammad's uncle in retaliation for my uncle Ṭuʿaymah b. ʿAdī, you are free." Quraysh set out armed and determined

165. These Aḥābīsh (meaning "group of people not all of one tribe") were a confederacy of small clans or subtribes. The most important was Banū al-Ḥarith b. ʿAbd Manāt b. Kinānah; others were al-Muṣṭaliq and al-Hūn (with subdivisions ʿAḍal and al-Qārah). The assertion of Henri Lammens that they were Abyssinian slave mercenaries is mistaken. Cf. *EI*², art. Ḥabash. last section.

on battle, with their Aḥābīsh and those of the Banū Kinānah and the people of Tihāmah who were with them. They had taken their womenfolk with them in the hope that they would be spurred on by zeal to defend these and would not run away. Abū Sufyān b. Ḥarb, who was the leader of the army, had with him [1386]
Hind bt. ʿUtbah b. Rabīʿah; ʿIkrimah b. Abī Jahl b. Hishām b. al-Mughīrah had with him Umm Ḥakīm bt. al-Ḥārith b. Hishām b. al-Mughīrah; al-Ḥārith b. Hishām b. al-Mughīrah had with him Fāṭimah bt. al-Walīd b. al-Mughīrah; Ṣafwān b. Umayyah b. Khalaf had with him Barzah (Abū Jaʿfar [al-Ṭabarī] asserts that some say Barrah) bt. Masʿūd b. ʿAmr b. ʿUmayr al-Thaqafiyyah, the mother of ʿAbd Allāh b. Ṣafwān; ʿAmr b. al-ʿAṣ b. Wāʾil had with him Rayṭah bt. Munabbih b. al-Ḥajjāj, the mother of ʿAbd Allāh b. ʿAmr b. al-ʿĀṣ; Ṭalḥah b. Abī Ṭalḥah, who was ʿAbd Allāh b. ʿAbd al-ʿUzzā b.ʿUthmān b. ʿAbd al-Dār, had with him Sulāfah bt. Saʿd b. Shuhayd, the mother of Musāfiʿ, al-Julās, and Kilāb, sons of Ṭalḥah, who were killed on that day together with their father; Khunās bt. Mālik b. al-Muḍarrib, one of the women of the Banū Mālik b. Ḥisl, and the mother of Muṣʿab b. ʿUmayr, set out with her son Abū ʿAzīz b. ʿUmayr, and ʿAmrah bt. ʿAlqamah, one of the women of the Banū al-Ḥārith b. ʿAbd Manāt b. Kinānah, also set out.

Every time Hind bt. ʿUtbah b. Rabīʿah passed by Waḥshī, or he [1387]
passed by her, she would say, "Go to it, Abū Dusmah! Quench my thirst for vengeance, and quench your own!" Abū Dusmah was Waḥshī's *kunyah.*[166]

The Meccan force went forward, and halted at ʿAynayn on a hill in the valley of al-Sabkhah of Qanāt on the edge of the wadi nearest to Medina. When the Messenger of God and the Muslims

---

166. The *kunyah* or "parent name" is the name of the form "Abū M" or "Umm N" ("father of M," "mother of N"), and was a title of respect. M or N was usually the eldest son, but, especially in Medina, could instead be a daughter. Sometimes a *kunyah* seems to have been given to children as a first name, as in the case of Muḥammad's daughter Umm Kulthūm, and sometimes as a kind of nickname. While Waḥshī could conceivably have had a daughter called Dusmah (or Dasmah), it seems more likely that Abū Dusmah, "father of duskiness or blackness," was felt to be an appropriate name for an Abyssinian slave; but it does not seem to be a disrespectful mode of address, just as the name of Muḥammad's uncle Abū Lahab probably originally meant "father of brightness," although Sūrah 91 links it with the flame (*lahab*) of Hell.

heard that they were camped there, the Messenger of God said to the Muslims, "I saw in a dream some cattle, and interpreted them as a good omen; and I saw that the blade of my sword was notched, and I saw that I had put on an invulnerable coat of mail, and I interpreted that as Medina. If you see fit to remain in Medina and to leave them encamped where they are, well and good; for, if they remain there, they will be in the worst possible place, and if they enter Medina to fight us, we will fight them here."

Quraysh camped at Uḥud on Wednesday and remained there on that day, Thursday, and Friday. When the Messenger of God had led the Friday prayer, he went out and reached the gorge of Uḥud the following morning. Battle was joined on Saturday, halfway through Shawwāl (March 23, 625).

The opinion of ʿAbd Allāh b. Ubayy b. Salūl was the same as the opinion of the Messenger of God on this matter, that he should not go out to meet the enemy. Yet, although the Messenger of God had not wanted to go out of Medina, some men of the Muslims whom God ennobled with martyrdom on the day of Uḥud, and others who had missed Badr and the chance to be there, said,
[1388] "O Messenger of God, lead us out to our enemies so that they may not think that we are too cowardly and weak to face them." ʿAbd Allāh b. Ubayy b. Salūl said, "O Messenger of God, stay in Medina and do not go out to meet them. By God, we have never gone out of it to meet an enemy but that they have inflicted severe losses on us; and no enemy has ever entered it but that we have inflicted severe losses on them. Leave them alone, O Messenger of God, and if they remain, they will be in the worst possible place; and if they enter Medina, the men will fight them face to face, and the women and boys will hurl stones at them from above; if they then withdraw, they will withdraw disappointed in their hopes, as they came." Those who were eager to meet the enemy, however, continued to press the Messenger of God until he went into his house and put on his coat of mail. This was on Friday, after he had finished the prayer.

On that day there had died a man of the Anṣār called Mālik b. ʿAmr, one of the Banū al-Najjār. The Messenger of God prayed over him, and then went out to meet the enemy. By this time the people had repented; they said, "We have compelled the Messenger of God against his wishes, and we had no right to do this."

The narrative of al-Suddī.

Abū Ja'far (al-Ṭabarī) says that according to Muḥammad b. al-Ḥusayn—Aḥmad b. al-Mufaḍḍal—Asbāṭ—al-Suddī, when the Messenger of God heard that the polytheists of Quraysh and their followers had camped at Uḥud he said to his companions, "Advise me what I should do." They said, "O Messenger of God, lead us out to these dogs." The Anṣār said, "O Messenger of God, no enemy of ours has ever overcome us who came to us in our dwelling places, so how much more will this be the case now that you are among us." The Messenger of God called upon 'Abd Allāh b. Ubayy b. Salūl, although he had never called upon him before, [1389] and asked for his counsel. "O Messenger of God," he said, "lead us out to these dogs." The Messenger of God would have preferred that the enemy should enter Medina, so that the fighting could be in the alleyways. Al-Nu'mān b. Mālik al-Anṣārī came to him and said, "O Messenger of God, do not deprive me of Paradise! By him who sent you with the truth, I shall indeed enter Paradise!" "In what way?" the Messenger of God said. Al-Nu'mān replied, "By testifying that there is no deity but God and that you are the Messenger of God, and by not fleeing from the advancing enemy." "You have spoken the truth," the Messenger of God said. Al-Nu'mān was killed that day.

The Messenger of God then called for his coat of mail and put it on. When they saw him armed, the people repented and said, "What an evil deed we have done, giving the Messenger of God advice when inspiration comes to him!" They rose up and apologised to him, saying, "Do what you see fit!" The Messenger of God replied, "It is not fitting for a prophet to put on his coat of mail and take it off again before fighting." So the Messenger of God went out to Uḥud at the head of a thousand men, having promised them victory if they showed endurance. When he went out, however, 'Abd Allāh b. Ubayy b. Salūl returned with three hundred men. Abū Jābir al-Salimī followed them, calling them, but they did not heed him[167] and said to him, "We know of no battle; and if you take our advice, you will come back with us." On

167. Al-Ṭabarī's text does not quite make sense here, perhaps owing to a careless abridgement, and has been slightly changed in translation; see Ibn Isḥāq's version below.

this occasion God said, "When two parties of you almost fell away. . . ."[168] The two parties were the Banū Salimah and the Banū Ḥārithah, who were minded to go back when ʿAbd Allāh b. Ubayy went back; but God restrained them, and the Messenger of God remained at the head of seven hundred men.

Resumption of the narrative of Ibn Isḥāq.

When the Messenger of God went out to do battle with the en-
[1390] emy, the Muslims said, "O Messenger of God, we have compelled you against your will, and we had no right to do this. If you wish, stay here, may God bless you." The Messenger of God replied, "It is not fitting for a prophet when he has put on his coat of mail to take it off until he fights." So the Messenger of God went out at the head of a thousand men of his companions until, when they were at al-Shawṭ, between Uḥud and Medina, ʿAbd Allāh b. Ubayy b. Salūl split off from him with a third of the army, saying, "He obeyed them by setting out and disobeyed me. By God, we do not know why we should get ourselves killed here, men." So he went back to Medina with those of his people of the Hypocrites and doubters who followed him. ʿAbd Allāh b. ʿAmr b. Ḥarām, the brother of the Banū Salimah, followed them saying, "I call on you in God's name not to abandon your Prophet and your people when the enemy is here!" They replied, "If we knew that we were going to fight, we would not desert you, but we do not think that there is going to be a battle." When they thus refused to heed him and insisted on going back, he said, "God curse you, enemies of God! God will let us manage without you."

According to Abū Jaʿfar (al-Ṭabarī)—Muḥammad b. ʿUmar al-Wāqidī: ʿAbd Allāh b. Ubayy split off from the Messenger of God at al-Shaykhayn with three hundred men, and the Messenger of God remained with seven hundred. The polytheists numbered three thousand and their cavalry numbered two hundred horse. Their womenfolk numbered fifteen.

Among the polytheists there were seven hundred men wearing coats of mail, while among the Muslims there were only one hundred. The Muslims had no cavalry with them apart from two

168. Qur. 3.22.

horses, one belonging to the Messenger of God and one belonging to Abū Burdah b. Niyār al-Ḥārithī. The Messenger of God set out before daybreak from al-Shaykhayn, just as the sky was beginning [1391] to redden. Al-Shaykhayn received the name from two strongholds which were looked after by a blind Jew and a blind Jewess who used to talk to one another; they were called al-Shaykhayn (the two old people) because of this. They lie at the furthest extremity of Medina.

The Messenger of God had reviewed his troops at al-Shaykhayn after sunset, allowing some to go on and sending some back. Among those whom he sent back were Zayd b. Thābit, Ibn 'Umar, Usayd b. Ẓuhayr, al-Barā' b. 'Āzib, and 'Arābah b. Aws. The latter is the person of whom al-Shammākh said:

> I considered 'Arābah the Awsite a man of good deeds,
> one without equal
> When the banner of glory was raised aloft,
> 'Arābah accepted it with his right hand.

He also sent back Abū Sa'īd al-Khudrī, but allowed Samurah b. Jundub and Rāfi' b. Khadīj to go on. The Messenger of God had considered Rāfi' too young, but he stood on his pair of patched shoes and stretched himself on tiptoe to his full height, and when the Messenger of God saw him, he passed him.

According to Al-Ḥārith—Ibn Sa'd—Muḥammad b. 'Umar (al-Wāqidī): Samurah's mother was married to Murayy b. Sinān b. Tha'labah, the uncle of Abū Sa'īd al-Khudrī, and he was Samurah's stepfather. When the Messenger of God went out to Uḥud, reviewed his men and sent back those whom he thought too young, he sent back Samurah b. Jundub and passed Rāfi' b. Khadīj. Then Samurah b. Jundub said to his stepfather Murayy b. Sinān, "Father, the Messenger of God has passed Rāfi' b. Khadīj and sent me back, but I can throw Rāfi' b. Khadīj in wrestling." So Murayy [1392] b. Sinān said, "O Messenger of God, you have sent back my son and passed Rāfi' b. Khadīj, but my son can throw him in wrestling." The Messenger of God said to Rāfi' and Samurah, "Wrestle!" Samurah threw Rāfi', and so the Messenger of God passed him, and he was present at the battle with the Muslims. The Prophet's guide was Abū Ḥathmah al-Ḥārithī.

Resumption of the narrative of Ibn Isḥāq.

As the Messenger of God was proceeding across the *ḥarrah* of the Banū Ḥārithah, a horse swished its tail, hit the handle of a sword, and knocked it out of its scabbard. The Messenger of God, who liked omens, although he did not take auguries from the flight of birds, said to the owner of the sword, "Sheathe your sword, for I see that swords will be drawn today." Then the Messenger of God said to his companions, "Who can take us close to the enemy by a road which will not cause us to pass by them?" Abū Ḥathmah, the brother of the Banū Ḥārithah b. al-Ḥārith, said, "I can, O Messenger of God." He took him through the *ḥarrah* of the Banū Ḥārithah and between their property, until he brought him to the property of al-Mirbaʿ b. Qayẓī, who was a Hypocrite, and blind. When the latter became aware of the presence of the Messenger of God and the Muslims with him, he rose up and threw dust in their faces, saying, "Even if you are the Messenger of God, I will not allow you into my garden!" I was told that he
[1393] took a handful of dust and then said: "If only I knew that I would not hit anyone else, Muḥammad, I would throw it in your face." The people rushed up to kill him, but the Messenger of God said, "Do not do so, for this man who is blind of sight is also blind of heart." Saʿd b. Yazīd, the brother of the Banū ʿAbd al-Ashhal, had rushed up to al-Mirbaʿ as the Messenger of God uttered this prohibition, and he split al-Mirbaʿ's head open with his bow.

The Messenger of God proceeded until he came down into the gorge from Uḥud on the slope up from the wadi towards the mountain. He stationed his men with their backs and their camp towards Uḥud, and said, "Let no one fight until I command him to fight." Quraysh had set their camels and horses free to pasture in some crops in al-Ṣamghah of Qanāt belonging to the Muslims, and one of the Muslims said, when the Messenger of God ordered them not to join battle, "Are the crops of the Banū Qaylah[169] to be used as grazing before we come to blows?" Then the Prophet prepared to fight with his seven hundred men, and Quraysh prepared to fight with their three thousand men and two hundred horses. They put Khālid b. al-Walīd in command of the right wing of the

169. Banū Qaylah is the name for the two tribes of al-Aws and al-Khazraj together, Qaylah being ostensibly the mother of both.

cavalry and ʿIkrimah b. Abī Jahl in command of the left wing. The Messenger of God put ʿAbd Allāh b. Jubayr, the brother of the Banū ʿAmr b. ʿAwf, in comı and of the archers. He was distinguished on that day by white clothes, and the archers numbered fifty men. "Defend us against the cavalry with your arrows," he said, "and do not come up behind us whether the battle goes for us or against us. Hold firm to your position, so that we will not be attacked from your direction." Then the Messenger of God put on two coats of mail.

The Fighting Begins

According to Hārūn b. Isḥāq—Muṣʿab b. al-Miqdām—Isrā'īl; [1394]
and (also) Ibn Wakīʿ—his father—Isrā'īl—Abū Isḥāq—al-Barā': When it was the day of Uḥud and the Messenger of God met the polytheists, he stationed certain men as archers and put them under the command of ʿAbd Allāh b. Jubayr, with the order, "If you see us victorious over them, do not leave your position, and if you see them victorious over us, do not come to our assistance." When battle was joined, the polytheists were put to flight, and I saw the women tucking up their skirts in flight and exposing their anklets. A cry went up of "Booty, booty!" ʿAbd Allāh said, "Not so fast! Do you not know the orders the Messenger of God gave you?" They refused to listen to him, however, and left. When they reached the others, God turned away their faces and seventy of the Muslims were killed.

According to Muḥammad b. Saʿd—his father—his paternal uncle—his father—his father—Ibn ʿAbbās: Abū Sufyān arrived on 3 Shawwāl (March 19, 625) and camped at Uḥud. The Prophet marched out, called on the people to come to fight and assembled them round him. He ordered al-Zubayr, who had al-Miqdād b. al-Aswad al-Kindī with him on that day, to engage the cavalry, and gave the banner to a man of Quraysh called Muṣʿab b. ʿUmayr. Next Ḥamzah b. ʿAbd al-Muṭṭalib marched out at the head of those who had no armour; he sent Ḥamzah out immediately in front of himself.

When Khālid b. al-Walīd advanced with the polytheist cavalry, together with ʿIkrimah b. Abī Jahl, the Messenger of God dispatched al-Zubayr with the order, "Meet Khālid b. al-Walīd and [1395] engage him until I give you further orders." Then he gave orders concerning other (enemy) horsemen who were in another part of the field, and said, "Do not leave your positions until I give you further orders."

Abū Sufyān advanced, raising a cry of "Al-Lāt! Al-ʿUzzā!"[170] The Prophet sent al-Zubayr against the enemy, and when he attacked Khālid b. al-Walīd, God put Khālid and his companions to flight. With reference to this, God said, "Allah verily made good His promise unto you . . . after He had shown you that for which ye long." God had promised the believers that He would give them victory and that He would be with them.

The Messenger of God had sent certain people to take up positions behind his army, and said to them, "Stay here and turn back any of us who flees, and act as a guard for our rear." When the Messenger of God and his companions put the enemy to flight, those who had been posted to the rear said to one another, when they saw the enemy's women scrambling up the hill and saw the booty, "Let us go to the Messenger of God and get the booty before the others beat us to it." Another group said, "No, we should obey the Messenger of God and keep to our position." It is to this that God's words refer: "Whoso desireth . . . the world," i.e., those who desired the booty, "and whoso desireth . . . the Hereafter," i.e., those who said, "We should obey the Messenger of God and keep to our position."[171] Ibn Masʿūd used to say, "I never realised that any of the Prophet's companions desired the world and its goods until that day."

According to Muḥammad b. al-Ḥusayn—Aḥmad b. al-Mufaḍ-
[1396] ḍal—Asbāṭ—al-Suddī: When the Messenger of God took the field at Uḥud, he gave orders to the archers who then took up a position at the base of the mountain facing the polytheist cavalry. He said, "Do not leave your positions if you see that we have put them to flight, for we shall not cease to be victorious as long as you keep to your positions."

He put ʿAbd Allāh b. Jubayr, the brother of Khawwāt b. Jubayr, in command of them.

---

170. These are two goddesses worshipped by the Meccans; see Watt, *Mecca*, 102–4. The verse quoted below is Qur. 3.152.

171. Qur. 3.145.

Then Ṭalḥah b. ʿUthmān,[172] the polytheist's standard-bearer, rose up and said, "You companions of Muḥammad, you assert that God will hasten us to Hell by means of your swords, and that He will hasten you to Paradise by means of our swords. Is there one of you whom God will hasten to Paradise by means of my sword, or who will hasten me to Hell by means of his sword?" ʿAlī b. Abī Ṭālib rose up and said, "By him who holds my soul in his hand, I shall not separate from you until I have hastened you to Hell by means of my sword or until you have hastened me to Paradise by means of your sword." Then ʿAlī struck him, cutting off his foot, and Talhah b. ʿUthmān fell down, exposing his genitals. He said, "I call on you in the name of God and in the name of blood-relationship, cousin!" So ʿAlī left him, and the Messenger of God cried out, "God is great!" His companions said to ʿAlī, "What prevented you from finishing him off?" He said, "My cousin called on me in God's name with his genitals exposed, and I felt a sense of shame before him."

After this al-Zubayr b. al-ʿAwwām and al-Miqdād b. al-Aswad attacked the polytheists and put them to flight, while the Prophet and his companions charged and put Abū Sufyān to flight. When Khālid b. al-Walīd, who was in command of the polytheists' cavalry, saw this, he made a countercharge, but the archers rained arrows upon him, and his advance was checked. However, when the archers saw the Messenger of God and his companions in the heart of the polytheists' camp and plundering them, they hurried down to the booty. Some of them said, "Do not go against the command of the Messenger of God," but most of them went to the camp. When Khālid saw how few archers there were left, he [1397]
shouted to his cavalry, charged, and killed the archers, and then charged the Prophet's companions. When the polytheists on foot saw that their cavalry was in action, they called to one another and renewed their attack on the Muslims, defeating them and killing some.

According to Bishr b. Ādam—ʿAmr b. ʿĀṣim al-Kilābī—ʿUbayd

172. The person intended is Ṭalḥah b. ʿAbd Allāh b. ʿAbd al-ʿUzzā b. ʿUthmān, also known as Ṭalḥah b. Abī Ṭalḥah; see W, 225f. The exposure of the genitals was deliberate and was a way of asking for mercy. It is not clear what precise cousinship Ṭalḥah intended; his paternal aunt Barrah bt. ʿAbd al-ʿUzzā was Muḥammad's maternal grandmother.

Allāh b. al-Wāzi'—Hishām b. 'Urwah—his father—al-Zubayr: The Messenger of God displayed a sword in his hand on the day of Uḥud, and said, "Who will take this sword with its right?" I rose up and said, "I will, O Messenger of God." But he turned away from me, and said again, "Who will take this sword with its right?" I said again, "I will, O Messenger of God," but he turned away from me and said, "Who will take this sword with its right?" Then Abū Dujānah Simāk b. Kharashah rose up and said, "I will take it with its right. What is its right?" The Messenger of God replied,"Its right is that you should not kill a Muslim with it, and that you should not flee with it from an unbeliever." Then he gave it to him.

When he was eager for battle, Abū Dujānah used to wear a headband as a distinguishing mark, and I said to myself, "I shall see what he will do today." Thereafter if any one rose up before him, he slashed them down and ripped them apart. Finally, he came to some women on the lower slopes of a mountain who had tambourines with them; among them was a woman who was chanting:

> We are the daughters of Ṭāriq
> If you advance we will embrace you
> And spread cushions
> If you turn your backs we will leave you
> And show you no tender love.

He raised his sword to strike them, but then let them be. I said to him, "I saw all of your deeds. Why did you decide to lower your sword after raising it against the woman?" He replied, "I respected the Messenger of God's sword too much to kill a woman with it."

[1398] Resumption of the narrative of Ibn Isḥāq.

The Messenger of God said, "Who will take this sword with its right?" Various men rose up, but he withheld it from them. Finally Abū Dujānah Simāk b. Kharashah, the brother of the Banū Sā'idah, rose up and said, "What is its right, O Messenger of God?" The Messenger of God replied, "That you should strike the enemy with it until it bends." Abū Dujānah said, "I will take it with its right, O Messenger of God"; so he gave it to him. Abū

Dujānah was a brave but conceited man when war broke out, and whenever he bound a red headband on his head as a distinguishing mark, people knew that he was going to fight. When he took the sword from the hand of the Messenger of God, he took his headband and bound it on his head. Then he began to strut between the opposing ranks.

According to Ibn Ḥumayd—Salamah—Muḥammad b. Isḥāq —Ja'far b. 'Abd Allāh b. Aslam, the mawlā of 'Umar b. al-Khaṭṭāb—a man of the Anṣār from the Banū Salima: When the Messenger of God saw Abū Dujānah strutting he said, "That is a gait which God hates except on an occasion like this."

Abū Sufyān had sent a messenger saying, "Men of al-Aws and al-Khazraj, leave us to deal with our cousin, and we will leave you; for we have no need to fight you." But they gave him a disagreeable answer.

According to Ibn Ḥumayd—Salamah—Muḥammad b. Isḥāq [1399]
—'Āṣim b. 'Umar b. Qatādah: Abū 'Āmir 'Abd 'Amr b. Ṣayfī b. Mālik b. al-Nu'mān b. Amah, one of the Banū Ḍubay'ah, had gone to Mecca in order to distance himself from the Messenger of God, accompanied by fifty young men of al-Aws, including 'Uthmān b. Ḥunayf; some people say there were fifteen of them. He kept promising Quraysh that if he met Muḥammad, no two men of them would meet him. When battle was joined, the first man to meet the Muslims was Abū 'Āmir with the Aḥābīsh and the slaves of the Meccans. He called out, "Men of al-Aws, I am Abū 'Āmir." They replied, "God curse you, you evildoer!" In the Jāhiliyyah, Abū 'Āmir had been called "the monk," but the Messenger of God called him "the evildoer." When he heard their reply, he said, "Evil has befallen my people since my departure." Then he fought the Muslims vigorously and pelted them with stones.

Abū Sufyān had said to the standard-bearers of the Banū 'Abd al-Dār, urging them on to battle, "Banū 'Abd al-Dār, you had charge of our banner on the day of Badr, and you saw what a disaster befell us. Men are dependent on what happens to their banners; if their banners are destroyed, they are destroyed too. Either [1400]
you must take proper care of our banner or leave it to us, and we will take care of it for you." This disgraceful possibility worried them, and they furiously retorted, "Are we to hand our banner

over to you? You will see how we will act tomorrow when we join battle." That was what Abū Sufyān wanted.

When battle was joined, and the armies closed upon one another, Hind bt. ʿUtbah stood up among the women who were with her, and they took up their tambourines. They beat their tambourines behind the men and urged them on to fight. Hind chanted:

> If you advance we will embrace you
> And spread cushions;
> If you turn your backs we will leave you
> And show you no tender love.

She also chanted:

> On, Banū ʿAbd al-Dār!
> On, protectors of our rear!
> Strike with every sharp-edged sword!

The armies engaged one another and the battle grew hot. Abū Dujānah fought until he had penetrated deep into the enemy ranks. Ḥamzah b. ʿAbd al-Muṭṭalib and ʿAlī b. Abī Ṭālib fought at the head of a band of Muslims. God sent down his victory and made good his promise to them. They cut down the enemy with their swords until they put them to flight. There was no doubt about the defeat the Muslims had inflicted on the Meccans.

According to Ibn Ḥumayd—Salamah—Muḥammad b. Isḥāq —Yaḥyā b. ʿAbbād b. ʿAbd Allāh b. al-Zubayr—his father—his
[1401] grandfather, al-Zubayr: "By God, I found myself looking at the anklets of Hind bt. ʿUtbah and her companions as they tucked up their skirts and fled. There was nothing to prevent us taking them, but the archers turned aside to the (enemy) camp in search of plunder after we had driven the enemy away from it and thus left our rear exposed to the cavalry. These came upon us from behind, and somebody shouted out, 'Muḥammad has been killed!' We turned back, and the enemy turned back after us, but not before we had killed the men guarding the (Meccan) banner so that none of the enemy were near it."

According to Ibn Ḥumayd—Salamah—Muḥammad b. Isḥāq—certain scholars: The banner remained flung on the ground until ʿAmrah bt. ʿAlqamah al-Ḥārithiyyah took hold of it; she then raised it for Quraysh and they flocked to it.[173] It had previously been in the hands of Ṣu'āb, an Abyssinian slave belonging to the sons of Abū Ṭalḥah (the group responsible for the banner). He was the last of the group to take it. He had fought until his hands were cut off, and then he had knelt over it and clutched it to his chest and throat. Finally he was killed over it, saying all the while, "O God, am I forgiven?" Ḥassān b. Thābit said on the subject of Ṣu'āb's hand being cut off when they were exchanging mutual taunts:

You boasted of your standard: the worst possible
  boast is a standard handed over to Ṣu'āb.
You have made your boast of it over
  a slave, one of the lowliest men who walks the earth.
You supposed, though only a fool supposes,
  for it has nothing to do with the truth,
That fighting us on the day when we met, was [1402]
  like your selling red leather bags in Mecca.
It gladdened the eye to see his hands reddened,
  though they were not reddened by dye.[174]

According to Abū Kurayb—'Uthmān b. Sa'īd—Ḥibbān b. 'Alī—Muḥammad b. 'Ubayd Allāh b. Abī Rāfi'—his father—his grandfather: When 'Alī b. Abī Ṭālib had killed the (Meccan) standard-bearers, the Messenger of God saw a group of the unbelievers of Quraysh and said to 'Alī, "Attack them." So 'Alī attacked them, dispersed them, and killed 'Amr b. 'Abd Allāh al-Jumaḥī. Then the Messenger of God saw another group of the unbelievers of Quraysh and said to 'Alī, "Attack them." So 'Alī attacked them, dispersed them, and killed Shaybah b. Mālik, one of the Banū 'Āmir b. Lu'ayy. Then Gabriel said, "O Messenger of God, this is for consolation." The Messenger of God said, "Verily he is of me

---

173. This woman was the wife of Ghurāb, son of Sufyān b. 'Uwayf, the leader of the Banū 'Abd Manāt b. Kinānah; in W, 203 she is called 'Amrah bt. al-Ḥārith b. 'Alqamah. Several sons and grandsons of Abū Ṭalḥah (of Banū 'Abd al-Dār) were killed defending the banner. Ṣu'āb is the reading of the slave's name by Wüstenfeld, Marsden Jones and Arafat.

174. See *Dīwān* of Ḥassān, i.367f.

and I am of him," and Gabriel said, "And I am of both of you." And they heard a voice saying,

> There is no sword but Dhū al-Faqār,
> and no brave young man but ʿAlī.

The Muslims Retreat

Abū Jaʿfar (al-Ṭabarī) says: When the Muslims were attacked from behind and put to flight, the polytheists killed many of them. When this catastrophe befell the Muslims, they were afflicted in three ways; some were killed, some wounded, and some put to flight. The latter were so exhausted by battle that they did not know what they were doing. The Messenger of God's lower
[1403] lateral incisor was broken, his lip was split, and he was wounded on the cheeks and on the forehead at the roots of his hair. Ibn Qamī'ah stood over him to his left with his sword. The person who wounded him was ʿUtbah b. Abī Waqqāṣ.

According to Ibn Bashshār—Ibn Abī ʿAdī—Ḥumayd—Anas b. Mālik: On the day of Uḥud, the Messenger of God's incisor was broken and he was wounded in the head. Blood began to pour down his face, and he kept wiping it away, saying, "How can a people prosper who stain the face of their Prophet with blood while he is calling them to God?" God revealed concerning this,"It is no concern at all of thee, (Muḥammad), whether He relent toward them or punish them: for they are evildoers."[175]

Abū Jaʿfar (al-Ṭabarī) says: When the enemy overwhelmed him, the Messenger of God said, "Who will sell his life for us?"

According to Ibn Ḥumayd—Salamah—Muḥammad b. Isḥāq—al-Ḥuṣayn b. ʿAbd al-Raḥmān b. ʿAmr b. Saʿd b. Muʿādh—Maḥmūd b. ʿAmr b. Yazīd b. al-Sakan:[176] Then Ziyād b. al-Sakan rose up with five of the Anṣār (some people say it was ʿUmārah b. Ziyād b. al-Sakan), and they fought to protect the Messenger of God. Man after man of them was killed in front of him until only Ziyād—or ʿUmārah b. Ziyād b. al-Sakan—was left; and he fought

---

175. Qur. 3.128; only the first clause is quoted in the text.
176. Maḥmūd's grandfather Yazīd appears to be the brother of Ziyād.

until his wounds made him incapable of further fighting. By this time a group of Muslims had come back and driven the enemy away from Ziyād. The Messenger of God said, "Bring him close to [1404]
me." They brought Ziyād close to him, and the Messenger of God made his foot a pillow for him so that he died with his cheek on the Messenger of God's foot.

Abū Dujānah shielded the Messenger of God with his body, bending over him while arrows struck his back until it was full of them.

Sa'd b. Abī Waqqāṣ used his bow in defence of the Messenger of God. He said, "I saw him handing me arrows and saying, 'Shoot, may my father and mother be your ransom.' He even handed me an arrow without a head and said, 'Shoot this.'"

According to Ibn Ḥumayd—Salamah—Muḥammad b. Isḥāq—'Āṣim b.'Umar b. Qatādah: The Messenger of God shot from his bow until its end broke. Qatādah b. al-Nu'mān took it and kept it. (Qatādah's) eye was so badly injured that day that it fell out onto his cheek. The Messenger of God put it back with his hand, and it was his best and keenest eye (thereafter).

Abū Ja'far (al-Ṭabarī) says: Muṣ 'ab b. 'Umayr fought in defence of the Messenger of God and bore his banner until he was killed. The man who killed Muṣ'ab was Ibn Qamī'ah al-Laythī, who thought it was the Messenger of God, and went back to Quraysh announcing that he had killed Muhammad. After Muṣ'ab b. 'Umayr was killed, the Messenger of God gave the banner to 'Alī b. Abī Ṭālib. Ḥamzah b. 'Abd al-Muṭṭalib fought until he killed Arṭāt b. 'Abd Shuraḥbīl b. Hāshim b. 'Abd Manāf b. 'Abd al-Dār b. Quṣayy, who was one of those who were carrying the (Meccan)
banner. Then Sibā' b. 'Abd al-'Uzzā al-Ghubshānī, whose *kunyah* [1405]
was Abū Niyār, passed by him, and Ḥamzah b. 'Abd al-Muṭṭalib said to him, "Come over here, you son of a cutter-off of clitorises." His mother was Umm Anmār, the *mawlāt* of Sharīq b. 'Amr b. Wahb al-Thaqafī, who was a female circumciser in Mecca. When they met, Ḥamzah struck him and killed him.

Waḥshī, the slave of Jubayr b. Muṭ'im, said, "By God, I saw Ḥamzah cutting down men with his sword, not sparing anyone who went past him; he was like an ash-colored camel (in size). When Sibā' b. 'Abd al-'Uzzā reached him before me, Ḥamzah said to him, 'Come over here, you son of a cutter-off of clitorises.' He then struck him so swiftly that he could not be seen striking his head. I balanced my javelin until I was satisfied with it, and then I hurled it at Ḥamzah. It struck him in the lower part of the belly with such force that it came out between his legs. He came towards me, but was overcome and fell. I waited until he was dead and then went and recovered my javelin; after that I returned to the camp, since there was nothing else I wanted to do there."

ʿĀṣim b. Thābit b. Abī al-Aqlaḥ, the brother of the Banū ʿAmr b. ʿAwf, killed Musāfiʿ b. Ṭalḥah and his brother Kilāb b. Ṭalḥah (son of Abū Ṭalḥah), hitting each of them with an arrow; each went to his mother Sulāfah and put his head in her lap. When she asked, "My son, who has wounded you?" each replied, "I heard a
[1406] man saying, when he shot me, 'Take that! I am Ibn al-Aqlaḥ.'" "The Aqlaḥī!" she exclaimed, and vowed that if God put her in possession of ʿĀṣim's skull she would drink wine from it. ʿĀsim had made a compact with God that he would never touch a polytheist and that no polytheist should touch him.

According to Ibn Ḥumayd—Salamah—Muḥammad b. Isḥāq—al-Qāsim b. ʿAbd al-Raḥmān b. Rāfiʿ, the brother of the Banū ʿAdī b. al-Najjār: Anas b. al-Naḍr, the paternal uncle of Anas b. Mālik, went to ʿUmar b. al-Khaṭṭāb and Ṭalḥah b. ʿUbayd Allāh, who were with some of the Emigrants and the Anṣār who had given up the fight. "Why have you stopped fighting?" he asked. "Muḥammad, the Messenger of God, has been killed," they replied. "What will you do with life after him?" he said. "Rise up and die as the Messenger of God has died!" Then he went towards the enemy and fought until he was killed. Anas b. Mālik was named after him.[177]

According to Ibn Ḥumayd—Salamah—Muḥammad b. Isḥāq—Ḥumayd al-Ṭawīl—Anas b. Mālik: That day we found seventy cuts and stab wounds on Anas b. al-Naḍr, and nobody but his sister could recognise him. She recognised him by the beauty of his fingertips.

According to Ibn Ḥumayd—Salamah—Muḥammad b. Isḥāq: The first man to recognise the Messenger of God after the defeat and the rumour that the Messenger of God had been killed was, according to Ibn Shihāb al-Zuhrī, Kaʿb b. Mālik the brother of the

177. Anas b. Mālik was an important Companion, source of many Ḥadīth.

Banū Salimah. (He said,) "I recognised his eyes shining beneath his helmet and I called out at the top of my voice, 'Muslims, rejoice! This is the Messenger of God!'" The Messenger of God [1407] signed to me to be silent. When the Muslims recognised the Messenger of God, they went up with him towards the gorge.[178] With him were ʿAlī b. Abī Ṭālib, Abū Bakr b. Abī Quḥāfah, ʿUmar b. al-Khaṭṭāb, Ṭalḥah b. ʿUbayd Allāh, al-Zubayr b. al-ʿAwwām, al-Ḥārith b. al-Ṣimmah, and a number of other Muslims. As the Messenger of God was climbing up the gorge, he was overtaken by Ubayy b. Khalaf, who was saying, "Where is Muḥammad? May I not escape if you escape!" They said, "O Messenger of God, shall one of us go over and deal with him?" "Leave him," he said. When he drew close, the Messenger of God took a javelin from al-Ḥārith b. al-Ṣimmah. I have been told that some people say that when the Messenger of God took it, he shook us off, so that we flew off from him like camel-flies from a camel's back when it shakes itself. Then he confronted (Ubayy) and gave him such a thrust in the neck that he swayed in the saddle several times.

According to Ibn Ḥumayd—Salamah—Muḥammad b. Isḥāq—Ṣāliḥ b. Ibrāhīm b. ʿAbd al-Raḥmān b. ʿAwf: Ubayy b. Khalaf used to meet the Messenger of God in Mecca and say to him, "Muḥammad, I have a horse called al-ʿAwd, whom I feed every day on a measure (*faraq*) of millet. I shall kill you on it." "Not so," said the Messenger of God. "I shall kill you, if God wills." When he went back to Quraysh with a scratch on his throat which was not particularly large and in which the blood had stopped flowing, he said, "By God, Muḥammad has killed me." "By God, you have lost heart," they answered, "by God, there is [1408] nothing wrong with you." He replied, "He said to me in Mecca, 'I will kill you,' and, by God, even if he spat on me he would kill me." The enemy of God died at Sarif as they were taking him back to Mecca.

When the Messenger of God got to the mouth of the gorge, ʿAlī went out and filled his shield from al-Mihrās and brought it to the Messenger of God so that he could drink from it. He thought it

---

178. The gorge was some feature of the lower slopes of the hill of Uḥud where the Muslims were safe from the Meccan cavalry; the place called "the rock" was presumably nearby.

had an unpleasant smell, however, and he felt so disgusted by it that he would not drink. He washed the blood from his face and poured the water over his head, saying, "May God's anger be intense against those who have bloodied the face of His Prophet."

According to Ibn Ḥumayd—Salamah—Muḥammad b. Isḥāq—Ṣāliḥ b. Kaysān—somebody who told him from Sa'd b. Abī Waqqāṣ: Sa'd used to say, "By God, I never thirsted to kill anyone as I thirsted to kill 'Utbah b. Abī Waqqāṣ.[179] Even if I had not known that he was evil of character and hated among his own people, the Messenger of God's saying, 'May God's anger be intense against those who have bloodied the face of the Messenger of God,' would have been enough for me."

According to Muḥammad b. al-Ḥusayn—Aḥmad b. al-Mufaḍḍal—Asbāṭ—al-Suddī: Ibn Qamī'ah al-Ḥārithī, one of the Banū al-Ḥārith b. 'Abd Manāt b. Kinānah, came and threw a stone at the Messenger of God, breaking his nose and his lateral incisor, splitting his face open, and stunning him. His companions dispersed and abandoned him, some of them going to Medina and some of them climbing up the mountain (of Uḥud) to the rock, and standing there. The Messenger began calling out to his army, "To me, servants of God! To me, servants of God!" Thirty men
[1409] gathered round him and moved forward ahead of him, but none stood their ground except Ṭalḥah and Sahl b. Ḥunayf. Ṭalḥah protected him from behind and was wounded in the hand by an arrow, as a result of which his hand withered. Ubayy b. Khalaf al-Jumaḥī—who had sworn to kill the Prophet, and to whom the latter had replied, "No, I will kill you"—advanced saying, "Where will you flee to now, you liar!" He charged at him, but the Prophet gave him a thrust in the collar of his coat of mail which wounded him lightly. He fell down bellowing like an ox, and they picked him up and said, "You are not wounded, so there is nothing to worry about." He replied, "Did he not say, 'I will kill you'? If this wound had been inflicted on the whole of Rabī'ah and Muḍar[180] it would have killed them." In no more than a day or so he died of that wound.

---

179. 'Utbah was Sa'd's brother but had remained a pagan, whereas Sa'd was one of the earliest Muslims.

180. Two great groups of tribes.

The rumour spread among the army that the Messenger of God had been killed. Some of the people on the rock began to say, "Would that we had an envoy to ʿAbd Allāh b. Ubayy, so that he could secure our safety from Abū Sufyān! Muḥammad has been killed, so go back to your people before the Meccans come and kill you." Anas b. al-Naḍr, however, called out, "Men, if Muḥammad has been killed, the Lord of Muḥammad has not been killed, so fight as Muḥammad fought. O God, I apologise to you for what these people are saying, and I disavow before you what they have done." Then he rushed at the enemy with his sword and fought until he was killed.

The Messenger of God set off uphill, calling upon his men to follow, and soon reached the people on the rock. When they saw him, one man put an arrow in his bow and would have shot him, but he said, "I am the Messenger of God." They rejoiced when they realised that the Messenger of God was alive, and the Messenger of God rejoiced when he saw companions among whom he [1410]
could hold out.

When they regrouped with the Messenger of God among them, their sorrow vanished, and, as they climbed up, they spoke of how the victory had eluded them and of their companions who had been killed. To those who said, "Muḥammad has been killed, so go back to your people," God said, "Muḥammad is but a messenger, messengers (the like of whom) have passed away before him. Will it be that, when he dieth or is slain, ye will turn back on your heels! He who turneth back doth no hurt to Allah, and Allah will reward the thankful."[181]

Then Abū Sufyān advanced until he was nearly upon them. When they saw him, they forgot what they had been about and directed their attention to Abū Sufyān. The Messenger of God said, "These men must not get to a higher position than ours! O God, if this band of people is killed, you will have no worshippers!" Then his companions bestirred themselves and threw stones at the enemy which forced them to retreat downhill.

On that day Abū Sufyān said, "Hubal be exalted! A Ḥanẓalah for a Ḥanẓalah, and a day for the day of Badr."[182] On the day (of

181. Qur. 3.144.
182. Hubal was a prominent Meccan deity. Muḥammad is alleged to have said

Uḥud) they had killed Ḥanẓalah b. al-Rāhib, who was in a state of ritual impurity and was cleansed by the angels, while Ḥanẓalah b. Abī Sufyān had been killed on the day of Badr. Abū Sufyān said, We have "Al-'Uzzā, and you have no 'Uzzā."[183] The Messenger of God said to 'Umar, "Say, 'God is our Lord, and you have no Lord.'" Abū Sufyān said, "Is Muḥammad among you? Some of your dead have been mutilated. I neither commanded this nor forbade it, and it neither gave me pleasure nor saddened me."

God spoke of Abū Sufyān's approaching them and said, "Therefore, He rewarded you with grief upon grief that (He might teach) you not to sorrow either for that which ye missed or for that which befell you."[184] The first grief is the victory and booty which eluded them, and the second grief is the enemy's approaching
[1411] them; they were not to grieve for the booty which eluded them, nor the memory of the killing which was inflicted upon them. Abū Sufyān distracted them from this.

According to Abū Ja'far (al-Ṭabarī)—Ibn Ḥumayd—Salamah —Ibn Isḥāq: While the Messenger of God was in the gorge with those companions of his, suddenly a group of Quraysh came up the mountain. The Messenger of God said, "They should not be above us," so 'Umar and a group of Emigrants with him fought until they forced them to retreat down the mountain. The Messenger of God went up to the rock on the mountain to get on top of it. He had become stout with age and was wearing two coats of mail. When he tried to climb up, he could not manage to do so, and Ṭalḥah b. 'Ubayd Allāh bent down beneath him and then rose up until the Messenger of God was settled on the rock.

According to Ibn Ḥumayd—Salamah —Muḥammad (b. Isḥāq) —Yaḥyā b. 'Abbād b. 'Abd Allāh b. al-Zubayr—his father —'Abd Allāh b. al-Zubayr —al-Zubayr: I heard the Messenger of God saying on that day, "Ṭalḥah performed an action deserving of reward when he did what he did for the Messenger of God."

Abū Ja'far (al-Ṭabarī) says: The army had fled and abandoned the Messenger of God, some of them getting as far as al-Munaqqā,

---

after the death of Ḥanẓalah b. Abī 'Amir (al-Rāhib) that he was being washed by the angels (1412 below and IH, 568).

183. The name of the goddess al-'Uzzā means "the mighty one."

184. Qur. 3.153; Pickthall's translation has been lightly modified to correspond to al-Ṭabarī's understanding of the verse.

near al-Aʿwaṣ. ʿUthmān b. ʿAffān, together with ʿUqbah b. ʿUthmān and Saʿd b. ʿUthmān, two men of the Anṣār, fled as far as al-Jalʿab, a mountain in the neighbourhood of Medina, near al-Aʿwaṣ.[185] They stayed there for three days, and then came back to the Messenger of God. They claimed that he said to them, "On that day you were scattered far and wide." [1412]

Abū Jaʿfar (al-Ṭabarī) says: Ḥanẓalah b. Abī ʿĀmir, he whom the angels cleansed, met Abū Sufyān b. Ḥarb in battle. He had gained the better of Abū Sufyān when Shaddād b. al-Aswad, who was known as Ibn Shaʿūb, seeing him poised over Abū Sufyān, struck and killed him. The Messenger of God said, "Your companion (meaning Ḥanẓalah) is being cleansed by the angels. Ask his family what this is about." When they asked his wife, she replied, "He went out to battle in a state of ritual impurity when he heard the call to battle." The Messenger of God said, "That is why the angels were cleansing him."

Shaddād b. al-Aswad said of his killing of Ḥanẓalah:

> Verily I protect my companion and myself
> with a thrust swift as a sunbeam.

Extolling his endurance on that day and the way in which Ibn Shaʿub Shaddād b al-Aswad came to his assistance against Ḥanẓalah, Abū Sufyān said:

> Had I wished, my thoroughbred bay horse could have rescued me,
> and I should owe no thanks to Ibn Shaʿūb.
> My colt kept a short distance from them
> from morning until near sunset
> I was fighting them and calling out, "Men of Ghālib!"
> and driving them off with unbending strength[186]
> So weep, and pay no attention to those who reprove you, [1413]
> And do not weary of tears and lamentation.

185. There is a reference to the conduct of ʿUthmān, the later caliph, in W, 278f. W,277 says Saʿd b. ʿUthmān, an Anṣārī, was the first to inform those in Medina that Muḥammad was dead.

186. Ghālib was the son of Fihr (Quraysh) from whom nearly all the clans of Mecca were descended; see Watt, *Mecca*, 7.

For your father and his brothers who followed one another to death,
for they are worthy of their share of tears
My soul's grief has been consoled by the fact that
I have killed every noble of the Banū al-Najjār
A noble stallion of Hāshim, and Muṣʿab
who was not fearful in war.[187]
If I had not slaked my soul's thirst for vengeance on them,
my heart would have been grieved and scarred
They retired, their companies dead,
covered with sword wounds, bleeding and dejected.
Stricken by those who were not equal to them in blood,
nor similar to them in quality.[188]

He was answered by Ḥassān b. Thābit:[189]

[1414] You have spoken of the proud-necked stallions of the people of Hāshim
but you have not hit the mark in the falsehood you have uttered
Do you marvel that you have killed Ḥamzah from them,
a noble, whom you name a noble?
Did they not kill ʿAmr, ʿUtbah and his son,
Shaybah, al-Ḥajjāj and Ibn Ḥabīb
On the morning when al-ʿĀṣ challenged ʿAlī,
and he surprised him with a sharp blow which drenched him with blood?

Shaddād b. al-Aswad, speaking of the benefit he had conferred upon Abū Sufyān b. Ḥarb in coming to his rescue, said:

If not for my being present and defending you, Ibn Ḥarb,

---

187. The claim to have killed the nobles of the clan of al-Najjār (of Medina) seems exaggerated. The stallion of Hāshim is Ḥamzah, and Musʿab is a Muslim from the Meccan clan of ʿAbd al-Dār.

188. He presumably means that the Muslims were inferior in quality to those who killed them.

189. See *Dīwān*, ed. Arafat, i.446; ii.315. The Meccans killed at Badr and mentioned here by Ḥassān include ʿAmr (who is Abū Jahl), ʿUtbah b. Rabīʿah, al-Walīd b. ʿUtbah, Shaybah b. ʿUtbah, and al-ʿĀṣ b. Saʿīd; but the others are not clearly identifiable.

you would have been found speechless on the day when
we fought in the mountain valley.
If I had not wheeled my horse round in the mountain
valley,
hyenas and rabid dogs would have mangled your limbs.

Replying to Abū Sufyān's words, "My colt kept a short distance from them," al-Ḥārith b. Hishām,[190] who thought he was alluding to him as he had fled from Badr, said:

If you had seen what they did at the pool of Badr, [1415]
You would have gone back with a heart which would be
terror-struck as long as you lived.
Or mourning-women would have risen up to bewail you,
and you would not care about the loss of a loved one.
I requited them later for Badr with its like,
mounted on a swift, smoothly-moving, galloping
horse.

Mutilation of the Muslim Dead

According to Abū Jaʿfar (al-Ṭabarī)—Ibn Ḥumayd—Salamah—Muḥammad b. Isḥāq—Ṣāliḥ b. Kaysān: Hind bt. ʿUtbah and the women who were with her stopped to mutilate the Messenger of God's dead companions, cutting off their ears and noses until Hind was able to make anklets and necklaces of them. She gave her own anklets, necklaces, and earrings to Waḥshī, the slave of Jubayr b. Muṭʿim. Then she ripped open Ḥamzah's body for his liver and chewed it, but she was not able to swallow it and spat it out. Then she climbed a high rock and screamed at the top of her voice the lines of verse which she had spoken when they took possession of the booty they had seized from the companions of the Messenger of God.

According to Ibn Ḥumayd—Salamah—Muḥammad b. Isḥāq—Ṣāliḥ b. Kaysān: ʿUmar b. al-Khaṭṭāb said to Ḥassān, "Ibn al- [1416]

190. Al-Ḥārith b. Hishām b. al-Mughīrah, a full brother of Abū Jahl, had fled from Badr; he became a Muslim at the conquest of Mecca.

Furayʿah,[191] I wish you had heard what Hind was saying and seen her insolence as she stood on a rock reciting *rajaz*-poetry against us and recounting how she had treated Ḥamzah." Ḥassān said, "By God, I was watching the javelin falling as I was on top of Fāriʿ (meaning his 'stronghold'), and I said to myself, 'By God, this is a weapon which is not one of the weapons of the Arabs.' It seemed to be falling towards Ḥamzah, but I did not know. Tell me some of what she said, and I will deal with her for you." ʿUmar recited part of what she had said to him, and he satirized Hind as follows:[192]

The vile woman was insolent, and she was habitually base,
    since she combined insolence with disbelief.
May God curse Hind, distinguished among Hinds, she with the large clitoris,
    and may he curse her husband with her.
Did she set out for Uḥud on an ambling camel,
    among the army on a saddled camel-colt?
A slow-paced camel which would not move,
    whether scolded or rebuked.
Spur on your mount with your backside, Hind,
    and soften sinews, pounding them with a stone
Her backside and her genitals are covered with ulcers
    as a result of prolonged swift travel in the saddle.
[1417] Her companion continued to treat her
    with water which she sprinkled and with *sidr*-leaves.
Did you set out hastily in search of vengeance
    for your father and your son on the day of Badr?
And for your uncle, who was wounded in the backside, lying in his blood,
    and your brother, all of them coated in dust in the well?
And did you forget a foul deed which you committed?
    Hind, woe to you, the shame of the age.

191. Al-Furayʿah bt. Khunays was the mother of Ḥassān b. Thābit. The form of address is respectful and is a relic of the former matriliny at Medina.

192. *Dīwān*, ed. Arafat, i.384f. The kinsmen for whom she sought vengeance were her father ʿUtbah b. Rabīʿah, her stepson Ḥanẓalah b. Abī Sufyān, her uncle Shaybah b. Rabīʿah and her brother al-Walīd b. ʿUtbah.

And you went back humbled, without obtaining
vengeance on us and without victory.
Slave girls claim that they give birth
to a small child as a result of fornication.

According to Abū Ja'far (al-Ṭabarī)—Hārūn b. Isḥāq— Muṣ'ab b. al-Miqdām—Isrā'īl: Then Abū Sufyān went up to the Muslims.

According to Ibn Wakī'—his father—Isrā'īl— Abū Isḥāq—al-Barā': Then Abū Sufyān came up to us and said, "Is Muḥammad among you?" The Messenger of God said, "Do not answer him the first two times." Then he said three times, "Is Ibn Abī Quḥāfah[193] among you?" but the Messenger of God said, "Do not answer him." Then he said three times, "Is Ibn al-Khaṭṭāb among you?" but the Messenger of God said, "Do not answer him." Then he turned to his companions and said, "These people must have been killed, for if they were alive they would have answered." Then 'Umar b. al-Khaṭṭāb could not restrain himself, and said, "You lie, enemy of God. God has preserved for you that which will disgrace you." Then Abū Sufyān said, "Be exalted, Hubal, be exalted, Hubal!"

Then the Messenger of God said, "Answer him!" "What shall we say?" they asked. "Say, 'God is most exalted and most lofty,'" he replied. Abū Sufyān said, "We have al-'Uzzā, and you have no 'Uzzā (mighty one)." The Messenger of God said, "Answer him." "What shall we say?" they asked. "Say, 'God is our Lord, and you have no lord,'" he replied. Abū Sufyān said, "A day for the day of Badr. War has its ups and downs. You will find that some of your dead have been mutilated. I did not command it, nor did it displease me." [1418]

According to Ibn Ḥumayd—Salamah—Ibn Isḥāq:[194] When 'Umar answered Abū Sufyān, Abū Sufyān said, "Come here, 'Umar." The Messenger of God said to him, "Go to him, and see what he wants." So he went, and Abū Sufyān said to him, "In God's name, 'Umar, tell me; have we killed Muḥammad?" "No, by God," said 'Umar, he is listening to what you are saying now."

193. Abū Bakr.
194. IH, 583; but the following passage about al-Ḥulays is on p.582.

He replied, "You are more truthful and more upright than Ibn Qamī'ah in my opinion." This was referring to Ibn Qamī'ah's having claimed that he had killed Muḥammad. Then Abū Sufyān called out and said, "Some of your dead have been mutilated. By God, I neither approved of this nor was I displeased with it, and I neither forbade it nor commanded it."

Al-Ḥulays b. Zabbān, the brother of the Banū al-Ḥarith b. ʿAbd Manāt, who was then the chief of the Aḥābīsh, had passed by Abū Sufyān b. Ḥarb as he was striking the side of Ḥamzah's mouth with the point of his spear and saying, "Taste that, you rebel!" Al-Ḥulays said, "Banū Kinānah, can this be the chief of Quraysh acting as you see with the dead body of his cousin?" "Keep it quiet," Abū Sufyān said. "It was a slip."

When Abū Sufyān and those with him left, he shouted out,
[1419] "Your rendezvous is Badr next year." The Messenger of God said to one of his companions, "Say, 'Yes, it is a rendezvous between us and you.'" Then the Messenger of God sent ʿAlī b. Abī Ṭālib, saying, "Go out following in the tracks of the enemy, and see what they are doing and what they intend doing. If they are leading their horses and riding their camels, they are making for Mecca, but if they are riding their horses and leading their camels, they are making for Medina. By the one who has my soul in his hands, if they are making for Medina, I shall go to them there and take the field against them!"

ʿAlī said, "So I went out in their tracks to see what they were doing. They mounted their camels, led their horses and set off for Mecca.[195] The Messenger of God had said, 'Whichever it is, keep it to yourself until you come to me.' But when I saw them setting off for Mecca, I came shouting, unable to conceal what the Messenger of God had commanded me to conceal because of the joy I felt at seeing them leaving Medina for Mecca."

According to Ibn Ḥumayd—Salamah—Muḥammad b. Isḥāq—Muḥammad b. ʿAbd Allāh b. ʿAbd al-Raḥmān b. Abī Ṣaʿṣaʿah al-Māzinī, the brother of the Banū al-Najjār: While the people were occupying themselves with their dead, the Messenger of God said, "Who will look for me to see weather Saʿd b. al-Rabīʿ is among the living or the dead?" Saʿd was the brother of the Banū

195. The following words spoken by ʿAlī are not found in IH.

al-Ḥārith b. al-Khazraj. A man of the Anṣār offered to look on behalf of the Messenger of God. When he found Sa'd lying wounded [1420] among the dead, and himself at the point of death, he said to him, "The Messenger of God has commanded me to see for him whether you are among the living or the dead." He replied, "I am among the dead. Give the Messenger of God my greetings, and tell him that Sa'd b. al-Rabī' says to him, 'May God give you the best reward that any prophet has been given in his community.' Give your people my greetings, and tell them that Sa'd b. al-Rabī' says to them, 'You have no excuse in God's sight if anybody reaches your Prophet while you have an eye that blinks.'" Sa'd died soon after, and the man went to the Messenger of God and told him the story.

Then, as I (Ibn Isḥāq) have been told, the Messenger of God went out in search of Ḥamzah b 'Abd al-Muṭṭalib, and found him at the bottom of the wadi; his belly had been ripped open and his liver removed, and he had been mutilated by the cutting off of his nose and ears.

According to Ibn Ḥumayd—Salamah—Ibn Isḥāq—Muḥammad b. Ja'far b. al-Zubayr: When the Messenger of God saw Ḥamzah in that condition, he said, "If it were not that Ṣafiyyah[196] would grieve, or that it would become a *sunnah* (standard practice) after me, I would leave him so that he would find his way into the bellies of wild beasts or the crops of birds. If God gives me victory over Quraysh at any time, I shall mutilate thirty of their men!" When the Muslims saw the grief and rage of the Messenger of God at what had been done to his uncle, they said, "By God, if one day we are victorious over them, we shall mutilate them in a way which none of the Arabs has ever mutilated anybody." [1421]

According to Ibn Ḥumayd—Salamah—Muḥammad b. Isḥāq—Buraydah b. Sufyān b. Farwah al-Aslamī—Muḥammad b. Ka'b al-Quraẓī—Ibn 'Abbās; and (also) Ibn Ḥumayd—Salamah—Muḥammad b. Isḥāq—al-Ḥasan b. 'Umārah—al-Ḥakam b. 'Utaybah—Miqsam —Ibn 'Abbās: God revealed concerning these sayings of the Messenger of God and his companions, "If ye punish, then punish with the like of that wherewith ye were afflicted.

196. Ṣafiyyah bt. 'Abd al-Muṭṭalib was Ḥamzah's full sister and Muḥammad's aunt.

But if ye endure patiently, verily it is better for the patient . . ." to the end of the Sūrah.[197] So the Messenger of God forgave, was patient, and forbade mutilation.

Ibn Isḥāq says: I have been told that Ṣafiyyah bt. ʿAbd al-Muṭṭalib came up to look at Ḥamzah, who was her full brother. The Messenger of God said to her son, al-Zubayr b. al-ʿAwwām, "Go to meet her and turn her back so that she does not see what has happened to her brother." Al-Zubayr met her and said to her, "Mother, the Messenger of God commands you to go back." She said, "Why? I have heard that my brother has been mutilated, but that is a small thing for the sake of God, and I am fully resigned to what has happened. I shall accept God's will and be patient if God will." Al-Zubayr went to the Messenger of God and told him this, and he said, "Let her come." She came to (Ḥamzah), looked at him, prayed over him, exclaimed, "We belong to God and to him do we return," and prayed for his forgiveness. Then the Messenger of God gave orders for him to be buried.

[1422] According to Ibn Ḥumayd—Salamah—Muḥammad b. Isḥāq: ʿAbd Allāh b. Jaḥsh, the son of Umaymah bt. ʿAbd al-Muṭṭalib, who had Ḥamzah as his maternal uncle, was mutilated in the same way as Ḥamzah, except that his liver was not ripped out. Some of his family claim that the Messenger of God buried him along with Ḥamzah in one grave; but I have only heard that from his family.

Various Accounts Concerning Uḥud

According to Ibn Ḥumayd—Salamah—Muḥammad b. Isḥāq —ʿĀṣim b. ʿUmar b. Qatādah—Maḥmūd b. Labīd:[198] When the Messenger of God went out to Uḥud, Ḥusayl b. Jābir—who was al-Yamān, the father of Ḥudhayfah b. al-Yamān —and Thābit b. Waqsh b. Zaʿūrāʾ, who were very old men, were sent up into the strongholds with the women and children. One of them said to

197. Qur. 16.126–8. Al-Ṭabarī has a fuller *isnād* for this section than IH.

198. IH, 577. Al-Yamān was a nickname (*laqab*) given to Ḥusayl because he (or an ancestor) had incurred blood-guilt in his own tribe and fled to Medina, where he became a confederate of the clan of ʿAbd al-Ashhal, which like all the Anṣār was reckoned to the group known as al-Yamān. See Ibn al-Athīr, *Usd al-ghābah*, s.v. Ḥudhayfah b. al-Yamān.

the other, however, "What are you waiting for, confound you? By God, neither of us has more of his life left than it takes a donkey to drink. We will both be corpses today or tomorrow, so let us take our swords and join the Messenger of God, and perhaps God will grant us martyrdom with the Messenger of God." So they took their swords and went out, entering the ranks without anyone being aware of them. Thābit b. Waqsh was killed by the polytheists, but Ḥusayl b. Jābir al-Yamān was killed by Muslims who failed to recognise him and rained sword blows on him. Ḥudhayfah said, "This is my father." They said, "By God, we did not recognise him," and they spoke the truth. "May God forgive you," said Ḥudhayfah, "for he is the most merciful of the merciful." The Messenger of God wanted to pay him blood-money, but [1423]
Ḥudhayfah distributed his blood-money as alms to the Muslims, which increased the Messenger of God's high regard for him.

According to Ibn Ḥumayd—Salamah—Muḥammad b. Isḥāq—'Āṣim b. 'Umar b. Qatādah:[199] One of the (Anṣār) called Ḥāṭib b. Umayyah b. Rāfi' had a son called Yazīd b. Ḥāṭib, who was wounded on the day of Uḥud and brought dying to his people's settlement. The people of the settlement gathered round him and the Muslim men and women began to say, "Rejoice, Ibn Ḥāṭib, at the good news of Paradise." Ḥāṭib was an elderly man who had grown old in the Jāhiliyyah, and his being a Hypocrite appeared that day, for he said, "What are you congratulating him on? A Garden of rue?[200] By God, you have deluded this lad into losing his life, and stricken me with grief at his death."

According to Ibn Ḥumayd—Salamah—Muḥammad b. Isḥāq—'Āṣim b. 'Umar b. Qatādah: There was among us a stranger, whose origins were unknown, called Quzmān. When anybody mentioned his name, the Messenger of God used to say, "He is one of the people of Hell-fire." On the day of Uḥud he fought hard, and killed eight or nine polytheists with his own hand, being bold, brave, and redoubtable. Finally he was disabled by his wounds and was carried to the settlement of the Banū Ẓafar. Some Muslims began to say, "You have fought valiantly today,

199. IH, 578; W, 263. Ḥāṭib and his son belonged to the clan of Ẓafar, but Ḥāṭib seems to have had some connection with the Jewish clan of Qurayẓah (W, 511).

200. Rue (*ḥarmal*) was placed in tombs at the feet of the dead.

Quzmān, so rejoice!" "What have I to rejoice about?" he answered. "By God, I only fought for the honour of my people; but for that, I would not have fought." When the pain of his wounds
[1424] became too severe, he took an arrow from his quiver,[201] slit his wrists, and bled to death. The Messenger of God was told of this, and said, "I testify that I am truly the Messenger of God."

Among those who were killed on the day of Uḥud was Mukhayrīq the Jew. He was one of the Banū Thaʿlabah b. al-Fiṭyawn.[202] On that day he said, "O Jews, by God you know that it is your duty to go to Muḥammad's aid." They replied, "Today is the Sabbath." He said, "There is no Sabbath," and took up his sword and his equipment. Then he said, "If I am killed, I leave my property to Muḥammad to do with as he will." Then he went out to the Messenger of God and fought along with him until he was killed. The Messenger of God said, as I have been told, "Mukhayrīq is the best of the Jews."

According to Ibn Ḥumayd—Salamah—Muḥammad b. Isḥāq:[203] Some of the Muslims carried their dead to Medina and buried them there. Then the Messenger of God forbade that and said, "Bury them where they fell."

According to Ibn Ḥumayd—Salamah—Muḥammad b. Isḥāq—his father, Isḥāq b. Yasār—some *shaykhs* of the Banū Salimah:[204] The Messenger of God said on that day when he ordered the burial of the dead, "Look out for ʿAmr b. al-Jamūḥ and ʿAbd Allāh b. ʿAmr b. Ḥarām. They were close friends in this world, so

---

201. The rest of this sentence and also the following sentence are not in IH, 578. Al-Wāqidī has two accounts of the death of Quzmān (223f.; 263) and gives more information. He was reckoned to the clan of Ẓafar but his origin was unknown, and he had no wife or child. Like Ḥāṭib b. Umayyah he was reckoned a Hypocrite. He went out to fight because the women of Ẓafar taunted him with cowardice. By committing suicide he condemned himself to Hell. There are many references to the story in theological contexts because it is taken as an example of predestination and of Muḥammad's foreknowledge of that. This is the reason for Muḥammad's testifying below.

202. Thaʿlabah was an important group of Jews in Medina, but they may have been Arabs who had accepted Judaism, since they also had links with the tribe of Ghassān; see Watt, *Medina*, 193.

203. IH, 585f.

204. IH, 586; the sentence about Muʿāwiyah, the later caliph, is not in IH.

put them in one grave." When Muʿāwiyah dug the canal, they were exhumed, and their bodies were as supple as though they had been buried the day before.

Then the Messenger of God left to go back to Medina. He was met, as I have been told, by Ḥamnah bt. Jaḥsh, who was given the [1425] news of the death of her brother ʿAbd Allāh b. Jaḥsh. She said, "We belong to God and to him do we return," and prayed for his forgiveness. Then she was given the news of the death of her maternal uncle Ḥamzah b. ʿAbd al-Muṭṭalib, and repeated these words. Then she was told of the death of her husband Muṣʿab b. ʿUmayr, and she screamed and wailed. The Messenger of God said, "The woman's husband occupied a special place in her heart," because he saw her steadfastness at the death of her brother and uncle and her screaming over her husband.

The Messenger of God passed by a settlement of Anṣār of the Banū ʿAbd al-Ashhal and Ẓafar and heard sounds of lamentation and women weeping. The Messenger of God's eyes filled with tears and he wept, but then he said, "Yet Ḥamzah has no women weeping for him." When Saʿd b. Muʿādh and Usayd b. Ḥuḍayr came back to the settlement of the Banū ʿAbd al-Ashhal, they told their women to gird themselves up and to go and weep for the Messenger of God's uncle.

According to Ibn Ḥumayd—Salamah—Muḥammad b. Isḥāq—ʿAbd al-Wāḥid b. Abī ʿAwn—Ismāʿīl b. Muḥammad b. Saʿd b. Abī Waqqāṣ: The Messenger of God passed by a woman of the Banū Dīnār whose husband, brother, and father had been killed fighting along with the Messenger of God at Uḥud. When she was told of their deaths, she said, "What about the Messenger of God?" They said, "He is well. God be praised, he is as you would wish him to be." She said, "Show him to me, that I may look upon him." He was pointed out to her, and when she saw him she said, "Every loss is bearable now that I have seen you safe." Abū Jaʿfar (al-Ṭabarī) says: When the Messenger of God got [1426] back to his family, he gave his sword to his daughter Fāṭimah and said, "Wash the blood off this, my daughter." Then ʿAlī gave her his sword and said, "Wash this one too, for by God it has served me well today." The Messenger of God said, "If you have fought well, Sahl b. Ḥunayf and Abū Dujānah Simāk b. Kharashah fought well with you."[205] They assert that when ʿAlī b. Abī Ṭālib gave Fāṭimah his sword, he said:

Fāṭimah, take the sword which is not blameworthy,
for I am neither cowardly nor blameworthy.
By my life, I fought for love of Muḥammad
and in obedience to a Lord who is merciful to his servants.
With my sword in my hand which I was brandishing like a meteor,
hacking with it freedman and noble alike.
I continued in this way until my Lord dispersed them,
and until we had slaked the thirst for vengeance of every forbearing man.

When Abū Dujānah took the sword from the hand of the Messenger of God, he fought fiercely with it. He used to say, "I saw a person stirring up the enemy to a fury, so I made my way over there and attacked with my sword; then she wailed, and I realised that it was a woman. I respected the Messenger of God's sword too much to strike a woman with it." Abū Dujānah said:

I am he with whom my friend made a compact
as we were at the foot of the mountain near the date-palms
[1427] That I would not stand forever among those in the rear ranks,
so strike with the sword of God and the Messenger!

The Messenger of God returned to Medina on Saturday, the day of the battle at Uḥud.

The Expedition of Ḥamrā' al-Asad

According to Ibn Ḥumayd—Salamah—Muḥammad b. Isḥāq—Ḥusayn b. ʿAbd Allāh—ʿIkrimah:[206] The day of Uḥud was on

205. It is not clear why these two men are singled out for mention. They are named together as receiving some of the goods of the clan of al-Naḍīr because they were poor (1453 below; IH,654).

206. IH, 588–90, but without the first *isnād*; W, 334–40. The retreat of the Meccans showed that they had been roughly handled by the Muslims, even if the Muslim casualties had been higher, and that they were not in a position to attack the "strongholds" of Medina and so benefit from such advantage as they had gained. Muḥammad presumably realized this, and his march out to Ḥamrā' al-Asad was primarily a display of strength to the enemy and a way of boosting the morale of the Muslims after their losses; see Watt, *Medina*, 28f.

Saturday, halfway through Shawwāl. On the following day, which was Sunday, 16 Shawwāl (March 24, 625), the Messenger of God's crier called out to the people to go in pursuit of the enemy, but added that nobody was to join the force except those who had been present at the battle the day before. Jābir b. ʿAbd Allāh b. ʿAmr b. Harām[207] spoke to him and said, "O Messenger of God, my father left me behind to look after my seven sisters and said to me, 'My son, it is not right for me and you to leave these women without a man among them, and I am not one to give you the precedence over myself in fighting along with the Messenger of God; you must stay behind to look after your sisters.' So I stayed behind to look after them." The Messenger of God gave him permission, and he went out with him. The Messenger of God's only purpose in this expedition was to lower the morale of the enemy; by going out in pursuit of them, he wanted to give them the impression that his strength was unimpaired, and that the Muslims' casualties had not weakened their ability to engage [1428]
in fighting.

According to Ibn Ḥumayd—Salamah—Muḥammad b. Isḥāq—ʿAbd Allāh b. Khārijah b. Zayd b. Thābit—Abū al-Sā'ib, the *mawlā* of ʿĀ'ishah bt. ʿUthmān: One of the Messenger of God's companions from the Banū ʿAbd al-Ashhal said, "I and my brother were present at the battle with the Messenger of God, and we came back wounded. When the Messenger of God's crier called on us to go out in pursuit of the enemy, I said to my brother and he said to me, 'Shall we miss the chance of taking part in an expedition with the Messenger of God? We have no beast to ride, and both of us are badly wounded.' So we went out with the Messenger of God. I was less severely wounded than he was, and at times when his wounds were too much for him I carried him, while at other times he walked, until we reached the spot where the other Muslims were."

The Messenger of God went out until he reached Ḥamrā' al-Asad, which is eight miles from Medina, and stayed there three days—Monday, Tuesday, and Wednesday (March 25–27, 625)—and then went back to Medina.

---

207. Jābir's father had been killed at Uḥud and, as recorded above (1414), buried in one grave with ʿAmr b. al-Jamūḥ. Jābir took part in many later expeditions.

According to Ibn Ḥumayd—Salamah—Ibn Isḥāq —ʿAbd Allāh b. Abī Bakr b. Muḥammad b. ʿAmr b. Ḥazm: Maʿbad al-Khuzāʿī passed by (the Messenger of God). The Khuzāʿah, both Muslims and polytheists, were trusted allies of the Messenger of God in Tihāmah, having made an agreement with him that they would not conceal from him anything that happened there. At that time Maʿbad was a polytheist. "O Muḥammad," he said, "the losses among your companions which you have endured are grievous to
[1429] us, and we hope that God will preserve you despite these losses." Then he left the Messenger of God at Ḥamrāʾ al-Asad and went to Abū Sufyān b. Ḥarb and his men at al-Rawḥāʾ. They had decided to return to the attack against the Messenger of God and his companions. They argued, "We killed a proportion of Muḥammad's companions, including leaders and nobles, and now we have turned back home before exterminating them. Let us return to Medina for the rest of them and finish them off." When Abū Sufyān saw Maʿbad, be said, "What is going on over there, Maʿbad?" He replied, "Muḥammad has come out at the head of his companions in pursuit of you, leading an army the like of which I have never seen. They are burning with anger against you. Those who stayed away on the day when you fought and have repented of what they did have gathered round him. I have never seen the like of their fury against you." "What are you saying, confound you?" he said. "By God," replied Maʿbad, "I do not think you will leave here before seeing the forelocks of their cavalry." "By God," he said, "we have decided to attack them again to exterminate the remainder of them." "I advise you against that," said Maʿbad. "By God, what I saw has prompted me to compose some verses about it." "What are they?" Abū Sufyān asked. Maʿbad said:

My riding-camel was almost knocked over by the noise
 when the earth was flowing with troops of short-haired horses,
Pounding along carrying noble lions who are not idle
 in battle, nor clumsy or weak.
[1430] I continued running, thinking that the earth was tilting,
 when they brought up a leader who is never deserted,

And I said, "Woe betide Ibn Ḥarb when he meets them,
when the valley is seething with men."
I give an open warning to the people of the sanctuary (of Mecca),
to every intelligent and reasonable man of them,
Of the army of Muḥammad, whose riders are far from contemptible,
and my warning is no idle prattle.

This was enough to turn back Abū Sufyān and his men.

When a party of riders from (the tribe of) ʿAbd al-Qays went past (Abū Sufyān), he said to them, "Where are you making for?" They replied, "We are making for Medina." "Why?" he asked. "For provisions," they said. "Will you give Muḥammad a message from me," he said, "and I will load these camels of yours with raisins in ʿUkāẓ later on, when you get there?" They agreed, so he said, "When you go to him, tell him that we have resolved to march against him and his companions and to exterminate the remainder of them."

The party of riders passed by the Messenger of God while he was in Ḥamrāʾ al-Asad and told him what Abū Sufyān had threatened, but he only said, "God is sufficient for us, the best in whom to trust."

Abū Jaʿfar (al-Ṭabarī) says: Then the Messenger of God left for Medina after the third day. Some specialists in historical reports (*akhbār*) claim that the Messenger of God captured Muʿāwiyah b. al-Mughīrah b. Abī al-ʿĀṣ and Abū ʿAzzah al-Jumaḥī on his way to Ḥamrāʾ al-Asad.[208] When he went on that expedition he left Ibn [1431]
Umm Maktūm in charge of Medina.

208. There is no mention of this in Ibn Isḥāq, but IH has a long addition to Ibn Isḥāq in which he gives several variants (590f.). According to W, 332–4, and one of IH's accounts this Muʿāwiyah, who was maternal grandfather of the Umayyad caliph ʿAbd al-Malik, had fled from the battle of Uḥud and taken refuge with ʿUthmān the later caliph, to whom Muḥammad granted security for him for three days; but he mistook the route back to Mecca and after the three days were over fell into the hands of some Muslims and was killed. Abū ʿAzzah ʿAmr b. ʿAbdallāh b. ʿUthmān (or ʿUmayr) was captured at Badr, but, because he was a poor man with five daughters, Muḥammad allowed him to go free without a ransom on condition

The Sons of 'Alī, etc.

In this year, al-Ḥasan b. 'Alī b. Abī Ṭālib was born, halfway through the month of Ramaḍān (about March 1, 625).

In this year also, Fāṭimah became pregnant with al-Ḥusayn; it is said that there were only fifty days between her giving birth to al-Ḥasan and her conceiving al-Ḥusayn.

In this year also, it is said that Jamīlah bt. 'Abd Allāh b. Ubayy conceived 'Abd Allāh b. Ḥanẓalah b. Abī 'Āmir, in Shawwāl (which began March 17, 625).[209]

---

he did not fight against him (IH, 471). Before the battle of Uḥud, the Meccan leader Ṣafwān b. Umayyah prevailed on him to join the expedition, promising to enrich him or, of he was killed, to provide for his daughters (1385 above; IH, 556). It is not stated how he came to be captured by the Muslims, but when he was brought to Muḥammad the latter ordered his execution because he had given his word and broken it (IH, 591, from Ibn Hishām only). On p.1402 'Alī is said to have killed him. See also W, 101f., 201, 308f.

209. Jamīlah, the daughter of the leading Hypocrite 'Abdallāh b. Ubayy, was the wife of the Ḥanẓalah killed at Uḥud and washed by the angels (1412 above). His death occurred only six days after the month began.

The Events of the Year 4 (June 13, 625–June 1, 626)

Then the fourth year of the Hijrah commenced.

The Expedition of al-Rajīʿ, in Ṣafar (July–August, 625)[210]

According to Ibn Ḥumayd—Salamah—Muḥammad b. Isḥāq—ʿĀṣim b. ʿUmar b. Qatādah: After Uḥud a group of men from ʿAḍal and al-Qārah came to the Messenger of God and said to him, "O Messenger of God, some of us are good Muslims; please send a few of your companions back with us to instruct us in the faith, teach us to recite the Qur'ān, and teach us the laws of Islam." The Messenger of God agreed and sent six men back with them, Marthad b. Abī Marthad al-Ghanawī, the confederate of Ḥamzah b. ʿAbd al-Muṭṭalib, Khālid b. al-Bukayr, the confederate of the Banū [1432]
ʿAdī b. Kaʿb, ʿĀṣim b. Thābit b. Abī al-Aqlaḥ, the brother of the

210. IH, 638–48; W, 354–63; Watt, *Medina*, 33f. According to al-Wāqidī, the tribe of Liḥyān were seeking vengeance for the killing of their chief Sufyān b. Khālid al-Hudhalī, and they paid the men of ʿAḍal and al-Qārah to ask for instructors; but this raises difficulties about dating. ʿAḍal and al-Qārah were subclans of al-Hūn b. Khuzaymah and included in the Aḥābīsh.

Banū ʿAmr b. ʿAwf, Khubayb b. ʿAdī the brother of the Banū Jaḥjabā b. Kulfah b. ʿAmr b. ʿAwf, Zayd b. al-Dathinnah, the brother of the Banū Bayāḍah b. ʿĀmir, and ʿAbd Allāh b. Ṭāriq, a confederate of the Banū Ẓafar from (the tribe of) Balī. The Messenger of God put Marthad b. Abī Marthad in charge of them, and they set out with the delegation. When they got to al-Rajīʿ, a watering place belonging to (the tribe of) Hudhayl, in a district of Ḥijāz in the upper part of al-Had'ah, the (delegation) betrayed the (Muslims) and called Hudhayl to their assistance against them. The (Muslims) who had bivouacked for the night were taken completely by surprise by men with swords in their hands; they took up their swords to fight them, but the (men) said, "By God, we do not want to kill you. We only want to get some (money) for you from the people of Mecca. We swear to you by God's covenant that we will not kill you." Marthad b. Abī Marthad, Khālid b. Bukayr, and ʿĀṣim b. Thābit b. Abī al-Aqlaḥ said, "By God, we will never accept a compact or contract from a polytheist," and then fought until they were all killed. Zayd b. al-Dathinnah, Khubayb b. ʿAdī, and ʿAbd Allāh b. Ṭāriq, however, were soft and
[1433] yielding, desiring life, and surrendered; they were made prisoners and taken to Mecca to be sold there.

When they got as far as al-Ẓahrān, ʿAbd Allāh b. Ṭāriq broke loose from his bonds, and seized his sword. His captors kept well back from him, but threw stones at him until they had killed him. They buried him at al-Ẓahrān. As for Khubayb b. ʿAdī and Zayd b. al-Dathinnah, their captors took them to Mecca and sold them there. Khubayb was bought by Ḥujayr b. Abī Ihāb al-Tamīmī, the confederate of the Banū Nawfal, on behalf of ʿUqbah b. al-Hārith b. ʿĀmir b. Nawfal, Ḥujayr being the brother of al-Ḥārith b. ʿĀmir by his mother; this was so that ʿUqbah might kill him in revenge for his father. Zayd b. al-Dathinnah was bought by Ṣafwān b. Umayyah in order to kill him in revenge for his father, Umayyah b. Khalaf.

When ʿĀṣim b. Thābit was killed, Hudhayl had wanted his head in order to sell it to Sulāfah bt. Saʿd b. Shuhayd,[211] because she had

211. See 1405 above. Sulāfah was the wife of Ṭalḥah b. Abī Ṭalḥah, whose clan ʿAbd al-Dār were responsible for guarding the Meccan standard. In defence of the standard Ṭalḥah and four sons were killed.

vowed, when he killed her son at Uḥud, to drink wine from his skull if she ever got hold of his head. He was protected by hornets, however, and when these prevented the men from reaching him, they said, "Leave him until evening; then the hornets will leave him and we can take him." But God sent a flood in the wadi which lifted up ʿĀṣim's body and carried it away. ʿĀṣim had made a covenant with God that no polytheist should touch him and [1434] that he would never touch a polytheist, for fear of being defiled. When the news that the hornets had protected him reached ʿUmar b. al-Khaṭṭāb, he used to say, "How wonderful! God protected his believing servant! ʿĀṣim swore that no polytheist would ever touch him, and that he would never touch a polytheist in his life, and God protected him from this after his death just as he abstained from contact in his life."

Abū Jaʿfar (al-Ṭabarī) says: Other authorities than Ibn Isḥāq have a different account of this expedition. One variant version is that of Abū Kurayb—Jaʿfar b. ʿAwn al-ʿAmrī—Ibrāhīm b. Ismāʿīl—ʿAmr or ʿUmar b. Asīd—Abū Hurayrah: The Messenger of God sent out a group of ten men, putting ʿĀṣim b. Thābit in command of them, and they travelled until they reached Hadʾah. There somebody told a clan of (the tribe of) Hudhayl called the Banū Liḥyān about them. The latter sent a hundred archers against the Muslims. This force found the remains of the Muslims' food, which had consisted of dates. "These are the date-stones of Yathrib," they said, and followed the Muslims' tracks. When ʿĀṣim and his companions became aware of them, they withdrew to a hill, but the others surrounded them and called on them to surrender, giving them their word that they would not kill them. ʿĀṣim said, "By God, I will not surrender on the word of an infidel. O God, inform your prophet about us." Ibn al-Dathinnah al-Bayāḍī, Khubayb, and another man gave themselves up, and the enemy removed the bowstrings from their bows and tied them up with them. When they wounded one of the three, he said, "By God, is this the beginning of treachery? By God, I will not follow you!"—they beat him until he died. Then they took Khubayb and Ibn al-Dathinnah to Mecca. Khubayb they handed over to the [1435] sons of al-Ḥārith b. ʿĀmir b. Nawfal b. ʿAbd Manāf, as it was he who had killed al-Ḥārith at Uḥud. While he was with al-Ḥārith's daughters, he borrowed a razor from one of them to shave himself with before being killed. The woman, who had a son who was just beginning to walk, was thunderstruck to see Khubayb with the boy on his knee and the razor in his hand. She screamed, but Khubayb said, "Are you afraid that I will kill him? Treachery is not one of our customs."

The woman said later, "I never saw a more virtuous captive than Khubayb. At a time when there was no fruit in Mecca, I saw him with a bunch of grapes in his hand which he was eating; it was indeed sustenance which God bestowed on Khubayb."

One section of Quraysh sent asking for a part of ʿĀṣim's body to be brought to them, since he had left his mark on them at Uḥud; but God sent a swarm of hornets which guarded his body, and they were not able to take any part of him.

When they took Khubayb out of the *ḥaram* (sacred area round Mecca) to kill him, he asked to be allowed to pray two *rakʿahs;* they left him, and he prayed two prostrations. After that, it be-
[1436] came the *sunnah* for those about to be executed to pray two *rakʿahs*. Khubayb said, "If it were not that they would say I did not want to die, I would have prayed longer.

I do not care which side it comes from; my death is for God."

Then he said:

"This is for God himself, and if he will
he will bless the limbs of a mangled corpse.
O God, count them by number and take them one by one!"

Then Abū Sirwaʿah b. al-Ḥārith b. ʿĀmir b. Nawfal b. ʿAbd Manāf took him out and beheaded him.

According to Abū Kurayb—Jaʿfar b. ʿAwn—Ibrāhīm b. Ismāʿīl—Jaʿfar b. ʿAmr b. Umayyah—his father—his grandfather:[212] The Messenger of God sent him alone to Quraysh as a spy. He said, "I came to the cross to which Khubayb was bound, frightened that someone might see me, climbed up it, and untied Khubayb. He fell to the ground, and I withdrew a short distance. Then I turned round, and I could not see a trace of Khubayb—it was as though

212. According to the isnād on 1437f. the great-grandfather (*jadd*) is ʿAmr b. Umayyah al-Ḍamrī. The subtribe of Ḍamrah was part of Banū Bakr b. ʿAbd Manāt b. Kinānah and had grounds close to Mecca.

the earth had swallowed him up. Nothing has been heard of Khubayb to this day." [1437]

According to Abū Ja'far (al-Ṭabarī)—Ibn Ḥumayd—Salamah—Ibn Isḥāq: Zayd b. al-Dathinnah was sent to al-Tan'īm by Ṣafwān b. Umayyah along with a *mawlā* of his called Nisṭās who was to take him outside the *ḥaram* and then kill him. A group of Quraysh, among whom was Abū Sufyān b. Ḥarb, gathered around Zayd, and when he was brought forward to be killed Abū Sufyān said to him, "I call on you in God's name to tell me the truth, Zayd; do you not wish that Muḥammad was here in your place, so that we could execute him, and that you were at home among your family?" "By God," he replied, "I do not even wish that Muḥammad, at home as he is now, should be hurt by a thorn prick in order that I could be at home among my family." Abū Sufyān used to say, "I never saw anyone love another person so completely as Muḥammad's companions love Muḥammad." Finally Nisṭās killed him.

The Mission of 'Amr b. Umayyah against Abū Sufyān[213]

The story of 'Amr b. Umayyah al-Ḍamrī, when he was sent by the Messenger of God to kill Abū Sufyān b. Ḥarb.

When the men whom the Prophet had sent to 'Aḍal and al-Qārah were killed at al-Rajī' and the news reached the Messenger of God, he sent 'Amr b. Umayyah al-Ḍamrī and one of the Anṣār to Mecca, ordering them to kill Abū Sufyān b. Ḥarb.

According to Ibn Ḥumayd—Salamah b. al-Faḍl—Muḥammad b. Isḥāq—Ja'far b. al-Faḍl b. al-Ḥasan b. 'Amr b. Umayyah al-
Ḍamrī—his father—his great-grandfather, that is 'Amr b. Umay- [1438]
yah, whose account is as follows: After the death of Khubayb and his companions, the Messenger of God sent me together with one of the Anṣār, saying, "Go to Abū Sufyān b. Ḥarb and kill him." I and my companion set out. I had a camel and he had not, and he had a weakness in his foot, so I carried him on my camel until we

213. This story is not in our text of Ibn Isḥāq, and Ibn Hishām (992) says the latter omitted it and gives a version from another unspecified source. Al-Ṭabarī, however, ascribes his version (1437–41) to Ibn Isḥāq. See also Guillaume, xlii, 790n.

reached the valley of Ya'jaj. Then we hobbled our camel in the bottom of a ravine and climbed up. I said to my companion, "Come with me to Abū Sufyān's house, as I am going to try to kill him. You keep watch, and if a patrol comes or something alarms you, get back to your camel, mount it, return to Medina, and go to the Messenger of God and tell him what has happened. You can leave me to my own devices, because I know the town well, am bold, and have strong legs."

When we entered Mecca I had with me the like of an eagle's secondary feather—meaning his dagger—which I had ready to kill anybody who laid hold of me. My companion said to me, "Shall we make a start by circumambulating the Kaʿbah seven times and praying two *rakʿah*s?" I said to him, "I know the people of Mecca better than you do. When it gets dark, they sprinkle their courtyards with water and sit in them; and I am better known there than a piebald horse."

But he kept on pestering me until in the end we went to the Kaʿbah, circumambulated it seven times, and prayed two *rakʿah*s. When we came out we went past a group of men sitting together, and one of them recognized me and shouted out at the top of his voice, "That is ʿAmr b. Umayyah!" The Meccans rushed after us, saying "By God, ʿAmr b. Umayyah has not come here for any good purpose! By the God by whom we swear, he has never come here except for some evil purpose!" (ʿAmr had been a cutthroat and a desperado before accepting Islam).

They set out in pursuit of my companion and myself, and I said
[1439] to him, "Let us get out of here! This is just what I was afraid of! We will never reach Abū Sufyān now, so save your own skin." We left at full speed, took to the hills, and hid in a cave, where we spent the night. In this way we gave them the slip, and they had to return without us. As we went into the cave, I concealed the entrance with stones, saying to my companion, "Let us wait here until the hue and cry has died down; they are sure to hunt for us the rest of the night and all tomorrow until the evening." I was still in the cave when, by God, ʿUthmān b. Mālik b. ʿUbayd Allāh al-Taymī came up riding proudly on his horse. He kept coming nearer and nearer, riding proudly on his horse, until he reached the entrance to our cave. I said to my companion, "This is Ibn Mālik. By God, if he sees us, he will tell everyone in Mecca about

us!" So I went out and stabbed him below the breast with my dagger. He gave a shout which all the Meccans heard, and they came up to him while I went back to my hiding place, went in and said to my companion, "Stay where you are!" The Meccans hastily followed the shout, and found him on the point of death. They asked him, who had wounded him. "ʿAmr b. Umayyah," he replied, and died. They could not find anything to show them where we were, and merely said, "By God, we knew that he came for no good purpose." The death of their companion impeded their search for us, for they carried him away. We remained in the cave for two days until the pursuit had died down and then went out to al-Tanʿīm, where Khubayb's cross was. My companion said to me, "Shall we take Khubayb down from his cross?" "Where is he?" I said. "You can see him over there," he said. "Very well," I [1440]
said, "but leave it to me, and keep well away from me." The cross was watched over by a guard, so I said to the Anṣāri, "If you are afraid of anything, make your way to your camel, mount it, go to the Messenger of God, and tell him what has happened." I went quickly to Khubayb's cross, untied him, and carried him on my back, but I had gone no more than forty paces when they spotted me. At once I threw him down, and I will never forget the sound his body made when it fell. They ran after me, and I took the path to al-Ṣafrā' and managed to throw them off. They went back, while my companion made his way to his camel, mounted it, went to the Prophet and told him what had happened to us. I proceeded on foot until I was overlooking Ghalīl Ḍajnān. There I went into a cave with my bow and arrows. While I was in it a tall one-eyed man from the Banū al-Dīl b. Bakr came in driving some sheep. He said, "Who is there?" and I said, "One of the Banū Bakr."[214] He said, "I am from the Banū Bakr, one of the Banū al-Dīl." Then he lay down next to me, and raised his voice in song:

I will not be a Muslim as long as I live,
and will not believe in the faith of the Muslims.

I said, "You will soon see!" Before long the beduin went to sleep and started snoring, and I went to him and killed him in the most

214. ʿAmr's tribe of Ḍamrah was part of Bakr, as was also al-Dīl.

dreadful way that anybody has ever killed anybody. I leant over him, stuck the end of my bow into his good eye, and thrust it down until it came out of the back of his neck. After that I rushed
[1441] out like a wild beast and took to the highway like an eagle, fleeing for my life. First, I came to such and such a village, then to Rakūbah, and then to al-Naqīʿ. At this place there were two Meccans whom Quraysh had sent to spy out how things were with the Messenger of God. I recognized them and called on them to surrender. "Shall we surrender to you?" they said; so I shot an arrow at one of them and killed him, and then called on the other to surrender. He did so and I tied him up and took him to the Messenger of God.

According to Ibn Ḥumayd—Salamah—Ibn Isḥāq—Sulaymān b. Wardān—his father—ʿAmr b. Umayyah: When I came to Medina, I went past some shaykhs of the Anṣār. "By God," they said, "that is ʿAmr b. Umayyah!" Some boys heard what they were saying and rushed to the Messenger of God to tell him. I had tied my prisoner's thumbs together with my bowstring, and the Messenger of God looked at him and laughed so that his back teeth could be seen. Then he questioned me and I told him what had happened. "Well done!" he said, and prayed for me to be blessed.

Muḥammad's Marriage to Zaynab bt. Khuzaymah[215]

In this year, in the month of Ramaḍān (which began February 4, 626), the Messenger of God married Zaynab bt. Khuzaymah, known as "the Mother of the Poor," a woman of the Banū Hilāl. He consummated his marriage to her in the same month and settled twelve *ūqiyyah*s and a *nashsh* on her as a dowry. She had previously been married to al-Ṭufayl b. al-Ḥārith, who had divorced her.[216]

---

215. This Zaynab, who is not to be confused with Zaynab bt. Jaḥsh, belonged to Banū Hilāl, part of the nomadic tribe of ʿĀmir b. Ṣaʿṣaʿah. After her divorce from Ṭufayl, a Muslim of the Meccan clan of al-Muṭṭalib, she married his brother ʿUbaydah, who was killed at Badr. See i.1775f. below and Watt, *Medina*, 396.

216. The *ūqiyyah* is usually rendered "ounce" and the *nashsh* is half of that. Zaynab's dowry consisted of this weight of gold or silver presumably.

The Story of Bi'r Maʿūnah[217]

Abū Jaʿfar (al-Ṭabarī) says: In this year there occurred the disaster of the expedition sent out by the Messenger of God which was killed at Bi'r Maʿūnah.

According to Ibn Ḥumayd—Salamah—Muḥammad b. Isḥāq: [1442] (After the battle of Uḥud) the Messenger of God remained in Medina for the rest of Shawwāl, and Dhū al-Ḥijjah (of year 3) and Muḥarram (of year 4) (late March 625 to early July 625). The polytheists had charge of the pilgrimage that year. Then in Ṣafar (which began July 13, 625), four months after Uḥud, he sent out the men of Bi'r Maʿūnah. The reason was as follows.

According to (Ibn Isḥāq)—my father, Isḥāq b. Yasār—al-Mughīrah b. ʿAbd al-Raḥmān b. al-Ḥārith b. Hishām, and also ʿAbd Allāh b. Abī Bakr b. Muḥammad b. ʿAmr b. Ḥazm and other scholars: Abū Barā' ʿĀmir b. Mālik b. Jaʿfar, the "Player with spear-heads," who was the chief of the Banū ʿĀmir b. Ṣaʿṣaʿah, came to the Messenger of God in Medina and presented him with a gift. The Messenger of God declined to accept it, saying, "Abū Barā', I do not accept presents from polytheists, so become a Muslim if you want me to accept it." Then he expounded Islam to him, explained its advantages for him and God's promises to the believers, and recited the Qur'ān to him. He did not accept Islam, but was not far from doing so, saying, "Muḥammad, this matter of yours to which you call me is good and beautiful. If you were to send some of your companions to the people of Najd to call them to your religion, I would hope that they would respond to you." The Messenger of God said, "I fear that the people of Najd would do them some harm." Abū Barā' replied, "I will guarantee their protection, so send them to call people to your religion." The Messenger of God thereupon sent al-Mundhir b. ʿAmr, the brother of the Banū Sāʿidah, "he who hastens to death," at the head of forty of the best Muslims from his companions; among them were al-Ḥārith b. Ṣimmah, Ḥarām b. Milḥān, the brother of the Banū ʿAdī b. al-Najjār, ʿUrwah b. Asmā' b. al-Ṣalt al-Sulamī, [1443] Nāfiʿ b. Budayl b. Warqā' al-Khuzāʿī, and ʿĀmir b. Fuhayrah, the

217. See also IH, 648–52; W, 346–52; Watt, *Medina*, 31–3; *EI*², art. Bi'r Maʿūna (C. E. Bosworth).

mawlā of Abū Bakr, together with other named men from the best of the Muslims.

According to Ibn Ḥumayd—Salamah—Muḥammad b. Isḥāq —Ḥumayd al-Ṭawīl—Anas b. Mālik: The Messenger of God sent al-Mundhir b. ʿAmr with seventy riders. They went on until they halted at Biʾr Maʿūnah, which lies between the territory of the Banū ʿĀmir and the *ḥarrah* of the Banū Sulaym, near to both of them but closer to the latter. After halting, they sent Ḥarām b. Milḥān to ʿĀmir b. al-Ṭufayl[218] with a letter from the Messenger of God. When Ḥarām arrived, ʿĀmir did not even look at the letter but rushed on him and killed him. Then he called on the Banū ʿĀmir to aid him against the Muslims, but they refused to do what he asked them, saying, "We will not betray Abū Barāʾ. He has entered into a compact with them and given them his protection." ʿĀmir then called on some clans of the Banū Sulaym, ʿUṣayyah, Riʿl, and Dhakwān, to come to his aid against the Muslims, and they responded to his request. They set out and took the Muslims by surprise, surrounding them while they were dismounted and encamped. The Muslims, on seeing them, snatched up their swords and fought them until they themselves were killed to the last man, except for Kaʿb b. Zayd, the brother of the Banū Dīnār b. al-Najjār. The enemy left Kaʿb at the point of death, but he was pulled out from among the slain and survived, eventually being killed at the battle of the Trench (in 5/627).

ʿAmr b. Umayyah al-Ḍamrī and one of the Anṣār belonging to the Banū ʿAmr b. ʿAwf were out with the grazing camels and only realized what had happened to their companions from the birds which were hovering over the camp. "By God," they said, "these birds mean something." They went up to see and found their companions lying in their blood, while the horsemen who had killed them stood close by. The Anṣārī said to ʿAmr b. Umayyah,
[1444] "What do you think we should do?" He said, "I think that we should go to the Messenger of God and tell him what has happened." The Anṣārī said, "I do not want to leave a place in which al-Mundhir b. ʿAmr has been killed, and I do not want people to

218. ʿAmir b. Ṭufayl was the nephew of Abū Barāʾ and also had a position of leadership in the tribe, but the precise details are not known. The tribe refused to support ʿĀmir in disregarding the protection (*ijārah*) granted by Abū Barāʾ.

say that I did so." He then fought against the enemy until he was killed. The latter took ʿAmr b. Umayyah prisoner, but when he told them that he was from Muḍar ʿĀmir b. al-Ṭufayl set him free, after cutting off his forelock. He freed him, so he claimed, because of an oath taken by his mother.

ʿAmr b. Umayyah proceeded towards Medina until, when he was at al-Qarqarah in the upper part of Qanāt, two men of the Banū ʿĀmir came up and halted next to him in the shade, where he was. The ʿĀmirīs had a compact of protection with the Messenger of God which ʿAmr b. Umayyah did not know about. When they dismounted he asked them who they were, and they replied that they were from the Banū ʿĀmir. He let them be until they were asleep, but then rushed on them and killed them, thinking that he had taken vengeance on them for the companions of the Messenger of God who had been killed by the Banū ʿĀmir. When he came to the Messenger of God he told him what had happened, and the Messenger of God said, "You have killed two men for whom I shall have to pay blood-money." Then he added, "This is the doing of Abū Barāʾ. I was opposed to sending out this party and apprehensive about it."[219] Abū Barāʾ heard of this and was distressed by ʿĀmir's betrayal of him and by the disaster which had befallen the Messenger of God as a result of his guaranteeing the protection of the party of Muslims. One of those who was killed was ʿĀmir b. Fuhayrah.

According to Ibn Ḥumayd—Salamah—Muḥammad b. Isḥāq—Hishām b. ʿUrwah—his father: ʿĀmir b. al-Ṭufayl used to say, "Which of them is the man whom I saw being raised up between heaven and earth after his death until I saw the heavens beneath him?" They said, "That was ʿĀmir b. Fuhayrah."

According to Ibn Ḥumayd—Salamah—Muḥammad b. Isḥāq [1445]
—one of the Banū Jaʿfar, one of the sons of Jabbār b. Sulmā b. Mālik b. Jaʿfar: Jabbār was one of those who were present that day

219. The reason why Muḥammad had to give blood-money for two to Banū ʿĀmir, while claiming none for the men he had lost, is presumably that the latter were actually killed by tribesmen of Sulaym, even if ʿĀmir b. al-Ṭufayl had asked them to do so and was "morally responsible" according to Western ideas. Abū Barāʾ was at most responsible for exaggerating his own ability to protect, but he felt disgraced because his grant of protection had been betrayed. Hence the poem below by Ḥassān b. Thābit.

with 'Amir, but he accepted Islam later on. He used to say, "One of the things which summoned me to Islam was that I struck one of them that day between his shoulders with my spear. I saw the spearhead coming out of his breast, and I heard him say as I speared him, "I have won, by God!" I said to myself, "What has he won? Have I not killed the man?" Later on I asked what he had said, and was told, "He meant he had won martyrdom." "By God," I said, "he has won."

Ḥassān b. Thābit said,[220] inciting the sons of Abū Barā' against 'Āmir b. al-Ṭufayl:

O sons of Umm al-Banīn, have you not been dismayed,
although you are the highest of the people of Najd,
By 'Āmir's scornful behaviour to Abū Barā'
in betraying his guarantee of protection; for a mistake is not like a deliberate act.
Say to Rabī'ah who ever strives,
what have you done in the course of time since I was with you?
Your father is the man of war Abū Barā'
and your maternal uncle, Ḥakam b. Sa'd, is glorious.

On the same subject, Ka'b b. Malīk said:

The betrayal of Abū Barā''s guarantee of protection
has spread far and wide in every direction
[1446] It is like Musahhab and his father's sons
by al-Radh in the region of Suwā'
O sons of Umm al-Banīn, did you not hear
the call for help at evening time
And the raising of the cry? Nay, you heard it,
but you knew that it was a true battle.
The bags of the Banū Kilāb are not empty
of blame for faithlessness, nor those of the Quraṭā'.
'Āmir, 'Āmir of shameful acts of old,
you have not gained comprehension or splendour

220. See his *Dīwān*, i.232f., ii.174–7; the verses are in a different order there. Umm al-Banīn ("mother of the sons") was the mother of Abū Barā' and had four other sons. Ḥakam b. Sa'd was her brother and Rabī'ah the son of Abū Barā'. The following verses by Ka'b b. Mālik are not in IH.

Have you betrayed the Prophet, when of old you used
to hasten to shameful acts under the open sky?
You are not like the protector of Abū Duwād,
nor like al-Asadī, the protector of Abū al-ʿAlā'
But your shame is an ancient sickness,
and the sickness of treachery, be assured, is worst of all.

When these words of Ḥassān and Kaʿb reached Rabīʿah, the son of ʿĀmir Abū Barā', he attacked ʿĀmir b. al-Ṭufayl and thrust at him with his lance, but the lance was deflected and failed to kill him. ʿĀmir fell off his horse and said, "This is the doing of Abū Barā'. If I die, I give the right to avenge my death to my uncle,[221] and he is not to be held to account for it; but if I live, I shall make my own decision about what has happened to me."

According to Muḥammad b. Marzūq—ʿAmr b. Yūnus—ʿIkrimah—Isḥāq b. Abī Ṭalḥah—Anas b. Mālik: The companions of the Prophet whom he sent to the people of Bi'r Maʿūnah, were either forty or seventy, I do not know. ʿĀmir b. al-Ṭufayl al-Jaʿfarī was in control of that watering place. This company of compan- [1447] ions of the Prophet travelled until they came to a cave overlooking the watering place. There they settled down, and then said to one another, "Which of us will deliver the Messenger of God's letter to the people of this watering place?" One of them, Ibn Milḥān the Anṣārī, I think, said, "I will deliver the Messenger of God's letter." He reached a group of tents, in front of which he sat down, and said, "People of Bi'r Maʿūnah, I am an envoy of the Messenger of God to you. I testify that there is no deity but God and that Muḥammad is His servant and His Messenger. So believe in God and His Messenger." A man came out of a tent flap with a spear and struck him with it in one side so that it came out at the other side. He said, "God is most great. I have won, by the Lord of the Kaʿbah." Then they followed his tracks backwards until they came to his companions in the cave, and ʿĀmir b. al-Ṭufayl killed them all.

According to Isḥāq—Anas b. Mālik: God revealed concerning them as part of the Qur'ān, "Tell our people of us. Verily we have

221. That is, to Abū Barā', presumably. If ʿAmir b. al-Ṭufayl lives, it will still be open to him to seek vengeance.

met our Lord, and He has been pleased with us and we have been pleased with Him." Later it was abrogated and removed from the Qur'ān, but for a time we had recited it.[222] God then revealed, "Think not of those, who are slain in the way of Allah, as dead. Nay, they are living. With their Lord they have provision, jubilant."

According to Al-ʿAbbās b. al-Walīd—his father—al-Awzāʿī—Isḥāq b. ʿAbd Allāh b. Abī Ṭalḥa al-Anṣārī—Anas b. Malīk: The Messenger of God sent to ʿĀmir b. al-Ṭufayl al-Kilābī seventy of the Anṣār. Their commander said, "Stay where you are until I bring you news of the people." When he came to them he said, "Will you grant me security so that I can tell you about the message of the Messenger of God?" They said, "Yes," but while he was with them one of them suddenly stuck his spear into him. He
[1448] said, "I have won, by the Lord of the Kaʿbah." ʿĀmir said, "I am sure that he must have companions," so they followed his tracks backwards until they came to them and killed them. Nobody escaped except for one man.

Anas says: We used to recite, as part of what was abrogated, "Tell our brethren of us, that we have met our Lord, and he has been pleased with us and we have been pleased with him."

The Expulsion of the Banū al-Naḍīr[223]

In this year, the fourth year of the Hijrah, the Prophet expelled the Banū al-Naḍīr from their settlements.

Abū Jaʿfar (al-Ṭabarī) says: The cause of this was, as we have mentioned above, that ʿAmr b. Umayyah, as he returned from the expedition sent out by the Messenger of God to Bi'r Maʿūnah, killed two men to whom had been given a promise of protection by the Messenger of God. It is said that ʿĀmir b. al-Ṭufayl wrote to the Messenger of God, "You have killed two men whom you had given a promise of protection, so send their blood-money." The Messenger of God went to Qubā' and then turned towards the Banū al-Naḍīr to seek help from them in the payment of the

---

222. For this revelation not in the Qur'ān see Th. Nöldeke, *Geschichte des Qorāns*,[2] Leipzig 1909, i.246–8. The following verse is Qur. 3.169.

223. IH, 652–61; W, 363–83; Watt, *Medina*, 211f.

blood-money. With him there were a group of Emigrants and Anṣār, including Abū Bakr, ʿUmar, ʿAlī and Usayd b. Ḥuḍayr.

According to Ibn Ḥumayd — Salamah — Muḥammad b. Isḥāq: The Messenger of God went out to the Banū al-Naḍīr to ask for their help in the payment of the blood-money for those two men of the Banū ʿĀmir whom ʿAmr b. Umayyah al-Ḍamrī had killed. This was because he had entered into an obligation to protect them, as I have been told by Yazīd b. Rūmān. The Banū al-Naḍīr and the Banū ʿĀmir were joined by a treaty and a compact, and when the Messenger of God came to them to ask for their help in the payment of the blood-money for those two men, they said, [1449] "Yes, Abū al-Qāsim,[224] we will give you the help which you want and which you have asked from us." Then they spoke privately with one another, and said, "You will never find this man in such a situation again." The Messenger of God was sitting by the wall of one of their houses, and they said, "Who will go on the roof of this house and drop a stone on him and kill him, and so relieve us of him?" ʿAmr b. Jiḥāsh b. Kaʿb, who was one of them, came forward to do this, and said, "I am your man." Then he went up to the roof to drop the stone on him as arranged. The Messenger of God was with a number of his companions, including Abū Bakr, ʿUmar, and ʿAlī, and news of what the people intended came to him from Heaven. He got up and said to his companions, "Do not leave until I come to you." He went back to Medina, and when his companions thought that he had been gone a long time they got up to look for him. Then they met a man coming from Medina and asked him about the Messenger of God. He said, "I saw him going into Medina." When his companions came to him, the Messenger of God told them the story of the treachery intended by the Jews and ordered them to get ready to fight them and march against them. He then led his men against the Banū al-Naḍīr and halted in their quarter. They fortified themselves against him in their strongholds, but he ordered the date-palms to be cut down and set fire to. They shouted, "Muḥammad, you have forbidden damage to property and have blamed those who

224. The *kunyah* of Muḥammad; al-Qāsim was the eldest of his sons by Khadījah but died at an early age.

perpetrated it: what is the idea of cutting down date-palms and setting fire to them?"

Abū Ja'far (al-Ṭabarī) says: As for al-Wāqidī, he says that when they conspired together to drop the stone on the Messenger of God, Sallām b. Mishkam told them not to do so, and warned
[1450] them that it would mean war, adding that Muḥammad knew what they intended. They ignored his advice, however, and 'Amr b. Jiḥāsh went up to the roof to roll the stone over. News of this came to the Prophet from Heaven, and he got up as though he wished to relieve himself. His companions waited for him, but he was gone for a long time. The Jews began to say, "What has delayed Abū al-Qāsim?" and his companions left. Kinānah b. Ṣūriyā' said, "News of what you intended has reached him."

When the Messenger of God's companions returned they went to him and found him sitting in the mosque. They said, "O Messenger of God, we waited for you but you did not come back." "The Jews intended to kill me," he replied, "and God informed me of it. Call Muḥammad b. Maslamah to me." When Muḥammad b. Maslamah came, he was told to go to the Jews and say to them, "Leave my country and do not live with me. You have intended treachery." Muḥammad b. Maslamah went to them and said, "The Messenger of God orders you to depart from his country." They said, "Muḥammad, we never thought that a man of al-Aws would come to us with such a message." "Hearts have changed," he replied, "and Islam has wiped out the old covenants." "We will go," they said.

'Abd Allāh b. Ubayy sent a message to the Banū al-Naḍīr saying, "Do not go. I have two thousand men from the beduin and those of my own people who are united around me. Stay, and they will enter battle with you, as will Qurayẓah." Ka'b b. Asad, however, the guarantor of the Banū Qurayẓah's compact with the Messenger of God,[225] heard of this and said, "No man of the Banū Qurayẓah shall break his compact as long as I am alive." Sallām b. Mishkam said to Ḥuyayy b. Akhṭab, "Ḥuyayy, we (our tribe) are eminent among our people (the Jews) by virtue of our wealth; accept what Muḥammad has proposed before you have to accept

225. Ka'b b. Asad had signed the agreement with Muḥammad on behalf of Banū Qurayẓah. Sallām and Ḥuyayy were leaders of al-Naḍīr.

what is worse than that." "What is worse than that?" he asked. "The seizure of our wealth, the enslavement of our children, and the killing of our fighting men," he replied. Ḥuyayy refused to accept his advice, however, and sent Judayy b. Akhṭab to the Messenger of God to say, "We will not leave our settlements; so do what you see fit." [1451]

The Messenger of God magnified God and the Muslims magnified God with him. Then he said, "The Jews have declared war." Judayy then went to Ibn Ubayy to ask for support from him. He said, "I found him sitting among a number of his companions while the Prophet's crier was calling men to arms. His son, ʿAbd Allāh b. ʿAbd Allāh b. Ubayy, came in as I was with him, took up his arms, and ran out.[226] I despaired of Ibn Ubayy's help, and told Ḥuyayy of all this. He said, "This is a clever trick of Muḥammad's." The Messenger of God marched against the Banū al-Naḍīr, and besieged them for fifteen days. In the end they made peace with him on the condition that the Messenger of God would not shed their blood and that their property and their coats of mail would be his.

According to Muḥammad b. Saʿd—his father—his paternal uncle—his father—his father—Ibn ʿAbbās: The Messenger of God besieged them (the Banū al-Naḍīr) for fifteen days until he had reduced them to a state of utter exhaustion, so that they gave him what he wanted from them and made peace with him. The terms were that he would not shed their blood, would expel them from their lands and their settlements, and would send them to Adhriʿāt in Syria, providing for every three of them a camel and a water-skin.

According to Ibn ʿAbd al-Aʿlā—Muḥammad b. Thawr—Maʿmar—al-Zuhrī: The Prophet fought them until he made peace with them on condition that they evacuated Medina. He expelled them to Syria but allowed them to keep what their camels could carry, except for their coats of mail ("coats of mail" means weapons).

Resumption of Ibn Isḥāq's narrative. [1452]

---

226. ʿAbdallāh, the son of ʿAbdallāh b. Ubayy, the leading Hypocrite, was a fervent Muslim who said he was ready to kill his father if Muḥammad commanded it; here he answers Muḥammad's call to arms.

A group of the Banū ʿAwf b. al-Khazraj, including ʿAbd Allāh b. Ubayy b. Salūl, Wadīʿah, Mālik b. Abī Qawqal, Suwayd, and Dāʿis had sent a message to the Banū al-Naḍīr saying, "Stand firm and hold out, for we will not desert you. If they fight you, we will fight along with you, and if you are driven out, we will leave with you." So they waited patiently, but the group with Ibn Ubayy did nothing, and God cast fear into the hearts of Banū al-Naḍīr so that they asked the Messenger of God to spare their lives and allow them to leave Medina. The condition was to be that they could keep as much of their property as their camels could carry, with the exception of their coats of mail. The Messenger of God agreed to this and they took away as much of their property as their camels could carry. Some of them were destroying their houses down to the lintel of the door, putting even that on the back of their camels, and going off with it.

They went to Khaybar, and some of them went to Syria. Among their nobles who went to Khaybar were Sallām b. Abī al-Ḥuqayq, Kinānah b. al-Rabīʿ b. Abī al-Ḥuqayq, and Ḥuyayy b. Akhṭab. When they settled in Khaybar its inhabitants submitted to them.

According to Ibn Ḥumayd—Salamah—Muḥammad b. Isḥāq—ʿAbd Allāh b. Abī Bakr: They loaded their camels with their wives, children and property, and there were tambourines, pipes, and singing girls behind them. Among them was Umm ʿAmr, wife of ʿUrwah b. al-Ward al-ʿAbsī, whom they had bought from him.[227] She was one of the Banū Ghifār. They went with a splen-
[1453] dour and a glory the like of which had never been seen from any tribe in their time.

The Banū al-Naḍīr left their property to the Messenger of God, and it became his personal property, to do with it as he wished. He divided it among the first Emigrants, to the exclusion of the Anṣār, except that Sahl b. Ḥunayf and Abū Dujānah Simāk b. Kharashah spoke of their poverty and he gave them some of it.[228] Only two of the Banū al-Naḍīr became Muslims, Yāmīn b. ʿUmayr b. Kaʿb, who was the nephew of ʿAmr b. Jiḥāsh, and Abū Saʿd b. Wahb; they were allowed to keep their property when they accepted Islam and in this way they preserved it.

227. IH, 653. The story of Umm ʿAmr Salmā is told more fully in W, 376.
228. See 1426 above and n.205.

Abū Ja'far (al-Ṭabarī) says: It is said that when the Messenger of God went out to fight the Banū al-Naḍīr he left Ibn Umm Maktūm in charge of Medina. His banner was borne on that occasion by 'Alī b. Abī Ṭālib.

Other Events

In this year, in Jumādā al-Ūlā (which began October 9, 625), there died 'Abd Allāh b. 'Uthmān b. 'Affān, who was six years old. The Messenger of God prayed over him, and 'Uthmān b. 'Affān went down into his grave.

In this year also, early in Sha'bān (which began January 6, 626), there was born al-Ḥusayn b. 'Alī.

The Expedition of Dhāt al-Riqā'

There is a difference of opinion as to which of his expeditions took place after that against the Banū al-Naḍīr.

According to Ibn Ḥumayd—Salamah—Ibn Isḥāq: The Messenger of God remained in Medina after the expedition against the Banū al-Naḍīr for the two months of Rabī' and part of the month of Jumādā (from August 11 to late October, 625). Then he went on an expedition into Najd, directed against the Banū Muḥārib and the Banū Tha'labah, part of Ghaṭafān, and reached Nakhl.[229] This [1454] was the expedition of Dhāt al-Riqā'. They met there a number of Ghaṭafān; the armies approached one another, but no fighting took place, because they feared one another. The Messenger of God then led the Muslims in the Prayer of Fear, and left with them.

As for al-Wāqidī, he asserts that the Messenger of God's expedition to Dhāt al-Riqā' was in Muḥarram in Year Five of the Hijrah (which began July 2, 626). He says that it was called Dhāt al-Riqā' because the mountain after which it was named, Dhāt al-Riqā' (the patchwork mountain) had black, white, and red patches on it. The Messenger of God left 'Uthmān b. 'Affān in charge of Medina during this expedition.

According to Ibn Ḥumayd—Salamah—Muḥammad b. Isḥāq

229. IH, 661–5; W, 395–402.

—Muhammad b. Jaʿfar b. al-Zubayr and Muḥammad (meaning b. ʿAbd al-Raḥmān)—ʿUrwah b. al-Zubayr—Abū Hurayrah: We went out with the Messenger of God to Najd. When we were at Dhāt al-Riqāʿ in the region of Nakhl he met a number of Ghaṭafān. No fighting took place between us, but our army was afraid of the enemy, and the rules for the Prayer of Fear were revealed. The Messenger of God divided his companions into two parts; one group stood facing the enemy while the other stood behind the Messenger of God. He magnified God and they all magnified God. Then he and those behind him performed a *rakʿah* and prostrated themselves. On standing up, they walked back to the ranks of their companions, while these returned and themselves prayed a *rakʿah*. When this party stood up (after their first *rakʿah*), the Messenger of God prayed a further *rakʿah* with
[1455] them, and at the end of it they sat down. Those who had been facing the enemy then came back and prayed the second *rakʿah*. When they had all sat down, the Messenger of God pronounced the greeting to both parties together.[230]

Abū Jaʿfar (al-Ṭabarī) says: The accounts of the way in which the Messenger of God led this prayer at the valley of Nakhl vary so much that I do not like to mention them here, for fear that this book may be unduly prolonged. We shall mention them, God willing, in our book entitled *The Simple Exposition of the Provisions of the Laws of Islam*,[231] in the chapter on the Prayer of Fear.

According to Muḥammad b. Bashshār—Muʿādh b. Hishām—his father—Qatādah—Sulaymān al-Yashkurī: I asked Jābir b. ʿAbd Allāh about the shortening of the prayer, on which day it was revealed or on which day it took place. Jābir said, "We set off to intercept a caravan belonging to Quraysh which was coming from Syria. When we got to Nakhl one of the enemy came to the

230. The details can be followed in a general account of Ṣalāt such as that in *EI*[1], section 2. To "magnify" God is to say "God is very great" (*Allāhu akbar*). The *rakʿah* is the cycle of acts and words which is repeated two, three, or four times according to the hour of the day—only twice for obvious reasons in the Prayer of Fear. The Ṣalāt also has an introductory section and a closing section, the latter concluding with the greeting ("Peace be with you") pronounced first to one's right then to one's left.

231. This work does not appear to be extant, if indeed it was ever written; see *GALS*, i.218.

Messenger of God and said, 'Muḥammad!' 'Yes?' he said. 'Are you afraid of me?' 'No.' 'Who will protect you from me?' he asked. 'God will protect me from you,' he said. Then the man drew his sword and threatened him.

"After this the Messenger of God gave the command to leave that place and take up arms, and then the call to prayer was made. The Prophet of God led one group of the army in prayer while another group guarded them. Those nearest to him he led in prayer for two *rak'ah*s, and then this group went back and occupied the positions of the other group. This second group meanwhile came and were led in prayer for two *rak'ah*s while the others guarded them. Then the Prophet gave the greeting to all. In this way the Prophet performed four *rak'ah*s while each half of his army performed only two *rak'ah*s. This was the day on which God gave a revelation concerning the shortening of prayer when the believers were ordered to take up arms."

According to Ibn Ḥumayd—Salamah—Muḥammad b. Isḥāq [1456] —'Amr b. 'Ubayd—al-Ḥasan al-Baṣrī—Jābir b. 'Abd Allāh al-Anṣārī: A man of the Banū Muḥārib called so-and-so b. al-Ḥārith said to his people of Ghaṭafān and Muḥārib, "Shall I kill Muḥammad for you?" They said, "Yes, but how are you going to kill him?" "I will do it by surprise," he said. He went to the Messenger of God as the latter was sitting with his sword in his lap, and said, "Muḥammad, may I have a look at your sword?" He said, "Yes." So the man took it and unsheathed it, and then started brandishing it, intending to kill him with it; but God restrained him. Then he said, "Muḥammad, are you not afraid of me?" "No," he said, "why should I be afraid of you?" "Are you not afraid of me with the sword in my hand?" he asked. "No," he replied, "God will defend me from you." At that he sheathed the sword and returned it to the Messenger of God. On this event, God revealed, "O ye who believe! Remember Allāh's favor unto you, how a people were minded to stretch out their hands against you but He withheld their hands from you. . . ."[232]

According to Ibn Ḥumayd—Salamah—Muḥammad b. Isḥāq —Ṣadaqah b. Yasār—'Aqīl b. Jābir—Jābir b. 'Abd Allāh al-Anṣārī:

232. Qur. 5.11.

We went out with the Messenger of God on the expedition to Dhāt al-Riqāʿ in the neighbourhood of Nakhl. At one point, one of the Muslims killed a polytheist woman. When the Messenger of God was on his way back to Medina, her husband, who had been away and had returned, on being told what had happened, swore that he would not rest until he had wrought bloodshed among Muḥammad's companions. He set out, following the Messenger of God's tracks. When the Messenger of God halted for the night
[1457] he said, "Who will keep watch for us tonight?" One of the Emigrants and one of the Anṣār volunteered, saying, "We will, O Messenger of God." He told them to station themselves at the top of the pass. The Messenger of God and his companions had halted further down the pass towards the valley bottom. When the two reached the top of the pass, the Anṣārī asked the Emigrant, "Which part of the night would you like me to stand watch for you—the first part or the second part?" "Stand watch for the first part for me," he said, and lay down and went to sleep, while the Anṣārī stood up to pray. The woman's husband now came, saw the standing figure, realised that he was the lookout for the army, and shot an arrow which hit him. The Anṣārī pulled the arrow out, put it down, and remained standing in prayer. The man shot a second and a third arrow at him, but exactly the same thing happened. Finally the Anṣārī, after bowing and prostrating himself, woke up his companion with the words, "Sit up, I have been wounded." The Emigrant leapt to his feet. When the man saw the two of them, he knew that they were alerted to his presence, (and fled).[233] When the Emigrant saw the Anṣārī's bloodstained condition he exclaimed, "God Almighty! Why did you not wake me up the first time he shot at you?" "I was in the middle of reciting a *Sūrah,*" he replied, "and I did not want to break off without finishing it. When he kept shooting at me I completed a *rakʿah* and woke you up. By God, but for the fact that I would have lost an outpost which the Messenger of God had ordered me to hold, the man could have killed me before I would have broken the *Sūrah* off uncompleted."

---

233. The words "and fled" have been added from IH's text; he also has a dual instead of the plural in al-Ṭabarī.

The Expedition of al-Sawīq (or Badr al-Maw'id)[234]

This is the Prophet's second expedition to Badr, which he undertook to keep his appointment with Abū Sufyān.

According to Ibn Ḥumayd—Salamah—Ibn Isḥāq: After the Messenger of God had returned to Medina from Dhāt al-Riqā', he remained there for the rest of Jumādā al-Ūlā, Jumādā al-Ākhirah, and Rajab (late October 625 to early January 626). Then in Sha'bān (which began January 6, 626) he went out to Badr to meet Abū Sufyān and halted there for eight days, waiting for him. Abū Sufyān came out with the Meccans and halted at Majannah in the region of Murr al-Ẓahrān—or, according to some people, went through 'Usfān, after which he decided to go back. "Men of Quraysh," he said, "only a fertile year in which you can pasture your animals on the bushes and drink their milk will be any good to you. This is a year of drought, and I am going to go back, so you go back too." They all went back, and the people of Mecca called them "the army of *sawīq* (barley-meal)," saying, "You only went out to drink barley-gruel."[235] [1458]

The Messenger of God stayed at Badr waiting to keep his rendezvous with Abū Sufyān. Makhshī b. 'Amr al-Ḍamrī, who had made a treaty with him on behalf of the Banū Ḍamrah during the expedition to Waddān, came to him and said, "Have you come to meet Quraysh at this watering place, Muḥammad?" "Yes, O brother of the Banū Ḍamrah," he said; "nevertheless, if you wish, we will release you from your treaty with us and then fight you until God decides between us." "No, by God, Muḥammad," he replied, "we want no such thing from you."

The Messenger of God remained, waiting for Abū Sufyān, and Ma'bad b. Abī Ma'bad al-Khuzā'ī passed by him, having seen where he was as he galloped past on his she-camel, and said:

> She was frightened away by Muḥammad's two companies [1459]

---

234. IH, 666–8; W, 384–91.
235. See n.153 above.

and a date-stone from Yathrib like a raisin,
Hurrying along in the hereditary faith of her fathers,
having made the water of Qudayd my meeting place
And the water of Ḍajnān hers tomorrow morning.

As for al-Wāqidī, he says that the Messenger of God urged his companions to take part in an expedition to Badr in order to meet Abū Sufyān, whom he had promised on the day of Uḥud to meet there for battle in a year's time. This was in Dhū al-Qaʿdah (which began April 4, 626). Nuʿaym b. Masʿūd al-Ashjaʿī had come to Mecca to perform the *ʿumrah* (lesser pilgrimage) and was asked by Quraysh which direction he had come from. When he said, "From Yathrib," Abū Sufyān asked, "Did you see Muḥammad making any movements?" He replied, "I left him making preparations for an expedition against you." This was before Nuʿaym became a Muslim.

Abū Sufyān said to him, "Nuʿaym, this is a year of drought, and only a year in which our camels can graze on shrubs and we can drink their milk will be suitable for us. Since the time for our rendezvous with Muḥammad has come, go to Medina, delay them, and make them think that we are coming with such a huge army that they will not be able to withstand us. In that way it will be they who break the agreement; and I would prefer that to our breaking it. Do this, and you shall have ten camels which I shall place in Suhayl b. ʿAmr's custody for safekeeping." So Suhayl b. ʿAmr came to them, and Nuʿaym said to Suhayl, "Abū Yazīd, will you be responsible for these camels so that I can go to Muḥammad and delay him?" He agreed, and Nuʿaym set out. When he arrived in Medina he found the people preparing themselves, so he mingled unobtrusively with them and would say, "This is not sensible. Was not Muḥammad personally wounded? Were his companions not killed?" In this way he delayed them, and when
[1460] the Messenger of God heard of it, he said, "By him in whose hand my soul rests, even if nobody goes out with me, I shall go out alone." Then God set the Muslims' understanding on the right path, and they set out to trade, earning two *dirhams* for every *dirham* laid out. They did not meet any enemy, and this expedition was known as *"Badr al-mawʿid"* (Badr of the Rendezvous).

Badr was the site of one of their markets in pre-Islamic times, and they assembled there for eight days once a year.

Abū Ja'far (al-Ṭabarī) says: The Messenger of God left 'Abd Allāh b. Rawāḥah in charge of Medina.

Other Events

Al-Wāqidī says: In this year, the Messenger of God married Umm Salamah bt. Abī Umayyah[236] and consummated the marriage in Shawwāl (which began March 6, 626). In this year also, the Messenger of God commanded Zayd b. Thābit to study the Book of the Jews, saying, "I fear that they may change my Book."

In this year, the polytheists were in charge of the Meccan Pilgrimage.

---

236. Umm Salamah Hind belonged to the Meccan clan of Makhzūm; her previous husband, Abū Salamah, also of Makhzūm, had been killed at Uḥud.

Abbreviations

EI[1], *EI*[2]: *Encyclopaedia of Islam*, London and Leiden, first edition, second edition.
GALS: C. Brockelmann, *Geschichte der arabischen Literaturs*, Supplementband I, Leiden 1937.
IH: Ibn Hishām, *Sīrah*, ed. F. Wüstenfeld, Göttingen 1859, 1860.
Qur.: Qur'ān (Pickthall's translation—see Bibliography).
W: Al-Wāqidī, *Kitāb al-Maghāzī*, ed. Marsden Jones, 3 vols. with continuous paging, London 1966.
Watt, *Mecca*: W.M. Watt, *Muhammad at Mecca*, Oxford 1953.
——, *Medina*: ——, *Muhammad at Medina*, Oxford 1956.

Bibliography of Cited Works

Aḥmad b. Ḥanbal, *Musnad*, 6 vols., Cairo 1893.

Goldziher, I., *Muslim Studies*, ed. S.M.Stern, vol.1, London 1967.

Guillaume, A., *The Life of Muhammad: a Translation of (Ibn) Isḥāq's Sīrat Rasūl Allāh*, London 1955; contains Ibn Hishām's editorial notes as an appendix.

Ḥassān b. Thābit, *Dīwān*, ed. W.Arafat, 2 vols., London 1971.

Ibn al-Athīr, *Usd al-ghābah*, 5 vols., Cairo 1864.

Ibn Hishām, *Sīrat Rasūl Allāh*, ed. F.Wüstenfeld, Göttingen 1859, 1860 (incorporates the *Sīrah* of Ibn Isḥāq).

al-Mas'ūdī, *Murūj adh-dhahab*, ed. and tr. C.Barbier de Meynard and Pavet de Courteille, vol.1, Paris 1861.

Nöldeke, Th., *Geschichte des Qorāns*,[2], vol.1 ed. F. Schwally, Leipzig 1909.

Qur'ān: quoted from *The Meaning of the Glorious Koran*, by Marmaduke Pickthall, London 1930.

Sezgin, F., *Geschichte des arabischen Schrifttums*, vol.1, Leiden 1967.

Watt, W. Montgomery, *Bell's Introduction to the Qur'ān*, Edinburgh 1970.

———, *Muhammad at Mecca*, Oxford 1953.

———, *Muhammad at Medina*, Oxford 1956.

Wagtendonk, K., *Fasting in the Koran*, Leiden 1968.

Wellhausen, J., *Reste arabischen Heidentums*[2], Berlin 1897.

Index

The index contains all proper names of persons, places, tribal and other groups, as well as topographical data, occurring in the introduction, the text, and the footnotes. However, as far as the footnotes are concerned, only those names that belong to the medieval or earlier periods are listed.

The definite article, the abbreviation b. (for ibn, son) and bt. (for bint, daughter), and everything in parentheses are disregarded for the purposes of alphabetization. Where a name occurs in both the text and the footnotes on the same page, only the page number is given.

(The Arabic article al- is neglected in the alphabetical arrangement. Abbreviations: ʿAA. = ʿAbd Allāh; M. = Muḥammad. An asterisk after a name indicates that it occurs only in the isnāds, the chains of transmitters.)

A

Abān al-ʿAṭṭār * 28
Abān b. Saʿīd 74
ʿAbbād b. ʿAA. * 58, 70, 74, 118, 126
ʿAbbād b. Bishr 95
al-ʿAbbās b. ʿAA. b. Maʿbad * 56, 69
al-ʿAbbās b. ʿAbd al-ʿAẓīm * 103f.
al-ʿAbbās b. ʿAbd al-Muṭṭalib xxxvii, 34–7, 55–7, 68–72, 82
al-ʿAbbās b. al-Walīd * 156
ʿAA. b. ʿAA. b. Ubayy 159
ʿAA. b. Abī Bakr (son of caliph) 8
ʿAA. b. Abī Bakr * 5, 18, 35, 47, 58, 60f., 66, 72, 75, 77, 94, 140, 151, 160
ʿAA. b. Abī Rabīʿah 105
ʿAA. b. ʿAmr b. al-ʿĀṣ 107
ʿAA. b. ʿAmr b. al-Ḥarām 110, 136
ʿAA. b. ʿAtīk 100–4
ʿAA. b. Ḥanẓalah 142
ʿAA. b. Jaḥsh 18–22, 29, 134, 137
ʿAA. b. Jubayr 62
ʿAA. b. Kaʿb b. Mālik * 101
ʿAA. b. Kaʿb b. Zayd 65
ʿAA. b. Khārijah * 139
ʿAA. b. Masʿūd 61f., 83, 114
ʿAA. b. al-Mubārak * 54
ʿAA. b. al-Mughīrah 21
ʿAA. b. al-Mughīth * 94f.
ʿAA. b. M. b. al-Mughīrah * 40
ʿAA. b. Rawāḥah 52, 64, 82, 94, 167
ʿAA. b. Ṣafwān 7, 107
ʿAA. b. Ṭāriq 144f.
ʿAA. b. Thaʿlabah * 56
ʿAA. b. Ubayy xxiv, xxviii, xxxi, 14, 86, 108–10, 125, 158–60
ʿAA. b. ʿUmar 84, 111
ʿAA. b. Unays 101–4
ʿAA. b. ʿUqbah 100
ʿAA. b. Urayqiṭ 8
ʿAA. b. ʿUrwah * 8
ʿAA. b. ʿUthmān xxxvi, 161
ʿAA. b. al-Zubayr 9f., 118, 126
ʿAbd al-Ashhal, clan in Medina 95, 112, 137, 139
ʿAbd al-ʿAzīz b. Abī Ḥāzim * 17
ʿAbd al-Dār, clan in Mecca xxxi, 67, 117f.
ʿAbd al-Ḥamīd * 7
ʿAbd al-Malik, caliph xxxvii, 28
ʿAbd al-Malik al-Yarbūʿī * 50
ʿAbd al-Muṭṭalib, sons of 33, 36
ʿAbd al-Qays, tribe 141
ʿAbd al-Raḥmān b. ʿAA. * 60

'Abd al-Raḥmān b. Abī al-Ḍaḥḥāk * 7
'Abd al-Raḥmān b. al-Aswad * 27
'Abd al-Raḥmān b. 'Awf 58–60
'Abd al-Raḥmān b. al-Ḥārith * 64
'Abd al-Raḥmān b. Ka'b * 103
'Abd al-Raḥmān b. Mahdī * 34
'Abd al-Raḥmān b. M. * 7
'Abd al-Razzāq * 40
'Abd al-Samad b. 'Abd al-Wārith * 28
'Abd Shams, clan in Mecca 50
'Abd al-Wahhāb al-Thaqafī * 54
'Abd al-Wāḥid b. Abī 'Awn * 59, 137
'Abd al-Wārith b. 'Abd al-Samad * 28
Abraham 82
Abū 'Abd al-Raḥmān al-Sulamī * 28
Abū 'Abs b. Jabr 95
Abū Aḥmad al-Zubayrī * 39
Abū 'Āmir * 39
Abū 'Āmir 'Abd 'Amr 117
Abū al-'Āṣ b. al-Rabī' 73–8
Abū al-Aswad * 10
Abū Ayyūb Khālid 4f.
Abū 'Azīz b. 'Umayr 67, 107
Abū 'Azzah 106, 141
Abū al-Bakhtarī 44, 56–8, 65, 67
Abū Bakr, caliph xviii, 6–8, 41, 53–5, 81f., 123, 131, 152, 157
Abū Bakr b. 'AA. b. Abī Sabrah * 18
Abū Bakr b. 'Abd al-Raḥmān * 60
Abū Bakr b. 'Ayyāsh * 39
Abū Bakr b. Ismā'īl * 11
Abū Barā' 'Āmir b. Mālik xxxivf., 151–5
Abū Burdah b. Niyār 111
Abū Dā'ūd al-Māzinī * 60
Abū Dujānah Simāk 116, 118, 121, 137f., 160
Abū Dusmah 107
Abū al-Ḥakam see: Abū Jahl
Abū Ḥathmah 111f.
Abū Ḥāzim * 17
Abū Hind 66
Abū Hurayrah * 84, 145, 162
Abū Isḥāq * 27, 32, 34, 39f., 100, 113, 131
Abū Jābir al-Salimī 109
Abū Ja'far * 18, 92
Abū Ja'far M. b. 'Alī * 53
Abū Jahl xxvi, 10, 13, 36, 44–6, 49–51, 61–3, 65, 67, 84, 128
Abū Kurayb * 27, 39, 119, 145f.
Abū Lahab xviii, 37f., 68, 73n., 107n.
Abū Lubābah 84, 86, 91
Abū Mālik * 24
Abū Mālik al-Janbī * 39
Abū Marthad 10
Abū Mu'āwiyah * 82
Abū Mubashshir * 87
Abū Nā'ilah see: Silkān
Abū Qatādah 101–3
Abū Qays b. al-Aslat xixf., 14
Abū Qubays 36
Abū Rāfi' (M.'s client) 8, 68
Abū Rāfi' * 119
Abū Rāfi' Sallām xxix, 99–104, 160
Abū Sa'd b. Wahb 160
Abū al-Sā'ib * 139
Abū Sa'īd al-Khudrī 111
Abū Salamah xxxvi, 16, 167n.
Abū Ṣāliḥ * 24, 71
Abū Sirwa'ah b. al-Ḥārith 146
Abū Sufyān b. Ḥarb xxvf., xxixf., xxxii –xxxiv, xxxvi, 11, 29–32, 37, 40, 43–5, 72f., 75n., 76, 89–91, 98f., 105–7, 113–5, 117f., 125–9, 131f., 140f., 147f., 165f.
Abū Sufyān b. al-Ḥārith 68
Abū Ṭālib 53
Abū al-Tayyāḥ * 5
Abū Turāb 16f.
Abū 'Ubaydah b. al-Jarrāḥ 22
Abū 'Ubaydah b. M. b. 'Ammār * 66, 82
Abū Uḥayḥah 6
Abū Umāmah al-Bāhilī * 64
Abū Umāmah b. Sahl * 60
Abū Wadā'ah 71
Abū Zam'ah al-Aswad xxx, 99
Abū al-Zinād * 27
Abū Zumayl * 80
al-Abwā' xix, 11f., 15
'Aḍal, tribe 106n., 143, 147
Aḍḥā', 87f.
Adhri'āt 159
'Adī * 27

'Adī, clan in Mecca 29, 46, 143
'Adī b. Abī al-Zaghbā' 40, 44
'Adī b. al-Najjār, clan in Medina 53, 55, 122, 151
'Afrā' 66
Ahābīsh 106f., 117, 132, 143n.
Aḥmad b. Isḥāq * 39
Aḥmad b. Manṣūr * 80
Aḥmad b. al-Mufaḍḍal * 108, 114, 124
Aḥmar (Thamūd) 17
Aḥyā' xix, 11f.
'Ā' ishah xviif., 6–8, 62, 74
al-Akhnas b. Sharīq 46
al-'Alā' b. Kathīr * 60
'Alī * 32, 34
'Alī b. Abī Ṭālib xxxvi, 14, 16–18, 33f., 39, 43, 52f., 65, 81, 89, 115, 118f., 121, 123, 132, 137f., 157, 161
'Alī b. Naṣr * 28
'Alī b. Umayyah 59
'Āliyah 84
'Alqamah * 27
al-A'mash * 82
'Āmir, tribe xxxiv–vi, 95, 150n., 151–3, 157
'Āmir, clan in Mecca 30, 71, 119
'Āmir b. Fuhayrah 21, 151, 153
'Āmir b. al-Ḥaḍramī 50f.
'Āmir b. Sa'd * 11
'Āmir b. al-Ṭufayl xxxv, 152–6
'Ammār b. Yāsir 16f., 21
'Amr b. 'AA. * 119
'Amr b. 'Abd Wudd 44
'Amr b. Abī Sufyān 72f.
'Amr b. 'Alī * 34
'Amr b. al-'Āṣ 107
'Amr b. 'Asīd * 145
'Amr b. 'Āṣim * 115
'Amr b. 'Awf, clan in Medina 66, 72, 84, 113, 122, 144, 152
'Amr b. al-Ḥaḍramī 19–22, 28f., 37, 49f.
'Amr b. Ḥammād * 21, 24, 40
'Amr b. al-Jamūḥ 136
'Amr b. Jiḥāsh 157f., 160
'Amr b. Murrah * 82
'Amr b. 'Ubayd * 163
'Amr b. Umayyah * 146f.
'Amr b. Umayyah al-Ḍamrī 16, 146–50, 152f., 156f.
'Amr b. Yūnus * 155
'Amrah bt. 'Alqamah 107, 118
Anas b. Mālik * 5f., 63, 120, 122, 155
Anas b. al-Naḍr 122, 125
'Anbasah * 26
Anmār 98
Anṣār xx, xxii, xxvf., xxix, xxxif., xxxiv, 4f., 33, 35, 39, 42, 52f., 56, 66f., 75, 79, 83f., 90, 100f., 108, 117, 120, 122, 127, 133, 137, 147, 150, 152, 157, 160, 164
al-'Aqabah xvii, 6n., 42
al-'Aqanqal 44, 47f.
'Aqīl b. Abī Ṭālib 34, 71, 81
'Aqīl b. al-Aswad 70
'Aqīl b. al-Jābir * 163
'Arābah b. Aws 111
'Arīḍ Abū Yasār 43
Arṭāt 121
al-'Āṣ b. Hishām 38, 68
al-'Āṣ b. Sa'īd 43, 128
al-'Āṣ b. Wā'il 6
As'ad b. Zurārah xviif., 5f.
Asbāṭ * 21, 24, 40, 108, 114, 124
'Āshurā' xxiii, 25n., 26
'Āṣim b. 'Adī 84
'Āṣim b. 'Alī * 80
'Āṣim b. Thābit 66, 122, 143–6
'Āṣim b. 'Umar b. Qatādah * 28, 35, 53, 55, 65, 85f., 94, 105, 117, 121, 134f., 143
Aslam 43
Aslam, tribe 102
Asmā' bt. Abī Bakr 9
al-Aswad * 27
al-Aswad b. 'Abd al-Asad 52
al-Aswad b. Khuzā'ī 101f.
al-Aswad b. al-Muṭṭalib 70
'Ātikah 35–7
'Ātikah bt. Asīd 94
al-A'waṣ 127
'Awf, clan in Medina 160
'Awf b. al-Ḥārith 52, 55

al-Aws, tribe in Medina xxix, 83, 90, 101, 117, 158
al-Awzā'ī * 156
Aymā' b. Raḥḍah 48, 50
'Aynayn 107

B

Badr, battle xxiv–vii, xxxii, 14, 16, 26–69
Badr al-Maw'id xxx, xxxv, 165–7
Bakr b. 'Abd Manāt, tribe 38, 149
Bakr b. Wā'il, tribe 99
Balī, tribe 144
Banū . . see under following name
Baqī' al-Gharqad 96
al-Barā' * 39f., 100, 113, 131
al-Barā' b. 'Āzib 84, 111
Barrah bt. 'Abd al-'Uzzā 115n.
Barzah (Barrah) bt. Mas'ūd 107
Basbas b. 'Amr 40, 44
Bayāḍah, clan in Medina 144
al-Bayḍā' 104
Bilāl 59
Bi'r Ma'ūnah xxxivf., 21, 151–6
Bishr b. Ādam * 115
Bishr b. Mu'ādh * 40
Bu'āth 97
Buḥrān 19, 21, 88, 93
Buraydah b. Sufyān * 133
Buwāṭ xixf., 13, 15

D

Dā'is 160
Ḍajnān 166
Damascus xx
Ḍamḍam b. 'Amr 35, 37
Ḍamrah, tribe 12, 14, 147, 149n., 165
Dā'ūd b. al-Ḥusayn * 78
Dhafirān 41f.
Dhāt 'Irq 99
Dhāt al-Riqā' xxxiv, 161–4
Dhū Amarr 93, 98
Dhū al-Faqār 84, 120
Dhū Ṭawā 76
Dhubāb 86
al-Dīl, tribe 61, 149
Dīnār, clan in Medina 137, 152
Ḍubay'ah, clan in Medina 117

E

Emigrants, xv, xviii, xx, xxiv, xxvi, xxxii, 5, 10, 12f., 16, 18, 35, 39, 83f., 122, 126, 157, 160, 164

F

al-Faḍl b. al-Ḥasan * 147
Farwah b. 'Amr 66
Fāṭimah xviii, xxxvi, 8n., 17f., 92, 137f., 142
Fāṭimah bt. al-Walīd 107
fatrah 2
fitnah 23
fiṭr, 26
Friday prayer, xvi, xxiii, 1–4, 108
al-Fur' 19, 88, 93
Furāt b. Ḥayyān 99
al-Furay'ah 130n.

G

Gabriel 7, 55, 86, 119f.
Gaza xx
Ghālib, clan-group in Mecca 127
Ghālib b. 'AA. 89
Ghamrah 99
Ghaṭafān, tribe 88f., 93, 161–3
Ghifār, tribe 41, 48, 60, 160
Guillaume, A. xxxvii

H

Habbār b. al-Aswad 76
al-Had'ah 144f.
Ḥafṣah xviii, 7, 105
al-Ḥajjāj * 25, 39

al-Ḥajjāj, subclan in Mecca 30, 43
al-Ḥakam b. Kaysān 19, 21, 29
al-Ḥakam b. Sa'd 154
al-Ḥakam b. 'Utaybah * 39, 60, 69, 133
Ḥakīm b. Ḥizām 44, 49–51
Hālah bt. Khuwaylid 73
Ḥammād b. Salamah * 5
Hammām b. Yaḥyā * 25
Ḥamnah bt. Jaḥsh 137
Ḥamrā' al-Asad xxxiif., 138–42
Ḥamzah xix, 10, 13, 15f., 33, 52, 59, 81, 87, 113, 118, 121f., 129f., 132–4, 137, 143
Ḥanẓalah b. Abī Sufyān 72, 125f.
Ḥanẓalah b. al-Rāhib 125-7, 142n.
Ḥaram of Mecca 19, 146f.
Ḥarām b. Milḥān 151f., 155
al-Ḥārith * 9f., 27, 85, 111
al-Ḥārith b. 'Abd Manāt, sub-tribe 106n., 107, 124, 132
al-Ḥārith b. 'Āmir 44, 144f.
al-Ḥārith b. al-Aswad 70
al-Ḥārith b. Aws 95, 97
al-Ḥārith b. Fihr 71
al-Ḥārith b. Ḥāṭib 84
al-Ḥārith b. Hishām 107, 129
al-Ḥārith b. al-Khazraj, clan in Medina 133
al-Ḥārith b. al-Ṣimmah 84, 123, 151
Ḥārithah, clan in Medina 95, 98, 110, 112
Ḥārithah b. Muḍarrib * 32, 34
Ḥārithah b. Surāqah 55
Hārūn b. Isḥāq * 32, 39, 100, 113, 131
Hārūn b. al-Mughīrah * 26
al-Ḥasan b. 'Alī 28, 91, 142
al-Ḥasan al-Baṣrī * 163
al-Ḥasan b. 'Umārah * 60, 69, 133
al-Ḥasan b. Yaḥyā * 40
Hāshim, clan in Mecca xxxvi, 46, 56f., 128
Ḥassān b. Thābit 103, 119, 128–30, 154f.
Ḥāṭib b. Umayyah 135
al-Ḥaysumān b. 'AA. 67
Ḥayzūm 60
Ḥibbān b. 'Alī * 119
Ḥibbān b. al-Wāsi' * 53
Ḥijāz 19, 144
Ḥijr 78f.
Hilāl * 84
Hilāl, tribe 150
Hind bt. 'Utbah 75, 107, 118, 129f.
Hishām b. al-Mughīrah 19
Hishām b. 'Urwah * 28, 116, 153
al-Ḥubāb b. al-Mundhir 47
Hubal 131
Ḥudhayfah b. al-Yamān 134f.
Hudhayl, tribe 144f.
Ḥujayr b. Abī Ihāb 144
Ḥujayr al-Tha'labī * 27
al-Ḥulays b. Zabbān 132
Ḥumayd al-Ṭawīl * 63, 120, 122, 152
al-Hūn b. Khuzaymah, tribe 106n., 143n.
Ḥunayn 61
Ḥusayl b. Jābir 134f.
al-Ḥusayn b. 'AA. * 68, 138
al-Ḥusayn b. 'Abd al-Raḥmān * 105, 120
al-Ḥusayn b. 'Alī xxxvi, 142, 161
Ḥusays, clan-group in Mecca 70
Ḥuwayyisah b. Mas'ūd 97f.
Ḥuyayy b. Akhṭab 90, 158–60
Hypocrites xvii, xxiv, xxxi, 57, 110, 112, 135

I

Iblīs 38
Ibn 'Abbās ('AA.) * xxvi, xxxi, 24, 35, 39, 54, 56, 60f., 69, 71, 78, 80, 82, 96, 113, 159
Ibn 'Abd al-A'lā * 159
Ibn Abī 'Adī * 120
Ibn Abī al-Ḥuqayq see: Abū Rāfi' Sallām
Ibn Abī Najīḥ * 38
Ibn Abī Sabrah * 92; and see: Abū Bakr b. 'AA.
Ibn Abī al-Zinād * 27f.
Ibn 'Afrā' see: 'Awf, Mu'ādh, Mu'awwidh b. al-Ḥārith

Ibn Hishām xvf., xxxvii, 55n.
Ibn Ḥumayd * 4f., 11f., 17f., 25f., 28, 34f., 38f., 43, 47, 49, 53, 55f., 58–67, 69–72, 74f., 77f., 83, 85, 88–90, 93–6, 105, 117f., 120–4, 126, 129, 131–40, 143, 147, 150–3, 157, 160f., 163, 165
Ibn Isḥāq * xix, xxv, xxx, xxxiii, xxxvif., 4f., 11f., 16–18, 21, 25, 34f., 38–40, 42f., 47, 49, 51, 53, 55f., 58–67, 69–72, 74f., 77f., 83, 85f., 88–90, 93–6, 105, 110, 112, 116–8, 120–4, 126, 129, 131–40, 143, 145, 147, 150–3, 157, 160f., 163, 165
Ibn al-Kalbī * 46, 71
Ibn Mas'ūd * 24, 27, 41
Ibn al-Muthannā * 27
Ibn al-Qamī'ah 120f., 124, 132
Ibn Sa'd * 9f., 25, 27, 84f., 111, 113, 159
Ibn Sha'ūb 127
Ibn Shihāb * see: al-Zuhrī
Ibn Sunaynah 97
Ibn Umm Maktūm 89, 141, 161
Ibn Wahb * 2, 25
Ibn Wakī * 8, 40, 54, 113, 131
Ibn Zayd * 25
Ibrāhīm * 27
Ibrāhīm b. 'Abd al-Raḥmān b. 'Awf * 59
Ibrāhīm b. 'Abd al-Raḥmān b. Ka'b * 103
Ibrāhīm b. Ismā'īl * 103, 145f.
'īd al-aḍḥā 87f.
'īd al-fiṭr 26
ijārah 77
'Ikrimah (*mawlā* of Ibn 'Abbās) * xxvi, 35, 54, 61, 68, 78, 138, 155
'Ikrimah b. Abī Jahl 12, 61, 105, 107, 112f.
'Ikrimah b. 'Ammār * 54, 80
Imāmah b. 'Amr * 50
Iraq 99
Isḥāq b. 'AA. b. Abī Farwah * 18, 92
Isḥāq (b. 'AA.) b. Abī Ṭalḥah * 155f.
Isḥāq b. Yasār * 49, 60, 136, 151
Ismā'īl * 11
Ismā'īl b. Abī Khālid * 7
Ismā'īl b. Ibrāhīm * 41
Ismā'īl b. Isrā'īl * 40
Ismā'īl b. M. b. Sa'd * 37
Ismā'īl b. Umayyah * 8
Isrā'īl * 27, 32, 34, 39, 100, 113, 131

J

Jabbār b. Sulmā 153f.
Jābir b. 'AA. 87, 139, 162f.
Ja'far b. 'AA. * 117
Ja'far b. 'Awn * 103, 145f.
Ja'far (b. al-Faḍl) b. 'Amr * 146f.
Ja'far b. M. al-Buzūrī * 34
Jāhiliyyah 79, 105, 117, 135
Jaḥjabā, clan in Medina 144
Jamīlah bt. 'AA. b. Ubayy 142
al-Jammā' 16
Jerusalem xxiii, 24f.
Jesus 82
Jews xv, xvii, xxiiif., xxvii–xxix, xxxvf., 9, 20, 84, 97, 102, 111, 136, 157–9, 167
Jubayr b. Muṭ'im 106, 129
Judayy b. Akhṭab 159
Juhaym b. al-Ṣalt 45
Juhaynah, tribe 13
al-Juḥfah 32, 45f., 50
al-Julās b. Ṭalḥah 107
Junādah b. Mulayḥah 57
Jundub b. 'AA. * 22

K

Ka'b b. 'Amr 69
Ka'b b. Asad 158
Ka'b b. al-Ashraf xxix, 94–7, 99, 103
Ka'b b. Luayy, clan-group in Mecca 29f.
Ka'b b. Mālik 91, 122, 154f.
Ka'b b. Zayd 152
Ka'bah 24f., 36, 148, 155f.
al-Khabār 13
Khadījah 7, 73f.
Khālid * 54
Khālid b. al-Bukayr 143f.
Khālid b. al-Walīd xxxii, 112–5

Khārijah b. Zayd * 27f.
al-Kharrār xix, 11
Khawwāt b. Jubayr 84, 114
Khaybar xxxvi, 101–3, 160
al-Khazraj, tribe in Medina 14, 83, 86, 90, 101, 117
Khubayb b. 'Adī 144–6, 149
Khufāf b. Aymā' 48
khums 20n., 87, 99
Khunās bt. Mālik 107
Khunays b. Hudhāfah 105
khuṭbah xvi
Khuzā'ah, tribe 140
Khuzā'ī b. al-Aswad 102
Kilāb, tribe 154
Kilāb b. Ṭalḥah 107, 122
Kinānah, tribe 38, 106f., 132
Kinānah b. al-Rabī 75f., 160
Kinānah b. Ṣūriyā' 158
Kulthūm b. Hidm xvii, 5
kunyah 107n.
al-Kudr 88f.
Kurz al-Fihrī 14, 16, 18

L

al-Lāt 114
Laylat al-Qadr 27
Layth, tribe 57
lex talionis xxvii
Liḥyān, clan 143n., 145

M

ma'āqil 92
Ma'bad b. 'Amr 91
Ma'bad al-Khuzā'ī xxiii, 140, 165
Maḥmūd b. 'Amr * 120
Maḥmūd b. Labīd * 134
Majannah 165
Majdī b. 'Amr al-Juhanī 10, 13, 44
Makhramah b. Nawfal 34, 46
Makhshī b. 'Amr 12, 165
Makḥul * 64
Makhzūm, clan in Mecca xxxvi, 19, 50, 62
mala' 65
Malal 21
Mālik b. Abī Qawqal 160
Mālik b. 'Amr 108
Mālik b. Dukhshum 71
Mālik b. Ḥisl, subclan in Mecca 107
Mālik b. Kinānah, subtribe 106
Mālik b. al-Najjār, subclan in Medina 84
Ma'mar * 6, 40, 159
al-Marah 10, 12
Marthad b. Abī Marthad 84, 143f.
Marwān b. al-Ḥakam 50
Mary, Maryam 7
Mas'ūd b. Sinān 101
mawlā (client) 19n.
Māzin b. al-Najjār, subclan in Medina 40, 60
Mihja' 55
al-Mihrās 123
Mikraz b. Ḥafṣ 11, 71
al-Miqdād b. 'Amr 11f., 41, 84
al-Miqdād b. al-Aswad 34, 113, 115
Miqsam * 39, 60, 69, 133
al-Mirba' al-Qayẓī 112
Mis'ar * 40
Misṭaḥ b. Uthāthah 10
Moses 26, 41, 83
mosque xvi, 4f.
Mu'ādh (b. 'Afrā') b. al-Ḥārith 4f.
Mu'ādh b. 'Amr 61
Mu'ādh b. Hishām * 162
Mu'āwiyah, caliph 137
Mu'āwiyah b. al-Mughīrah 141
Mu'awwidh b. al-Ḥārith 52, 61
Mudlij, tribe 14, 16
al-Mughīrah b. 'Abd al-Raḥmān * 151
al-Mughīrah b. 'Uthmān 21
Muḥammad:
- leads expeditions xix, xxix, 11–16, 26–69, 85–7, 89–91, 105–41, 156–67
- marriages xviii, 6–8, 105, 150, 167
- sermon 2–4
M. b. 'Abd al-A'lā * 6, 21

M. b. 'AA. b. 'Abd al-Raḥmān * 85, 132
M. b. 'Abd al-Raḥmān * 162
M. b. 'Amr * 18, 71
M. b. Bashshār * 162
M. b. al-Faḍl * 87
M. b. Hilāl * 84
M. b. al-Ḥusayn 108, 114, 124
M. b. Ja'far 27, 78, 89, 162
M. b. Ka'b al-Quraẓī * 16f., 133
M. b. Marzūq * 155
M. b. Maslamah 95, 97, 158
M. b. Salamah * 16
M. b. Ṣāliḥ * 27f., 86
M. b. Thawr * 159
M. b. 'Ubayd al-Muḥāribī * 17, 39, 41, 54
M. b. 'Ubayd Allāh b. Abī Rāfi' * 119
M. b. 'Ubayd Allāh al-Thaqafī * 28
M. b. 'Umar * see: al Wāqidī
M. b. 'Umārah al-Asadī * 27
M. b. Yaḥyā b. Ḥibbān * 43, 105
M. b. Yaḥyā al-Iskandarānī * 60
M. b. Yaḥyā b. Sahl * 9
M. (b. Yazīd) b. Khuthaym * 7, 16f.
Muḥārib, tribe 161, 163
Muḥayyiṣah b. Mas'ūd 97f.
Mujadhdhar b. Dhiyād 57f.
Mujāhid b. Mūsā * 5
Mukhayrīq 136
al-Mukhāriq * 41
al-Mukhtār b. Abī 'Ubayd 10
Munabbih b. al-Ḥajjāj 44, 65, 67, 84
munāfiqūn see: Hypocrites
al-Mundhir b. 'Amr 151f.
Murayy b. Sinān 111
Murrah al-Hamdānī * 24
Mūsā b. 'Abd al-Raḥmān * 103f.
Mūsā b. Hārūn * 21, 24, 40
Muṣ'ab b. al-Miqdām * 32, 39, 100, 113, 131
Muṣ'ab b. Thābit * 10
Muṣ'ab b. 'Umayr xvii, 67, 113, 121, 128, 137
Musāfi' b. 'Abd Manāt 106
Musāfi' b. Ṭalḥah 107, 122
Musahhab 154
al-Muṣallā 26, 65, 87
Muṣawwar * 50
al-Mushayrib 13
al-Mu'tamir b. Sulaymān * 22
al-Muthannā b. Ibrāhīm * 25
al-Muṭṭalib, clan of Mecca xxxvi, 45, 57
al-Muṭṭalib b. Abī Wadā'ah 71, 94

N

Nabhān, tribe 94
al-Naḍīr, Jewish clan xxxvf., 90, 94, 156–61
al-Naḍr b. al-Ḥārith 44, 65
Nāfi' b. 'Abd al-Qays 76
Nāfi' b. Budayl 151
Najd xxx, 90, 93, 98, 151, 154, 161f.
al-Najjār, clan in Medina xviif., 4–6, 13, 40, 108, 128, 132; see also: 'Adī, Dīnār, Mālik, Māzin
Nakhl 161f., 164
Nakhlah xx–xxii, 18–23, 29
al-Naqī' 91, 150
nashsh 150
nasī xxii, xxxviii
Nawfal, clan in Mecca 12, 21, 144
Nawfal b. 'AA. 19
Nawfal b. al-Ḥārith 34, 71
Nawfal b. Khuwaylid 44
Nisṭās 147
Noah 83
Nu'aym b. Mas'ūd 166
Nubayh b. al-Ḥajjāj 44, 65, 67
Nubayh b. Wahb * 67
al-Nu'mān b. Bashīr 9f.
al-Nu'mān b. Mālik 109
nuqabā' (sing. *naqīb*) xviii, 6

P

Pharaoh 26
Prayer of Fear 162f.

Q

Qanāt 107, 112, 153
al-Qaradah xxx, 98
al-Qārah, clan 106n., 143, 147
Qarqarat al-Kudr 88, 90, 153
al-Qāsim b. ʿAbd al-Raḥmān * 122
Qatādah * 25, 40, 162
Qatādah b. al-Nuʿmān 121
Qaylah, tribe in Medina 112
Qaynuqāʿ, Jewish clan in Medina xxvii-xxix, 85–7
Qays b. Abī Ṣaʿṣaʿah 40
qiblah xxiii, xxvii, 24f., 54
Qubā' xvii, xxxviii, 1, 5, 156
Qudayd 166
Quraysh *passim*
Qurayẓah, Jewish clan in Medina xxiv, 97, 135n., 158
Quzmān 135f.

R

Rābigh xix, 10
Rabīghah b. ʿĀmir 155
Raḍwā 13
Rāfiʿ b. Khadīj 84, 87, 111
al-Raḥmān 58
rakʿah 9, 146, 148, 162f., 164
al-Rajīʿ xxxivf., 144, 147
Rakūbah 150
Ramaḍān, fast of xxiiif., xxviii, 25–28
al-Rawḥā' xxxiii, 65, 84, 140
Rayṭah bt. Munabbih 107
Raqayyah xviii, xxxvi, 64, 73

S

sacred month, territory xxif.
Saʿd b. Abī Waqqāṣ xix, 11f., 14, 16, 19, 21f., 43, 121, 124
Saʿd. b. Ibrāhīm * 59
Saʿd b. Muʿādh xxivf., xxviii, 16, 42, 47, 56, 83, 137
Saʿd b. al-Nuʿmān 72f.
Saʿd b. Rabīʿ 132f.
Saʿd b. ʿUbādah 15, 39
Saʿd b. ʿUthmān 127
Saʿd b. Yazīd 127
Ṣadaqah b. Yasār * 163
Safawān xixf., 14
ṣafī 87
Ṣafiyyah 133f.
al-Ṣafrā' 40f., 65, 149
Ṣafwān b. Umayyah xxx, 67, 78–80, 99, 105–7, 144, 147
Sahl b. Abī Ḥathmah * 9
Sahl b. ʿAmr 4
Sahl b. Ḥunayf 60, 124, 137, 160
Sahl b. Saʿd * 17
al-Sā'ib b. Yazīd 98
Saʿīd * 40
Saʿīd b. ʿAbd al-Raḥmān * 2
Saʿīd b. al-ʿĀṣ 74
Saʿīd b. al-Musayyab * 50
Saʿīd b. Zayd 84
Sāʿidah, clan in Medina 40, 116, 151
Salamah b. al-Faḍl * 4f., 11f., 17f., 25, 34f., 38f., 43, 47, 49, 53, 55f., 58–67, 69–72, 74f., 77f., 83, 85, 88–90, 93–6, 105, 117f., 120–4, 126, 129, 131–40, 143, 147, 150–3, 157, 160f., 163, 165
Salamah b. Salamah 65
Ṣāliḥ b. Abī Umāmah * 94
Ṣāliḥ b. Kaysān * 124, 129
Sālim b. ʿAwf, clan in Medina 2, 71
Salimah, clan in Medina 47, 55, 61, 88, 101, 117, 123, 136
Sallām b. Abī al-Ḥuqayq see: Abū Rāfiʿ Sallām
Sallām b. Mishkam 90, 158
Salm b. Junādah * 82
Salmā bt. ʿAmr xvii, 6n.
Samurah b. Jundub 111
Saul 39f.
Sawād b. Ghaziyyah 53f.
Sawdah bt. Zamʿah xvii, 8, 66
sawīq (barley-meal raid) xxix, 89–91, 165f.

Shaddād b. al-Aswad 127f.
Shahādah 80
al-Shammākh 111
Sharīq b. ʿAmr 121
shawkah 6
Shaybah b. Mālik 119
Shaybah b. Rabīʿah 33, 44f., 52f., 63, 65, 67, 128
al-Shaykhayn 110f.
Shiʿb al-ʿAjūz 97
Shīʿites xviii, 17n.
Shuʿbah * 27, 34
Sibāʿ b. ʿAbd al-ʿUzzā 121
Sīf al-Baḥr xix, 10n., 13
Silkān b. Salāmah 95–7
Simāk al-Ḥanafī * 54
Ṣuʿāb 119
al-Suddī * xxi, 21, 24, 40, 109, 114, 124
Sufyān * 8, 39f.; see also: al-Thawrī
Sufyān b. Khālid 143n.
Suhayl b. ʿAmr 4, 44, 66f., 71, 166
Suhayl b. Bayḍā' 21, 83
Sulāfah bt. Saʿd 107, 122, 144
Sulaym, tribe xxxv, 88f., 93, 152
Sulaymān b. Mūsā * 64
Sulaymān b. ʿUmar * 16
Sulaymān b. Wardān * 150
Sulaymān al-Yashkurī 162
al-Sunḥ 8
sunnah 133, 146
Surāqah b. Juʿshum 38
Suwayd 160
Syria xxix, 29, 84, 98, 159f., 162

T

al-Ṭabarī xv, xix, xxi, xxiiif., xxvi–xxxi, xxxiii, xxxvif.
al-Ṭā'if 18
Ṭalḥah b. Abī Ṭalḥah 107, 115, 118, 144n.
Ṭalḥah b. ʿUbayd Allāh 8, 84, 122f., 124, 126
Ṭālib b. Abī Ṭālib 46
al-Tanʿīm 147, 149
Ṭāriq * 41
Ṭāriq 116
Ṭayyi', tribe 94
Thābit b. Waqsh 134f.
Thaʿlabah, Jewish clan in Medina 136
Thaʿlabah, Arab tribe 161
Thamūd, tribe 17
al-Thaqafī * see: ʿAbd al-Wahhāb
Thawr b. Zayd * 61, 96
al-Thawrī * 27
Tihāmah 106f., 140
Tuʿaymah b. ʿAdī 44, 106
al-Ṭufayl b. al-Ḥārith xxxvi, 150

U

ʿUbādah b. al-Ṣāmit 64, 87
ʿUbayd b. M. al-Muḥāribī * 27
ʿUbayd Allāh b. Abī Rāfiʿ * 119
ʿUbayd Allāh b. Kaʿb * 89
ʿUbayd Allāh b. Mūsā * 27, 34
ʿUbayd Allāh b. al-Wāziʿ * 116
ʿUbaydah b. al-Ḥārith xix, xxxvi, 10, 12f., 33f., 52f., 150n.
Ubayy b. Khalaf 123f.
Uḥud, battle xxvif., xxx–xxxiv, 105–38
ʿUkkāshah b. Miḥṣan 19
ʿUmar b. al-Khaṭṭāb xviii, xxvii, 21, 41, 55, 57, 71, 79–83, 122f., 126, 129–31, 145, 157
ʿUmārah b. Ziyād 120
ʿUmayr b. Abī Waqqāṣ 84
ʿUmayr b. al-Ḥumām 55
ʿUmayr b. Wahb 49, 78–80
Umaymah bt. ʿAbd al-Muṭṭalib 134
Umayyah b. Khalaf 16, 38, 44f., 58–60, 62f., 65, 67, 144
Umayyah b. Zayd, clan in Medina 97
Umm ʿAmr 160
Umm Anmār 121
Umm al-Faḍl 68, 72, 94
Umm Ḥakīm bt. al-Ḥārith 107
Umm Kulthūm bt. M. xviii, 8n., 73, 98, 107n.

Umm Rūmān 8
Umm Salamah xxxvi, 167
'umrah xxi, 72, 166
'Uqbah b. Abī Mu'ayṭ 32, 38, 65f., 72
'Uqbah b. al-Ḥārith 144
'Uqbah b. 'Uthmān 127
ūqiyyah 150
al-'Urayḍ 90f., 97
'Urwah b. Asmā' 151
'Urwah b. al-Ward 160
'Urwah b. al-Zubayr * xxv, xxxvii, 8, 18, 28, 38, 43, 62, 78, 86, 116, 153, 162
Usāmah b. Zayd 64
Usayd b. Ḥuḍayr 137, 157
Usayd b. Zuhayr 84, 111
'Usfān 165
al-'Ushayrah xix, 14, 16
'Utbah b. Abī Lahab 73f.
'Utbah b. Abī Waqqāṣ 120, 124
'Utbah b. 'Amr 71
'Utbah b. Ghazwān 12, 19, 21
'Utbah b. Rabī'ah 33, 36, 44f., 48–53, 63, 65, 67, 128
'Uthmān b. 'AA. b. al-Mughīrah 19, 21
'Uthmān b. 'Affān xviii, xxxvi, 61, 64, 74, 84, 98, 127, 161
'Uthmān b. Ḥunayf 117
'Uthmān b. Mālik 148
'Uthmān b. Maẓ'ūn 91
'Uthmān b. Sa'īd * 119
al-'Uzzā 114, 126, 131

W

Waddān xix, 12, 15, 165
Wādī al-Qurā xxix
Wādī Ranūnah 2n.
Wadī'ah 160
Wahb b. 'Umayr 78
Waḥshī 106f., 121, 129
Wā'il, clan in Medina 14n.
Wakī' * 8, 40, 131
al-Walīd * 156
al-Walīd b. al-Mughīrah 6
al-Walīd b. 'Utbah 33, 36, 52f., 128
Wāqid b. 'AA. 19–22, 28f.
al-Wāqidī (M. b. 'Umar) * xix–xxi, xxviii, xxx, xxxiii, xxxvii, 9–11, 14f., 18, 21, 25, 27f., 67, 83–7, 89, 91f., 94, 98f., 101, 110f., 143, 158, 161, 166f.
Wardān * 150

Y

Yaḥyā b. 'AA. b. 'Abd al-Raḥmān * 5, 66
Yaḥyā b. 'Abbād * 58, 70, 74, 118, 126
Yaḥyā b. Bukayr * 60
Yaḥyā b. Sahl * 9
Yaḥyā b. Sa'īd * 8
Yaḥyā b. Wāḍiḥ * 28
Yaḥyā b. Ya'qūb * 28
Ya'jaj 75, 148
al-Yamāmah 57
Yamīn b. 'Umayr 160
Yanbu' 14, 16
Yathrib 45, 49, 90, 104, 166
Yazīd * 40
Yazīd b. Hārūn * 5
Yazīd b. Ḥāṭib 135
Yazīd (b. M.) b. Khuthaym * 16f.
Yazīd b. Rūmān * 18, 28, 35, 38, 43, 62, 65, 77, 89, 157
Yazīd b. Zuray' * 6
Yūnus b. 'Abd al-A'lā * 2, 25

Z

Ẓafar, clan in Medina 135, 137, 144
al-Ẓahrān 144, 165
zakāt al-fiṭr 26
Zam'ah b. al-Aswad 44, 65, 67, 70
Zamzam 68
Zayd b. al-Dathinnah 144f., 147
Zayd b. Ḥārithah xxixf., 8, 16, 64, 75f., 94, 98f.

Zayd b. Thābit 27f., 84, 111, 167
Zaynab bt. Khuzaymah xxxvi, 150
Zaynab bt. M. 73–6
Ziyād b. al-Sakan 120f.
Ziyād b. Sumayyah 10
al-Zubayr * 27
al-Zubayr (b. al-ʿAwwām) xxxi, 26, 30, 43, 113–6, 118, 123, 126, 134
al-Zubayr b. Bakkār * 50
Zuhrah, clan in Mecca 12, 46, 56
al-Zuhrī (M. b. Muslim b. Shihāb) * 6, 18, 35, 56, 85f., 101, 105, 122, 159

www.ingramcontent.com/pod-product-compliance
Lightning Source LLC
Chambersburg PA
CBHW020654230426
43665CB00008B/432
* 9 7 8 0 8 8 7 0 6 3 4 5 9 *